Contemporary American Immigrants

CONTEMPORARY AMERICAN IMMIGRANTS

Patterns of Filipino, Korean, and Chinese Settlement in the United States

Luciano Mangiafico

New York
Westport, Connecticut
London

Library of Congress Cataloging-in-Publication Data

Mangiafico, Luciano.
  Contemporary American immigrants: patterns of Filipino, Korean,
  and Chinese settlement in the United States / Luciano Mangiafico.
  p.   cm.
  Bibliography: p.
  Includes index.
  ISBN 0-275-92726-1 (alk. paper)
  1. Asian Americans—Social conditions. 2. Filipino Americans—
Social conditions. 3. Korean Americans—Social conditions.
4. Chinese Americans—Social conditions. 5. Immigrants—United
States. 6. United States—Emigration and immigration. 7. Asia—
Emigration and immigration. I. Title.
E184. 06M26   1988   87-17752
305.8′95073—dc19

The preparation of this volume was financed in part through
a grant from the Una Chapman Cox Foundation. It was produced
during a period of sabbatical leave from the U.S. Department
of State.

Library of Congress Catalog Card Number: 87-17752

ISBN: 0-275-92726-1

First published in 1988

Praeger Publishers, One Madison Avenue, New York, NY 10010
A division of Greenwood Press, Inc.

Printed in the United States of America

∞™

The paper used in this book complies with the
Permanent Paper Standard issued by the National
Information Standards Organization (Z39.48-1984).

10 9 8 7 6 5 4 3 2 1

Contents

CHINA

List of Tables

Foreword

In early November 1984, while assigned to the U.S. Embassy in Manila as first secretary and consul, I received from my immediate superior—the consul general—a copy of a statistical report prepared by the U.S. Bureau of the Census.

The Consul General Vernon D. McAninch, instructed me to look through the report and determine whether it contained anything that might be of interest to the consular section of the embassy. As a professional consular officer and chief of the immigrant visa branch in Manila, I was actively involved in the issuance of visas to Philippine nationals planning to immigrate to the United States; and a quick look at the data in the report aroused my interest. The mimeographed report actually contained detailed sociodemographic statistical data on natives of the Philippines who were in the United States at the time of the 1980 census of the population. Attached to the report was a letter signed by the director of the Bureau of the Census, which indicated that similar data on natives of other countries had been collected by the Bureau of the Census—by means of a special tabulation of the 1980 census data—to meet heightened interest by organizations such as the UN Statistical Office and the International Union for the Scientific Study of Population.

Because of my professional concern in the matter, I took the report home and—over a period of several weeks—analyzed the data with a utilitarian purpose in mind: What message did these statistics hold for the embassy and for the work load of the consular section? What planning should be undertaken to meet demands for service? Were our consular officers in Manila too lenient or too hard in judging the likelihood that a visa applicant might become a "public charge," once settled in the United States? Were fraudulent attempts to obtain U.S. immigrant visas likely to increase?

With the above questions in mind, I prepared a short five-page report from the data. My report was used initially for internal purposes and subsequently as a source of various press releases in the Philippines. (In March 1985, it was telegraphically transmitted to the Department of State, since the embassy's deputy chief of mission felt that the information would be of value to a number of U.S. government agencies.)

Meanwhile, in late October 1984, the embassy had received a telegram from the Department of State, announcing the Una Chapman Cox Sabbatical Leave Program for 1985-86. The telegram solicted proposals from middle-level and senior Foreign Service officers for a year of work, travel, lecturing, teaching, research, writing, or other activities that might prove rewarding to the grantee and further his professional development—as well as being of interest to the Foreign Service.

Stimulated both by the Bureau of the Census report and by a summary report of a conference on Asian and Pacific immigration received from the East/West Population Institute of the University of Hawaii, I prepared a proposal and submitted it to the Department of State for consideration.

My application for the sabbatical leave and Cox grant proposed a study of U.S. immigrants from the Far East to the United States—including a review of the relevant literature and available data, and a survey of a nationwide sample of the most recent immigrants from that part of the world. The proposal was approved by the Selection Committee of the Department of State; and, in late December 1984, I received word that following my transfer from Manila and return to the United States, I would be attached to the Center of Study of Foreign Affairs of the Foreign Service Institute, Department of State—but would in effect, be working independently in a U.S. location of my choosing, to conduct the proposed study.

In April-May 1985, (while still in the Far East), I traveled to Hong Kong and Seoul to consult with my colleagues serving in those diplomatic posts—and to Taipei for discussions with the staff of the American Institute in Taiwan, so as to collect statistical data and discuss my proposal with local population and immigration experts. As a result of these visit and a review of the data collected up to that point, I decided to restrict my inquiry primarily to Filipino, Korean, and Chinese immigrants—the three Asian groups that provide most of the Far Eastern immigrants to the United States.

Returning to the United States in July 1985, I started work on the project in early August. My initial priorities were to establish an office; to construct the survey questionnaire and test it; to locate, recruit, and train interviewing assistants; and to do the appropriate background research for the study.

As part of the research and to set up interviewing schedules and procedures, I traveled to Washington, D.C., New York, Houston, Chicago, Seattle, Los Angeles, and San Francisco. Interviews were subsequently conducted in all those cities, except Washington, D.C. The result of this research and of the analyses of the survey is the present book.

While any faults found in this work are mine alone, I owe a debt of gratitude to a large number of people for their help, suggestions, ideas, encouragement, and support. First and foremost, my thanks to Consul General Vernon D. McAninch, who was my superior in Manila for three years; also to Samuel Baum, the now-retired chief of the Center for International Research, U.S. Bureau of the Census; Art Cresce and Edward Ferdandez of the Bureau of the Census; Robert Warren of the Immigration and Naturalization Service at the Washington Central Office; Canta Pian of the U.S. Department of Health and Human Services; and Daniel Levine of the National Research Council. My thanks also go to Dr. Cary D. Wintz of Texas Southern University in Houston; Professor Betty Lee Sung of the City University of New York; and James Fawcett of the East/West Population Institute in Honolulu. Last but not least, I am also grateful to Sheila Butch, who typed the manuscript; David M. Glixon, for editorial assistance; my children, who—despite their youth—provided valuable comments and typed some of my correspondence; and my wife Lina, for patience in bearing with me underfoot for close to a year.

Of course, none of this would have been possible without the encouragement, counsel, and assistance of Hans Binnendjik, who is the director of the Center for the Study of Foreign Affairs, Foreign Service Institute; Joseph Montville, the research director of the Center; and Dianna Wolridge, the Center's program assistant, who cheerfully provided valuable administrative support during the course of the year.

Introduction

The history, trials, and contribution of immigrants to the United States are an integral part of the American success story. Until recently, the symbol and reality of immigration was the Statue of Liberty in New York Harbor, which was the first sight in the new continent for the overwhelming majority of European immigrants. For the past 20 years, however, the symbol has no longer been part of the reality. In the 1970's immigrants from Europe comprised only 17.8% of the total admitted to the United States during that decade—while the number arriving from other countries in the Americas was 44.1%; and those coming from Asia, 35.3%. In 1981-83—whereas European immigration had further decreased to 11.1% of the total; and that from the Americas, to 36.8%—immigration from Asia had increased to 48.9%. A shift had clearly taken place. In the 1950's, immigrants from Asia accounted for only 4.9% of the total number of immigrants arriving in the United States; they now make up close to 50%.

Sixty-one percent of all Asian immigrants during the most recent period for which data are available (1981-83) were Filipinos, Koreans, and Chinese. By January 1, 1985, an additional 769,000 persons from these countries were registered as qualified intending immigrants at U.S. consulates and embassies in Manila, Seoul, Taipei, Hong Kong, and Canton —a number that accounted for 66% of all registered intending immigrants from Asia and 32.7% of all intending immigrants worldwide.

Since Chinese, Filipinos, and Koreans are—respectively—the largest, the second largest, and the fifth largest Asian ethnic groups in the United

States—and since the number of immigrants arriving from those countries is not likely to abate in the near future—these three groups seemed to make a worthwhile subject for an in-depth look.

This study is divided into three parts. Part I briefly explores the history of the immigration debate that has taken place in our country continuously throughout its history, surveys the ebb and flow of immigration, and looks at the sociodemographic characteristics of immigrants living in the United States in 1980. Part II comprises a closer examination of the history of immigration to the United States from the Philippines, Korea, and China. Its three sections deal respectively with immigration from these three countries and the sociodemographic characteristics of immigrants who were in the United States in 1980. Most of the statistical data in this part of the book have been extracted from the "Special Tabulations on the Foreign-Born" prepared in 1984 by the U.S. Bureau of the Census from data collected in 1980. Part III of the book consists of an analysis of data collected through a survey of post-1980 immigrants from the Philippines, China, and Korea—now residing in a number of cities throughout the United States.

The major aim of this book is to lay the groundwork for future studies on these three immigrant groups. Through a better understanding of immigrants' reasons for coming to this county, the problems they face, and how they adjust and take their places in society, we shall become better equipped to understand our own history and the dynamics of life in the United States.

I

Immigrants in the United States

1

The Ebb and Flow of Immigration to the United States

Since 1820, when the U.S. government started collecting statistical data on the arrival of immigrants, more than 51,000,000 persons have entered the United States to make it their home. This number, a tremendous influx of humanity for one single country, has been unequaled by movements to any other nation in the history of mankind. While no accurate statistical data are available of the numbers that remained in the United States permanently, some demographers have estimated that about 40–42 million did so. They have also estimated that about 9–11 million returned to their own countries—or, in any case, left the United States—after a period of stay as immigrants. In a study completed in 1985, Warren and Kraly estimated that, from 1900 to 1979 (when a total of 30,450,000 immigrants arrived here), 9,492,000 non–U.S. citizens left the United States. They also estimated that, during the same period, 789,000 U.S. citizens also left the country to take up residence abroad.[1]

Thus, we see that, at least for the period 1900-79 the impact of immigration on U.S. society—whether positive or negative—cannot be accurately gauged by the raw data on the number of arrivals. The data collected by Warren and Kraly indicate that approximately 31% of immigrants subsequently left the United States. If one adds the numbers of U.S. citizens who departed to the above figures, the data indicate that, for every 100 arrivals from 1900 to 1979, there were 34 departures. Thus, at least numerically as a net addition to our population, the impact of immigration has not been as severe as it is often thought to have been.

Immigration into the United States has been divided by historians into five periods: the Colonial Period (1609–1775); the Open Door Period (1776-1881); the Regulation Period (1882-1916); the Restriction Period (1917-64); and the Liberalization Period (1965 to the present).[2]

During the Colonial Period, immigration was regulated both by the British government and by the colonists themselves. The thrust of their policies was to encourage immigration, since it provided for the quicker economic development of the new land. Additionally, the results of these policies provided a bulwark against the encroachment of the French colonists and assisted in subjugating the area's native inhabitants, the Indians. Enticement in the form of land grants, transportation, loans to purchase tools, guarantees of religious and political freedom, and other similar inducements were offered to prospective immigrants by the colonies themselves.

While accurate statistical data are not available, and whatever records the various colonies did keep on immigration have not been systematically examined and studied, the first U.S. census—that of 1790—shows a total population of 3,929,214. Classification of the surnames of all those counted by the 1790 census by the approximate national origin indicates that a commanding majority of the U.S. residents were of English extraction (60.9%). They were followed by those of Irish extraction (9.7%), Germans (8.7%), and the Scotch (8.3%). The Dutch (3.4%), French (1.7%), and Swedish (0.7%) were also significant groupings.[3]

Following the Declaration of Independence and until the 1830s, while immigration on the whole was encouraged, the number of immigrants who took up the challenge and moved to the United States was very low: A reasonable estimate has put the yearly average until 1820 at less than 10,000 per year. The low numbers partly reflected the internal economic and political struggles of the new nation, but more importantly reflected international events: Poor U.S. relations with Great Britain and the wars of the Napoleonic period in continental Europe did not encourage immigration to the United States. Starting in 1820 (the year from which data on immigrant arrivals have been kept), the ethnic origin and composition of immigrants can be gauged more accurately, and more interesting trends can be observed.

First, peaks and valley in the volume of immigration followed the health and vitality of U.S. economic development. When the economy was strong, with business booming and economic development surging, the number of immigrants increased. Conversely, in periods of economic stagnation and decline, immigration tended to decline. This trend remained true throughout the nineteenth century and the beginning of the twentieth century, until the passage of restrictive legislation in the 1920s. However, to some extent, this factor continued to be important even after the passage of restrictive entry legislation. Rather than simply not coming—in fact—in periods of economic distress in the United States, individuals left the country and took up residence abroad. During the period 1930-34 at the height of the Great Depression, only 427,000 new immigrants arrived, but 336,000 aliens and 107,000 U.S. citizens left for abroad. The net population loss was 16,000.[4]

The second important trend in immigration was that of a large number of persons from any one country coming to the United States during a specific period of time. The trend was mainly caused by general development factors within Europe and specific events within each country of emigration. General factors that affected the large emigration exodus from Europe in the nineteenth century included rapid industrialization in the northwest and central portions of the continent, a number of medical discoveries that lowered the death rate and subsequently increased the population at an alarming rate, rapid urbanization and the concomitant creation of a poor proletariat, and technological advancements such as the invention of steam power and its use on ships and trains. Because of these last inventions, distances were greatly shortened, and the cost of transportation fell to a level which was more affordable to the middle and lower social classes of Europe.

Internal occurrences that made it necessary or highly advisable to emigrate included the potato famine in Ireland, internal strife and political problems in Central Europe, pogroms in Russia, ethnic frictions within the Austro-Hungarian Empire, and grinding poverty in the south of Italy.

Even though the United States was the haven for the largest number of immigrants, the European exodus was not confined to this country: Argentina, Canada, Brazil, Australia, New Zealand, and South Africa were also the destinations of countless numbers of emigrants from the Old World. Argentina provided a home to 5,500,000 Europeans, Canada to 4,500,000, and Brazil to 4,000,000.[5]

From 1821 to 1850, Ireland took the top spot as the sending country with the largest number of immigrants coming to the United States per decade. In the 1850s, 1860s, 1870s, and 1880s, the torch was passed to Germany. In the 1890s and the first two decades of the twentieth century, Italians were the largest group, with Russians being a close second. In the following decade (1921-30), the emphasis clearly shifted—primarily because of restrictive entry legislation—and Canada sent more immigrants than any other country. By 1921, large-scale European immigration to the United States had ended. During the decade 1951-60, Germany again regained the lead as the top sending country; but the U.S. neighbor to the immediate south, Mexico, dominated the two decades of the 1960s and 1970s. However, with the passage of the 1965 Immigration and Nationality Act, emigration from Asian countries increased tremendously, and the Philippines and Korea took the second and third spots in the 1970s. The source of U.S. immigration has clearly shifted, and, in this repect, the foreseeable future belongs to Asians and Latin Americans.

Table 1.1 gives an indication of this trend. While from 1820 to 1983 71% of all immigrants were from Europe, only 17.8% originated there in the decade from 1971 to 1980; 44.1% were from the Americas, and 35.3% from Asia. Since 1980, this trend had accelerated further. In fact, during the period 1981-83, only 11.1% of all immigrants were from Europe; a full 48.9% were Asians, and 36.8% came from the Americas. Only 3.2% were from Africa, Australia, New Zealand, and other parts of Oceania.

Table 1.2, which provides data on major U.S. immigration-source countries by decades, highlights this shift even more. The United Kingdom, which has provided a steady flow of immigrants since the seventeenth century, moved from a peak number of 607,000 in the decade 1861-70 to

Table 1.1
Distribution of Immigrants by Continent of Origin

Period	Total, Worldwide	Europe No.	%	Americas 1971–80 No.	%	Asia No.	%	All Others	%
1820–1983	51,406,446	36,534,209	71.0	10,096,536	19.7	4,131,176	8	654,525	1.3
1821–1830	143,439	98,797	68.9	11,564	8	30	.02	33,048	23
1831–1840	599,125	495,681	82.7	33,424	5.6	55	.009	69,965	11.7
1841–1850	1,713,251	1,597,442	93.2	62,469	3.6	141	.08	53,999	3.2
1851–1860	2,598,214	2,452,577	94.4	74,720	2.9	41,538	1.6	29,379	1.1
1861–1870	2,314,824	2,065,141	89.2	166,607	7.2	64,759	2.8	18,317	.8
1871–1880	2,812,191	2,271,325	80.8	404,044	14.4	124,160	4.4	12,062	.4
1881–1890	5,246,613	4,735,484	90.3	426,967	8.1	69,942	1.3	14,220	.3
1891–1900	3,687,564	3,555,352	96.4	38,972	1.1	74,862	2.0	18,378	.5
1901–1910	8,795,386	8,056,040	31.6	361,888	4.1	323,543	3.7	53,915	.6
1911–1920	5,735,811	4,321,887	75.3	1,143,671	19.9	247,236	4.3	23,017	.5
1921–1930	4,107,209	1,463,194	60.0	1,516,716	36.9	112,053	2.7	15,240	.4
1931–1940	528,431	347,552	65.8	160,037	30.3	16,081	3.0	4,761	.9
1941–1950	1,035,033	621,124	60.0	354,084	34.2	32,360	3.1	26,751	2.7
1951–1960	2,514,479	1,325,727	53.1	946,944	39.6	125,249	4.9	39,559	2.4
1961–1970	3,321,677	1,123,492	33.8	1,716,376	51.7	427,642	12.9	54,169	1.6
1971–1980	4,493,314	800,368	17.8	1,982,529	44.1	1,588,178	35.3	122,229	2.8
1981–1983	1,750,494	194,736	11.1	644,419	36.8	855,335	48.9	56,004	3.2

Note: From 1820 to 1867, totals represent alien passengers arrived; from 1868 to 1981 and 1895 to 1897, immigrant aliens arrived; from 1892 to 1894 and 1898 to 1983, immigrant aliens admitted.

Source: U.S. Department of Justice, *1983 Statistical Yearbook of the U.S. Immigration and Naturalization Service* (Washington, D.C.: Government Printing Office, 1984).

Table 1.2
Selected Major Immigrant Sending Countries (in thousands)

	United Kingdom	Italy	Ireland	Germany	Austria-Hungary	Russia	Scandinavian Countries	Mexico	Caribbean Countries	China	Canada	Korea*	Philippines
1821–1830	25	--	51	7	--	--	--	5	4	--	2	*	--
1831–1840	76	2	207	152	--	--	2	7	12	--	14	--	--
1841–1850	267	2	781	436	--	--	131	3	14	--	42	--	--
1851–1860	424	9	914	952	--	--	25	3	11	41	59	--	--
1861–1870	607	12	436	787	8	3	126	2	9	64	154	--	--
1871–1880	548	56	437	718	73	39	243	5	14	123	384	--	--
1881–1890	807	307	655	1453	354	213	656	2	29	62	393	--	--
1891–1900	272	652	388	505	593	505	372	1	33	15	4	--	--
1901–1910	526	2046	333	341	2145	1597	505	50	108	21	179	--	--
1911–1920	341	1110	146	144	896	921	204	219	123	21	742	--	--
1921–1930	340	455	210	412	64	62	215	459	75	30	925	--	--
1931–1940	32	68	11	114	11	1	13	22	16	5	109	--	--
1941–1950	139	58	20	227	28	1	29	61	50	17	172	--	--
1951–1960	204	185	48	478	104	1	59	300	123	10	378	6	19
1961–1970	215	214	33	191	26	2	46	454	470	35	413	35	98
1971–1980	137	129	11	74	16	39	18	604	741	125	170	268	354
1981–1983	44	12	3	20	3	30	6	216	214	105	33	98	130

*Data not kept before 1951.

Source: U.S. Department of Justice, 1983 Statistical Yearbook of the U.S. Immigration and Naturalization Service (Washington, D.C.: Government Printing Office, 1984).

137,000 in the decade 1971-80. Italy, which provided more than 2 million immigrants in the decade 1901-10, sent fewer in the 1970's than the United Kingdom—129,000. The same shift is evident in the data for the other European countries highlighted in this table; stabilized population, improved standards of living, and peace after World War II have kept Europeans at home. Immigrants from Europe are now likely to be the adventurous, those who are wishing to make a clean break with the past, entrepreneurs or businessmen who are transferred to the United States, and a few who are joining close family relatives.

On the other hand, Mexico and the Caribbean basin countries now provide an inordinately large percentage of immigrants: In the decade 1971-80, out of close to 4,500,000 total immigrants, 1,350,000 were from Mexico and the Caribbean. During 1981-83, this area accounted for 26% of all legal U.S. immigrants.

Some Asian countries show the same pattern of increase: The Philippines, Korea, and China—which, as late as the 1951–60 decade, accounted for only 2% of all U.S. immigrants—sent 19% of all legal immigrants entering the United States in the 1970s.

The increase from Latin America is primarily due to political developments in the area, major economic problems resulting in a drop in the standard of living in some cases, fast population growth, and the area's relative proximity to the United States. In the case of Asian countries, the major factor leading to immigration increase has been the Immigration and Nationality Act of 1965—which, by abolishing the previous discriminatory practices based on place of birth and national origin, has made Asians a major component of the immigration mix. Of course, rapid population growth, U.S. foreign-policy objectives, and a relatively low standard of living in the area have also encouraged emigration from Asia.

The effect of this altered composition of the immigrant stock is so recent that no definitive evaluation has yet been made. However, it is evident that by adding diversity, the new immigrants may be making the United States culturally richer and—it is hoped—more tolerant of different looks, points of view, diverse educational standards, and perspectives on life. At the same time, the newest immigrants present challenges to U.S. society, both to the different levels of government and to individuals: how to bring them into the mainstream of U.S. life and, in a process of give-and-take, use their energies and talents for the good of all U.S. residents—citizens and noncitizens alike.

2

Sociodemographic Characteristics of U.S. Immigrants

In analyzing U.S. immigrants, both those who came in the past and those who arrived more recently, several factors appear to be important: their education, occupation, family size, geographic distribution in the country, and earnings. It may also be significant to look at their impact in relieving population pressures in the sending country, and conversely, their effect on population increase in the United States.

EFFECTS OF MIGRATION ON THE POPULATION OF SENDING COUNTRIES

While many studies have been conducted on the impact of immigrants on U.S. society, limited attention has been paid to the effect of migration in relieving population pressures in the sending countries.

Generally, the emigration rate from a particular country tends to be related to the level of economic development within the country and the rate of natural increase of the population. These factors tended to be particularly true during the nineteenth century when emigration from one's country and entry into another country were fairly free; it is no longer true in the twentieth century. Government restrictions in both sending and receiving countries regulate the flow and composition of the movement of people, both qualitatively and quantitatively.

In the ninteenth century, however, the impact of immigration in relieving population pressures was significant for a number of sending countries. Ireland is the classic example: In the period from 1861 to 1910, an average of 11,400 persons per year emigrated from Ireland to the United States. The exodus reached its apogee in 1851, when close to 30,000 persons per million of the population of Ireland emigrated to the United States. Similarly, during the period 1901–10, Italians emigrated to the United States at the rate of 10,800 per million of population in Italy. Norwegians did so in the 1880s at the rate of 9,600 per million of population.[1] The above rates of emigration are thought to have had an impact in relieving both economic and population pressures in the sending countries.

But in 1980, the rate of emigration to the United States and its effect in relieving internal population and economic pressures on the sending countries were negligible: Just very small countries with a minute population but high population densities have had high rates of emigration to the United States. Only some of the small countries in the Caribbean islands have exceeded an immigration rate of 0.6% of their population per year.[2]

Thus, we see that the impact of emigration to the United States in relieving population and economic pressures is marginal for most countries, at best; however, when compared with emigration (both permanent and temporary) to a number of countries, it does help. This appears to be the case for the Philippines, which—while sending only an average of 40,000 immigrants per year to the United States—sends a much larger number of temporary workers to the Middle East. The remittances from these workers have a very clear impact on the economy of the Philippines, since the official remittances add up to about $1 billion annually. South Korea, on the other hand, benefits from its immigrants in the United States because they serve as a conduit for the enhancement of Korean foreign policy and trade.

In summary, while immigration appears to help a country with a rapidly increasing population and economic problems, its effects in alleviating population pressures are minimal—if noticeable at all.

IMPACT OF IMMIGRATION ON THE POPULATION OF THE UNITED STATES

While it is obvious that immigrants to the United States increase its total population, the impact is less predictable, since a number of variables must be considered: the country's total population, its rate of net increase, and the rate of net increase of the immigrants themselves. Some scholars have argued that, because of the low fertility of native-born Americans in the 1980s and the relatively young age of the new immigrants, immigration is a significant contributor to future population growth and may, in fact—if it continues unabated—literally change the complexion of U.S. society.

Historically, as shown on Table 2.1, the percentage of recent immigrants

Table 2.1
U.S. Population and Immigrants (in thousands)

Decade	Immigrants	U.S. Population At Decade's End	Immigrants as Percentage of Total U.S. Population
1821–1830	143	12,866	1.1
1831–1840	599	17,069	3.5
1841–1850	1,713	23,192	7.3
1851–1860	2,598	31,443	8.3
1861–1870	2,313	39,818	5.8
1871–1880	2,812	50,156	5.6
1881–1890	5,247	62,948	8.3
1891–1900	3,688	75,995	4.9
1901–1910	8,795	91,972	9.6
1911–1920	5,736	105,711	5.4
1921–1930	4,107	122,775	3.3
1931–1940	528	131,669	.4
1941–1950	1,035	151,326	.7
1951–1960	2,515	179,323	1.4
1961–1970	3,322	203,302	1.6
1971–1980	4,493	226,546	2.0

Sources: U.S. Department of Justice, *1983 Statistical Yearbook of the U.S. Immigration and Naturalization Service* (Washington, D.C.: Governement Printing Office, 1984); U.S. Bureau of the Census, *Historical Statistics of the United States* (Washington, D.C.: Government Printing Office, 1976) and *1980 Census of the Population* (Washington, D.C.: Government Printing Office, 1981).

in relation to the total U.S. population has not been large: In the decade when the largest number of immigrants arrived (1901-10), their number constituted only 9.6% of the total population of the United States at the end of that decade. The current rate of immigration is approximately 2% per decade. In 1983—when the U.S. population was 234.5 million—560,000 immigrants were admitted, at a decennial rate of 2.3% of the total U.S. population.

A different perspective in assessing the impact of the number of immigrants in U.S. society can be gained from data collected by the U.S. Bureau of the Census in 1980, a summary of which is given in Table 2.2.

Table 2.2
**Foreign-Born in the United States in 1980, by Continent and Period of
Immigration (in percentages)**

Continent	Total	Year of Immigration				
		%	1975-1980	1970-74	1960-1969	1959 or earlier
Total Foreign-Born	14,079,906	100	23.7	15.8	22.3	38.2
Africa	189,723	1.4	43.9	21.2	19.3	15.7
Asia	2,539,777	18.0	47.0	22.4	18.1	12.5
Europe	5,149,355	36.6	9.1	7.2	18.1	65.6
Latin America	4,372,487	31.0	29.2	24.3	30.4	16.1
North America	853,427	6.1	10.0	5.4	20.2	64.4
Oceania	77,577	0.6	36.6	16.7	19.5	27.7
Other areas	887,560	6.3	22.0	13.8	21.4	42.8

Source: U.S. Bureau of the Census, *1980 Census of the Population* (Washington, D.C.: Government Printing Office, 1981).

These data indicate that, in that year—out of a total U.S. population of 226,545,805—there were 14,079,906 (or 6.2%) foreign born. What is more startling is that 23.7% of the foreign-born had come to the United States within the past five years (1975-80)—compared with 15.8% during the previous five years (1970-74).

The long-term effect of the changes in the composition of the immigrant stock becomes more evident when the total number of the foreign-born is subdivided by continent of origin and year of immigration: Only 16.3% of the European immigrants had come to the United States during the period 1979-80. In contrast, 69.4% of the Asians and 53.5% of the Latin Americans had come here during the same period.

Because of the declining natural rate of increase in the U.S. population, the effect of immigration on population increase in the United States is becoming more pronounced. As late as 1960, net immigration constituted only 12.6% of the total natural rate of increase. However, because of a decreased birth rate and a stationary death rate, the immigration component of U.S. population increase is becoming greater: By 1970, it was 24.2%; and it has been estimated that, by the year 2000, it will be 38.6%.[3]

EDUCATION OF THE FOREIGN-BORN

Popular myth has it that immigrants to the United States have traditionally been largely illiterate and that their education, if any, has not been as extensive as that of native-born Americans.

Since 1917, when an entry bar against the admission of persons unable to read or write some language was passed by Congress over President Wilson's veto, all persons immigrating to the United States (with a few rare exceptions) have been literate. Otherwise, they would have been denied a visa and entry into the country.

But even in the case of immigrants who entered the United States prior to 1917, the available evidence indicates that a large majority could read and write. Data collected by the Dillingham Immigration Commission and published in 1911 indicates that, in fact, only 26.7% of the immigrants entering in the period 1899-1910 were illiterate. Of course, there were wide variations among the different ethnic groups, with the illiteracy rate ranging from 68.2% for Portuguese immigrants to 0.4% among the Scandinavian. Generally, the immigrants from southeastern Europe had a higher percentage of illiteracy, a factor that was used by restrictionists in passing, first, the literacy test requirement for entry and, subsequently, the various discriminatory quota laws.

Additional data collected by the Bureau of the Census for the decennial census indicate that, even though some immigrants may have been unable to read and write when they first arrived in the United States, they soon learned to speak English in order to be able to function. In fact, census data for the period 1890–1930 show that, while 15.6% of all foreign-born could not speak English in 1890, the rate was down to 12.2% by 1900. Because of the large influx of immigrants during the following decade, the rate of illiteracy among foreign-born was 22.8% in 1910. However, it had decreased to 11% by 1920, and had fallen further to 6.6% in 1930.[4] Detailed data from the 1980 census show that the foreign population are not far behind the native-born in terms of educational achievement. In fact, 15.8% of the former had completed at least four years of college, and 53.1% were high school graduates. Comparable figures for the U.S. population as a whole are 16.3% for college graduates and 67.7% for high school graduates.

Table 2.3 graphically shows the variations in education achievement among the foreign-born who came to the United States from different parts of the world and were in the United States in 1980. The Asians and Africans have more than twice the number of college graduates as the U.S. population at large, while European and Latin American percentages of college graduates are below those of the U.S. population. Detailed data for specific countries are even more interesting, since the number who have four or more years of college is above the 50% mark for the foreign-born from several countries. Kenya, Malawi, Tanzania, Zambia, Egypt, Taiwan,

Table 2.3
Educational Achievements of Foreign-Born in the United States in 1980
(in percentages)

	Persons Over Age 25, by Area	
	Percent High School Graduates	Percent Completed 4 or more yrs. college
Native-Born	67.7	16.3
Foreign-Born	53.1	15.8
Africa	81.9	38.7
Asia	73.0	35.9
Europe	51.4	12.3
Latin America	41.0	8.9
North America	61.8	14.3
Oceania	75.5	22.3
Others	50.0	11.8

Source: U.S. Bureau of the Census, *1980 Census of the Population* (Washington, D.C.: Government Printing Office, 1981).

Bangladesh, India, Nepal, and Pakistan are in this category. Surprisingly, the European sending country with the highest proportion of immigrants who were college graduates is Bulgaria with 27.9%. These data indicate the higher value placed on education by certain societies, the dearth of professional opportunities in some of the sending countries, and the high rate of nonreturn to the home country of persons from the Third World who obtained their college education in the United States.

GEOGRAPHIC DISTRIBUTION OF THE FOREIGN-BORN IN THE UNITED STATES

The geographic distribution of immigrants in the United States has been primarily affected by two historical movements. The first—the process of westward expansion—practically ended at the close of the nineteenth century; the second—the process of urbanization—continues to this day.

During the nineteenth century, approximately one-third of all immigrants appear to have settled in rural areas in the western and north-central part of the country. Two-thirds concentrated in the cities—forming the great pool of comparatively cheap, unskilled labor that provided the human energy necessary for the development of the U.S. industrial society. In 1890, when the foreign-born represented approximately one-third of the total U.S. population, 53% of the immigrants resided in an urban setting.[5]

The process of urbanization has continued from its inception in the mid-nineteenth century to the present—attracting a vast majority of immigrants to states that have large population centers and are generally highly urbanized.

Table 2.4 shows in some detail the distribution of the majority of foreign-born in ten selected states of the union. In 1980, these states had a total population of more than 121 million, or close to 54% of the total U.S. population. Yet, they were the home of more than 11 million, or close to 73%, of all foreign-born residing in the United States.

California, for example—with 10.5% of the total population of the United States—had 25.4% of all foreign-born, including 34.5% of all Asians and 36.6% of all Latin Americans. The two top states where Asians resided were California and New York. Latin Americans made their home primarily in California, New York, Texas, and Florida. Europeans were preeminent in New York, California, Illinois, and New Jersey.

Some general conclusions can be drawn from these data: (1) Immigrants tend to settle where other immigrants of the same sending country already reside. (2) Immigrants tend to settle in an area closest to their U.S. port of entry. (3) Economic opportunity and climate also appear to have some influence over the immigrant's choice of residence.

OCCUPATIONS OF FOREIGN-BORN

Another myth about immigrants has been that most of them were peasants who had been squeezed out of their land and that they moved to

Table 2.4
Selected States of Residence of Foreign-Born in the United States in 1980

Place of Residence	Total State Population	% of U.S. pop.	Total Foreign-Born Population	Total Foreign Born				
				% of Total State Pop.	% of Total Foreign-Born Pop.	Asians % of total in state	Latin Americans % of total in state	Europeans % of Total in State
California	23,667,902	10.5	3,580,033	15.1	25.4	34.5	36.6	13.4
New York	17,558,072	7.8	2,388,938	13.6	17.0	11.4	16.5	21.7
Florida	9,746,324	4.3	1,058,732	10.9	7.5	2.2	12.3	5.9
Texas	14,229,131	6.3	856,213	6.0	6.1	4.6	12.5	2.0
Illinois	11,426,518	5.0	823,696	7.2	6.9	5.8	5.2	7.1
New Jersey	7,364,823	3.3	757,822	10.3	5.4	3.8	4.2	8.0
Massachusetts	5,737,037	2	500,982	8.7	3.6	2.0	1.1	5.5
Michigan	9,262,078	4	417,152	4.5	3.0	3.0	.5	4.1
Pennsylvania	11,863,895	5.2	401,016	3.4	2.8	2.4	.6	5.2
Ohio	10,797,630	4.8	302,185	2.8	2.1	1.3	.4	3.8

Source: U.S. Bureau of the Census, "Foreign-Born Immigrants—Tabulations from the 1980 U.S. Census of the Population and Housing," mimeographed report, Washington, D.C., October 1984.

the United States for that reason. In fact, the vast majority of the nineteenth-century immigrants who reported an occupation at the time of their arrival were general laborers or in domestic service. On the average, not more than one-fourth were agricultural workers. Professionals generally averaged less than 2% of the total, between 1820 and 1920.[6]

Following passage of the 1965 Immigration and Nationality Act, an influx of Asian professionals came to the United States—bringing the average number of immigrant professionals very close to one-fourth of all immigrants during the decade and creating what became known as the "brain drain": highly educated and skilled individuals emigrating from their countries. This trend has now slowed down somewhat, since the overwhelming majority of immigrant visas are now being used by persons coming to the United States in the family reunification categories. In other words, relatives of the professionals who came to the United States shortly after passage of the 1965 act are now using most of the available visas; most enter not primarily because of their skills, but on the basis of their relationship to U.S. citizens or permanent residents.

The continuous changes and upgrading in the occupational qualities of immigrants can be seen by examining data collected by the U.S. Bureau of the Census and the U.S. Immigration and Naturalization Service. In the year 1900—of all immigrants reporting an occupation—only 0.8% were professionals or technical workers and a full 52.4% were general laborers; by 1960, 17.9% were professionals, and only 10.5% laborers. By 1977, the percentage of professionals had risen to 23.8%, and that of laborers dropped again to 6.5%.[7]

An additional dimension to this picture is provided by data on the foreign-born collected by the U.S. Bureau of the Census in 1980. Such data show that the percentage of persons 16 years of age or over who were employed in professional specialty occupations was about the same as that of the U.S. native population: 12.3% both for the U.S. native-born and the U.S. population at large, and 12% for the foreign-born.[8] More detailed data on the occupations of the foreign-born who entered the United States between 1970 and 1980 are given in Table 2.5. We see from this table that a larger percentage of Asian immigrants are in the managerial and professional category than are their U.S. counterparts. However, immigrants from North, Central, and South America brought down the percentage for all immigrants admitted during this period.

The data also indicate that the immigrant labor market for most groups is a dual one with a good percentage of persons employed at the top of the occupation scale and also with a large number employed in occupations where their earning power is limited. Obviously this split labor market has the tendency to decrease the median income level of all immigrant households.

Table 2.5
Major Occupations of Foreign-Born Admitted from 1970 to 1980

Occupation	U.S.	% U.S.	Total Foreign-Born	% Foreign-Born %	Europe %	Asia %	North & Central America %	South America %
U.S.-Employed over age 16	97,639,355	100	2,541,443	100	100	100	100	100
Managers and Professional Specialties	22,151,648	22.7	449,006	17.7	22.7	27.6	7.2	15.5
Technical, Sales and Administrative Support	29,593,506	30.3	533,262	21.0	19.3	28.2	14.4	23.7
Serving Occupations	12,629,425	12.9	458,692	18.0	16.2	17.0	19.7	18.5
Farming, Forestry, and Fishing	2,811,258	2.9	105,057	4.1	1.7	1.1	8.2	.5
Precision Production Crafts, and Repairs	12,594,175	12.9	300,652	11.8	15.1	8.5	13.5	12.3
Operators, Fabricators and Laborers	17,859,343	18.3	694,774	27.4	25.0	17.5	37.0	29.5

Source: U.S. Bureau of the Census, *1980 Census of the Population, U.S. Summary* (Washington, D.C.: Government Printing Office, 1981), pp. 1-13, table 255.

EARNINGS OF FOREIGN-BORN

It stands to reason that the earnings of immigrants should be lower than those of native-born Americans. In fact, many of them arrive in the United States with limited or no knowledge of the English language and are confronted with a new world and a myriad of problems. For most of them, starting life in a new country is like being born again: One must relearn the do's and don't's of society; learn how to find and keep a job; and, in general, cope with the hundreds of daily problems that are not problems at all to the native-born, but second nature. Given this set of initial handicaps, it is indeed amazing that immigrants do as well as they do.

Traditionally, immigrants have been relegated to the performance of tasks that pay a lower wage and require hard labor and stamina. In the nineteenth century and the first half of the twentieth, they invariably ended up laboring in the fields; building the railroads of the country and the subways of the cities; and constructing the public works, roads, and buildings of cities and towns.

In the past 20 years, this traditional picture has changed: While most immigrants still occupy low-paying positions upon their arrival in the United States, a significant number do not. Therefore, the income of the group as a whole is not significantly lower than the median income of U.S. workers. However, it must be kept in mind that tremendous variations exist—both among immigrant groups from different countries and within subgroups of immigrants from the same country. The dual occupational market is a reality obscured by statistics: The medical doctor from India who earns more than $100,000 per year has nothing in common with the Mexican laborer picking oranges in California, who has an income of less than $10,000 per year.

In 1980, the median household income for the entire U.S. population was $16,841. For the households of native-born Americans, it was $17,010, and for the households of the foreign-born, $14,588.

But the *distribution* of household incomes of immigrants who came to the United States between 1970 and 1980 is more meaningful than the *median* household income (Table 2.6). Among Asian immigrant households, 47.6% had incomes below $15,000—compared with 44.4% of U.S. households at large. At the other end of the scale, 27.7% of Asian households had an income over $25,000—compared with 29% of U.S. households.

Immigrants from North and Central America are economically worse off than any other group: A full 61% of these households have incomes below $15,000, while only 13.9% have incomes over $25,000.

However, the above analysis includes both immigrants who have been in the United States for a full decade and those who have been in the United States for only a few months; thus, it does not reflect an accurate picture of the immigrants' economic progress. By analyzing data from the 1970 census, Barry Chiswick—an economist who has extensively studied and written on this subject—ascertained that foreign-born men reach equality of earnings with native U.S. males in a little more than ten years, and tend to

Table 2.6
Household Income of Foreign-Born Admitted from 1970 to 1980

Income	Total U.S.	%	Total Foreign-Born	%	Europe %	Asia %	North & Central America %	South America %
Households	80,467,247	100	1,596,929	100	—	—	—	—
Less than $5,000	10,663,441	13.2	276,929	17.3	10.8	18.4	17.0	16.4
$5,000 – $7,499	6,439,024	8.0	144,801	9.1	6.2	7.3	11.4	9.3
$7,500 – $9,999	6,333,385	7.9	145,396	9.1	6.7	7.2	11.4	9.5
$10,000 – $14,999	12,342,073	15.3	280,94	17.6	15.0	14.6	21.2	20.0
$15,000 – $19,999	11,379,049	14.2	230,346	14.4	15.8	13.1	15.3	15.4
$20,000 – $24,999	10,004,409	12.4	173,873	10.9	13.8	11.6	9.8	10.5
$25,000 – $34,999	12,659,261	15.7	190,805	12.0	16.7	14.4	8.7	11.0
$35,000 – $49,999	6,954,720	8.7	96,189	6.0	9.2	8.2	3.5	4.9
$50,000 or more	3,692,065	4.6	57,704	3.6	5.8	5.1	1.7	3.0

Source: U.S. Bureau of the Census, *1980 Census of the Population, U.S. Summary* (Washington, D.C.: Government Printing Office, 1981), table 225.

subsequently surpass them in earning power. He also found that the foreign-born tend to surpass the income level of the native-born of the same ancestry after a period of 15–18 years in the United States.[9]

A more recent study by Seghal, who analyzed 1982-83 data from the Current Population Survey of the Bureau of the Census, confirms Chiswick's findings. The study revealed that the median earnings of foreign-born workers was similar to that of the native-born ($10,789 versus $11,250), and that the family income distribution was substantially the same for both groups. However, this study also revealed that the recent immigrants—those who arrived in the United States in 1980 and 1981—had higher unemployment rates and, when employed, generally held less remunerative jobs; therefore, their income was lower than that of U.S.-born workers of the earlier immigrants. On the other hand, immigrants who had arrived in the United States before 1960 or were naturalized as U.S. citizens had higher earnings than the native-born Americans, the later immigrant arrivals, and the immigrants who had not been naturalized.[10]

David North, who studied a group of 1970 immigrants for a number of years, reported that many immigrants generally obtained employment in occupations requiring lower skills than the jobs they had held in their country of origin. However, after a few years, the number of professionals in the group increased; and, by 1977, the percentage of such immigrants who were business owners, professionals, or managers was higher than the proportion among native-born Americans.[11]

In conclusion, it can be safely stated that, in general, immigrants do well economically in the United States—particularly, if they are educated. In such cases, their economic mobility is rapid; and, within a few years, they are on a par with or surpass the income of native-born Americans.

USE OF SOCIAL SERVICES AND PERCENTAGE BELOW POVERTY LEVEL

One of the controversies regarding recent immigrants concerns their utilization of social-services programs and their cost to society.

Use of such programs depends basically on several variables: (1) the legal status of the immigrant in the United States (immigrant or refugee); (2) the societal mores and traditions in the immigrant's country of origin; (3) the amount of knowledge about such programs available to immigrants; and (4) their degree of need—for example—the incidence of poverty in their midst.

While no definitive study has been completed on this subject, refugees—who are sponsored for entry and resettlement assistance by social and religious welfare organizations—generally make substantial use of social services. Legal immigrants do not do so, apparently for a number of reasons. They are too proud, are generally willing to accept employment that native-born Americans would not accept, may lack knowledge concerning their eligibility for social services or assistance, and use the kinship network for help.

Available evidence confirms this. The Seghal study found that 13.9% of all U.S.-born respondents had been recipients of selected government benefits in 1982, while the percentage of all foreign-born who had received the same benefits was 12.8. The percentage of foreign-born receiving such benefits tended to be inversely proportional to their length of residence in the United States: Immigrants who had arrived before 1960 had a rate of 8.7%, those who had come between 1960 and 1969 a rate of 14.5%; and the latest arrivals—those of 1980 and 1981—a rate of 17.5%.[12]

Distaste for the use of social services, limited knowledge of their availability, extensive use of social kinship networks, and the ability to survive on lower incomes than native-born Americans is evident when one compares the percentage of families with income below the poverty level with the percentage of those using social services. In 1979, 9.6% of families in the United States had an income below the poverty level; but, for foreign-born who had immigrated between 1970 and 1980, the percentage more than doubled: 20.7%. Yet the percentage of foreign-born using social services or getting assistance was not double that of the U.S. population at large. As a matter of fact, it was lower: 12.8% for the foreign-born versus 13.8% for the total U.S. population.

Wide fluctuations also exist in the percentage of foreign-born families from different continents who had immigrated between 1970 and 1980 and whose income in 1980 was below poverty level. This level was 10.1% for the Europeans, 19.2% for Asians, 25.1% for those born in North and Central America, and 18.4% for those from South America.[13]

The foreign-born, although they have a larger number of families below the poverty level, were not any more likely to use social services or obtain government assistance than the general U.S. population.

SEX RATIO AND AGE DISTRIBUTION OF FOREIGN-BORN

While the overall sex ratio of the U.S. population in 1980 was 94.5 males to 100 females, the ratio for foreign-born who had entered the country between 1970 and 1980 was 87.8 males to 100 females. The ratio varied according to the continent of origin: For Africa, it was 136.8 males to 100 females; for Asia; 96.5 males to 100 females; for North America, 70.5 males to 100 females; for Europe, 78.1 males to 100 females; for Latin America, 97.6 males to 100 females; and, for Oceania, 74.3 males to 100 females. These statistics suggest that, apart from Africa, females are more likely to immigrate than males.

The age distribution of those who immigrated to the United States between 1970 and 1980, as compared with that of the U.S. population at large, is given in Table 2.7. It shows that the foreign-born population who arrived

Table 2.7
Age Distribution of U.S. Population and Foreign-Born Who Immigrated
between 1970 and 1980 (in percentages)

		Percentages				
Age	U.S.	Total Foreign-Born	Asia	Europe	North and Central America	South America
Under 5	7.2	4.0	3.8	3.5	3.7	3.6
5–14	15.4	16.2	16.4	14.9	17.0	14.0
15–24	18.7	24.2	20.6	17.5	29.8	24.5
25–44	27.7	42.2	45.7	45.0	38.0	45.1
45–64	19.6	10.2	10.3	13.8	8.9	10.5
65 and over	11.3	3.2	3.2	4.3	2.6	2.3
Median Age	30.0	26.9	27.9	29.9 *	25.3	28.4 *

Source: U.S. Bureau of the Census, *1980 Census of the Population, U.S. Summary* (Washington, D.C.: Government Printing Office, 1981).

in the United States between 1970 and 1980 included a smaller percentage of children than the U.S. population at large. At the same time, the number of elderly was considerably lower—less than one-third of the U.S. percentage. The proportion of foreign-born in the age group between 15 and 64— the productive years—was much larger than that of the U.S. total population: 66.1% for the total U.S. population versus 76.6% for the foreign-born. Thus, three-fourths of all immigrants who came during the 1970's were of working age in 1980, as compared with the two-thirds of the U.S. population at large.

MARITAL STATUS

Several interesting factors are noticeable when one examines the data given in Table 2.8. Compared with native U.S. males and females, respectively, a smaller proportion of the immigrant males arriving between 1970 and 1980 were married, and a larger proportion of females.

The percentage of divorced immigrants was about half of that in the total U.S. population. Similarly, the proportion of widowed immigrants was approximately half of that in the total U.S. population. The number of widowed U.S. females, because of their statistically longer life span, was found to be 500% higher than that of U.S. males. For immigrants who

Table 2.8
Marital Status of U.S. Population and of Immigrants over Age 15 Who Entered the United States from 1970 to 1980

| Marital Status | U.S. Males | U.S. Females | Foreign–Born Who Entered U.S. from 1970 to 1980 | | | | | | | | | |
			All Immigrants Males	All Immigrants Females	Europe Males	Europe Females	Asia Males	Asia Females	North & Central America Males	North & Central America Females	South America Males	South America Females
Single	29.7	22.8	38.0	25.3	28.7	17.6	39.3	22.9	33.0	23.4	37.1	28.6
Married	60.6	55.2	56.4	62.3	62.2	70.3	56.3	67.0	55.5	57.5	55.7	56.3
Separated	1.9	2.6	2.2	3.2	1.7	1.3	1.3	1.7	2.3	4.6	3.2	4.3
Widowed	2.5	13.3	.9	5.5	1.0	6.1	.9	6.0	.7	4.5	.8	4.8
Divorced	5.3	7.1	2.5	3.7	3.4	4.1	1.6	2.4	2.3	4.0	3.2	4.8

Source: U.S. Bureau of the Census, *1980 Census of the Population, U.S. Summary* (Washington, D.C.: Government Printing Office, 1981).

arrived in the U.S. between 1970 and 1980, the number of widowed females was 600% higher than that of widowed males.

FERTILITY RATES AND FAMILY SIZE

The fertility rate of foreign-born women over the age of 15 who immigrated to the United States between 1970 and 1980 was found to be higher than the U.S. average for younger women, and slightly lower for older women. The same was true for foreign-born women who had immigrated to the United States prior to 1960. Table 2.9 gives a summary of the fertility rates for foreign-born females over age 15 who came to the United States between 1970 and 1980.

Family size—another demographic characteristic—is also slightly higher for the foreign-born. Whereas the average size of the U.S. family in 1980 was found to be 3.27 persons, that of the foreign-born who had immigrated

Table 2.9
Number of Children Born to U.S.- and Foreign-Born Women over Age 15 as of 1980 (per 1,000 women)

| Age | U.S. | Foreign–Born Who Immigrated Between 1970 and 1980 | | | | | Foreign–Born Who immigrated before 1960 |
		Total	Europe	Asia	North & South		
15–24	317	429	347	271	566	253	330
25–34	1,476	1,513	1,283	1,262	1,976	1,271	1,626
35–44	2,639	2,571	1,990	2,285	3,338	2,223	2,478

Source: U.S. Bureau of the Census, *1980 Census of the Population, U.S. Summary.* (Washington, D.C.: Government Printing Office, 1981).

between 1970 and 1980 was 3.81 persons, and that of foreign-born who had immigrated before 1960 was 3.30. By continent of origin, for those who immigrated between 1970 and 1980, the number of persons in the average family was as follows:

Europe 3.46

Asia 3.84

North and Central America 4.04

South America 3.58

These data suggest that immigrants—despite the propensity to have many children and consequently a larger family in their country of origin— tend to conform to the norm once they have settled in the United States, and limit their family size. The necessity for spouses to be employed and the cost of educating children are apparently having an effect on the family size of the foreign-born.

It also appears that the direct relationship between education, family size, and income applies to immigrants just as it does to native-born Americans. An interesting example is the case of Mexican immigrants: 32.9% have had less than five years of schooling, only 17% are high school graduates, and only 2.7% have had four or more years of college. The median family size of Mexican immigrants is 4.39 persons, and their median family income is $11,782—way below the median family income for all foreign-born families.

DEGREE OF ACCULTURATION

Two measureable indicators of the degree of acculturation of foreign-born who were residing in the United States in 1980 are the ability to speak English and the degree to which persons who have met the residency requirements for naturalization as U.S. citizens have done so. While spouses of U.S. citizens may apply for naturalization after three years of permanent residence, and children may be naturalized together with their parents, the majority of immigrants must wait until they have completed five years of residence before applying for naturalization.

The percentage of English-speaking foreign-born in the United States in 1980 is shown in Table 2.10. As the table makes clear, about two-thirds of all immigrants who arrived in the United States between 1970 and 1980 were found to speak English well or very well. This percentage was a little more than half for immigrants from North and Central America—principally because of the low level of English language skills of Mexican immigrants.

The data on naturalization given in Table 2.11 show that 66.2% of all immigrants who, by 1980, had been in the United States five years or longer

Table 2.10
English-Language Proficiency of Foreign-Born over Age 5, as of 1980
(in percentages)

Language Proficiency	Foreign Born Who Immigrated between 1970–1980				Foreign Born Who Immigrated Before 1970
	All	Europe	Asia	North & Central America	South America	All

Language Proficiency	All	Europe	Asia	North & Central America	South America	All
Speak English well or very well	66.1	76.3	74.8	52.1	67.8	85.7
Speak English not Very well or not at all	33.3	23.7	25.2	47.9	32.2	14.3

Source: U.S. Bureau of the Census, *1980 Census of the Population, U.S. Summary,* (Washington, D.C.: Government Printing Office, 1981), table 255(A).

were naturalized as citizens. The percentage of naturalization by selected continents indicates that, in this matter, Asians were more likely to become citizens than immigrants from other continents, once they had met the residency requirements. In fact, only 53% of the Asians residing in the United States in 1980 had immigrated prior to 1975; yet, 65.7% were naturalized by that date. On the other hand, 90.9% of the Europeans residing in the United States in 1980 had arrived before 1975; but only 79.5% were naturalized citizens in 1980. The poorest showing in this respect was made by immigrants from the Americas: For North and Central America, the percentage naturalized was 46.7; for South America, it was 42.8.

Table 2.11
Naturalization of Foreign-Born in 1980

	Totals	Europe	Asia	North & Central America	South America
Foreign Born	14,079,906	5,149,592	2,533,777	4,664,903	561,011
Immigrated prior to 1975	10,744,822	4,679,925	1,345,340	3,486,962	378,025
% who immigrated prior to 1975	76.3	90.9	53.0	74.7	67.3
% of those immigrating prior to 1975 Naturalized	66.2	79.5	65.7	46.7	42.8

Source: U.S. Bureau of the Census, *1980 Census of the Population, U.S. Summary* (Washington, D.C.: Government Printing Office, 1981), table 254.

CONCLUSIONS

While it cannot be denied that immigration is contributing and will continue to contribute a larger component of the population growth of the United States, the pessimistic observation that the country is being overrun by foreigners who will change U.S. society and impose unbearable burdens to its social and cultural life does not appear to stand up to careful scrutiny.

In fact, immigrants still contribute a very minor percentage of population growth; other countries, such as Canada take a larger percentage of immigrants every year—in relation to their population size—than the United States does. Furthermore, compared with the rest of the world, the United States does not appear to be an overpopulated country: U.S. population density of 65 persons per square mile compares very favorably with a density of 91 persons per square mile for the entire world. The annual rate of U.S. population growth is also lower than that of the entire world: 1% per year versus 1.7% for the world.

While fears have been expressed that continued population growth in the United States will accelerate the depletion of its natural resources, the answer to this concern does not lie in restricting population growth or immigration, but in managing such resources better and in avoiding their unnecessary use and waste. If pursued consistently, better management of resources works: Witness the efforts in the last decade to cut energy consumption—particularly, imported oil.

By all the data examined, immigrants do not appear to be a burden to U.S. society. On the average, they are either as well as or better educated than native-born Americans, do not use social services or obtain benefits from government programs any more than U.S. citizens do, and are as hardworking and productive as native-born Americans—if not more so. Indeed, if the immigrants were not available to fill certain low-paying, entry-level jobs, the results would be higher prices for everyone, perhaps more inflation, and a less competitive stance in world trade for the United States.

Immigrants—particularly recent ones—have also brought with them some valuable training and skills from which the United States has benefited immensely. Though U.S. society did not contribute to their education, it enjoys the fruits. Immigrants bring with them other characteristics that are less quantifiable but equally important for personal and societal success: a strong commitment to educational achievement, and a work and saving ethic that is not very common or widely practiced in the U.S. society.

Immigrants no longer tend to concentrate in ethnic neighborhoods or ghettos for long periods of time, as they did in the past. While there are still ethnic neighborhoods in virtually every large U.S. city, they are generally inhabited by the newest arrivals. As soon as the immigrants are financially able to do so, they purchase their own homes and tend to intermingle with the rest of the population. In time, like countless others before them, they become more and more like natives: Their family and household sizes become smaller; they intermarry and divorce; and they acquire other U.S. characteristics: credit cards, automobiles, cookouts, and a strong belief in the democratic ideals and in our own system of government. While dissimilarities will continue to exist, the sense of cultural insularity and special differences of the immigrants gradually disappear. After the second—and, at the latest, the third—generation, children and grandchildren of immigrants will no longer feel any peculiar attachment to their country of ancestry, and will no longer think and act differently from any native. They will be Americans both in spirit and in action, like everyone else.

"E Pluribus Unum" refers not only to sovereign states coming together to form "a more perfect union"; it also refers to a number of people from different countries coming together and, within their diversity, becoming one people fully committed to the ideals and way of life in the United States.

II

Asian Immigrants: Filipino, Korean, and Chinese

Following passage of the 1965 Immigration and Nationality Act amendments to the basic U.S. immigration laws, and the unexpected influx of South Asian refugees—particularly, Vietnamese—after the end of the Vietnam War in 1975, the character and composition of U.S. immigration also changed.

While European immigrants comprised 53.1% of the total number of immigrants in the decade ending in 1960, they accounted for 33.8% in the following decade, and only 17.8% by the period 1971-80. This share has fallen further; during 1981-83, Europeans comprised only 11.1% of the total number of immigrants. In the comparable time frame, immigrants from the countries in the Americas first increased their share of the total, then fell behind: In the 1950s, they comprised 39.6%; in the 1960s, 51.7%; and in the 1970s, 44.1%; and in the period 1981-83, 36.8%.

Conversely, Asian immigrants in the same time frame have consistently increased their share of the total number of legal immigrants. Between 1950 and 1960, they made up 4.9% of the immigrants; in the following decade, 12.9%; in the 1970s, 35.3%, and in the period 1981-83, 48.9%. Barring unforeseen changes in U.S. immigration laws, this trend is likely to continue: During the 1980s, the United States is likely to admit for permanent residence 2.85 million Asians, 2.15 million immigrants from Latin America and the Caribbean basin, and 650,000 Europeans.

In 1980, Asian immigrants and Asian-Americans already made up the third-largest ethnic racial group in the nation, after blacks and Hispanics. While their total number in relation to the entire U.S. population—1.5%— is small, this percentage is increasing fast because of sustained immigration. It has been estimated that the total Asian population in the United States rose from 3.5 million in 1980 to 5.1 million by 1985, and is likely to be close to 10 million by the year 2000—or 4% of the estimated total U.S. population by then.[1]

This increasing ethnic minority is extremely diverse—encompassing the descendants of Chinese immigrants who have been in the United States for more than 100 years, Japanese and Filipinos who came at the turn of the century as agricultural and plantation workers, refugees and immigrants from mainland China, Vietnamese refugees, Indian doctors and engineers, and many others who have come and are coming to the United States for a variety of reasons (principally, to improve their economic lot).

The cultures from which they come and the circumstances impelling their exodus from their homeland are just as varied. Three of the largest groups of Asian immigrants in the United States are the Filipinos, Koreans, and Chinese. They comprise close to 20% of the total number of legal immigrants admitted to the United States yearly, and nearly 50% of all the legal immigrants coming from the Asian continent every year. The percentage of Koreans, Filipinos, and Chinese becomes more impressive if one subtracts from the Asian total the Vietnamese, Kampucheans, and Laotians—the vast majority of whom are refugees, rather than immigrants. The Koreans, Filipinos, and Chinese would then comprise 61% of all Asian immigrants admitted during 1981–83 and 23.8% of the total worldwide number of immigrants admitted during the same period.

In addition, Manila, Seoul, Hong Kong (which also issues visas to residents of Taiwan), and Canton are among the top Foreign Service posts in issuing visas for immigrants to the United States. On January 1, 1985, the consulate files in those cities already had 769,007 qualified registered immigrants who were awaiting the availability of immigrant visa numbers to apply and—if eligible—to be issued such visas to move to the United States. This large number of intending immigrants comprise 66% of all intending Asian immigrants, and 32.7% of all intending immigrants to the United States registered worldwide at U.S. consulates and embassies.

These data explain why these three ethnic groups were chosen as the subject of the major portion of this study. Their number in the United States is already large—Chinese being the largest, Filipinos second, and Koreans fifth among all Asian ethnic groups in the United States. Apart from Mexico, the number coming every year from those three countries is larger than that from any other countries in the world; and the number awaiting their turn to come to the United States, ever larger.

THE PHILIPPINES

3

A Short History of Filipino Immigration to the United States

Filipino immigration to the United States can generally be divided into three periods: the early period, dating from 1906 to 1945; a middle period, which stretches from 1946 to 1964; and the current period, which goes from 1965 to the present.

However, the presence of Filipinos in the United States goes back much farther than 1906. During the period of the Manila Galleon Trade (1593-1815), Spanish ships crossed the Pacific from Manila to Acapulco and other Mexican ports—carrying spices and silk from the Orient for sale in the American continent and for transshipment to Europe. As most of the seamen on these ships were Filipinos, it seems highly probable that some remained behind in Mexico and eventually moved on to what subsequently became the states of California, Texas, and New Mexico.

Evidence exists that Filipino seamen settled in Louisiana in the 1830s and 1840s. Since the galleon trade had by then ceased, it is presumed that they must have come on sailing vessels directly to New Orleans, where they deserted. It is also possible that some were fugitives from Mexico, who arrived overland. However, what is known for sure is that, by 1833, they had gathered together in the fishing village of St. Malo at the mouth of the Mississippi. Most of them worked there seasonally as fishermen or hunters but maintained a permanent residence in New Orleans, where they kept their wives and children and where, by 1870, they had organized a benevolent association, La Unione Filipina. The village of St. Malo was completely destroyed by a strong hurricane in 1893, 60 years after its foundation. Some two-thirds of its 100 inhabitants died during the storm, and the rest fled to New Orleans.

In 1897, a Filipino seaman named Quintin de la Cruz established another fishing port, Manila Village, 40 miles south of New Orleans in Barataria Bay on the mouth of the Mississippi. The village—which, by 1933, had a Filipino population of 1,500—managed to survive by fishing shrimp in season, and by hunting muskrats for fur and fishing for trouts at other times.[1]

The first sizable groups of Filipinos to legally enter the United States came in 1903. After the United States had taken control of the Philippines in 1899—and the resistance movement to U.S. domination had died out— U.S. Governor-General William Howard Taft started a program that stressed educational development in the islands. In addition to bringing teachers from the United States, a program to send selected Filipino students to the United States to pursue higher education was started in 1903. By August 1903, 100 promising students out of 20,000 applicants traveled to the United States under the auspices of this program. Called "pensionados" because their expenses were fully paid by the colonial government, they graduated from U.S. universities and had returned to the Philippines by 1910. Filipino students continued to come to the United States until 1938. It has been estimated that their total number by then was approximately 14,000. While the overwhelming majority returned home after completing their education, some invariably remained behind and obtained employment mostly as unskilled laborers.

The first real wave of Filipino immigrants did not arrive in the United States until 1906. Changes occurring in U.S. agricultural techniques both on the West Coast and in Hawaii had created the need for larger numbers of agricultural workers to cut sugarcane and to plant and harvest grains, fruits, and flowers.

This need for cheap manpower was first met by Chinese immigrants. However, with passage in 1882 of the Chinese Exclusion Act (which forbade Chinese immigration for ten years, and was subsequently extended), the growers and planters encouraged Japanese to immigrate to the United States. By 1907, when the United States and Japan signed a gentleman's agreement severely restricting the immigration of Japanese, this source of cheap agricultural labor dried up. Koreans were the next Oriental group to be recruited, starting in 1903; but their numbers never filled the need for the large-scale agricultural development that had taken place.

After the acquisition of the Philippines and Puerto Rico from Spain as a result of the Spanish-American War, planters in Hawaii sponsored emigration of Puerto Rican laborers to their state. As these efforts did not produce the desired number of immigrants, plantation owners next turned to the Philippines for cheap labor.

At that time, sugar was king in Hawaii. Following annexation of the islands by the United States and the start of the tariff collected on the importation of foreign-produced sugar, sugarcane cultivation became very profitable; even marginal land in Hawaii was cleared and planted for sugar production. The number of laborers in sugarcane fields doubled in seven years to more than 48,000 by 1905. Sugar export comprised all but approximately 3% of the total Hawaiian exports in 1905.[2]

Labor problems with Japanese, Korean, and Chinese plantation laborers and the high cost of bringing in Portuguese laborers from Europe induced the Hawaii Sugar Planters Association (HSPA) to look elsewhere for sources of cheap, reliable field hands. They even induced 150 of the Russian immigrants who were living in California to move to Hawaii. But while the demand for field hands was increasing, the number of plantation workers was decreasing: Some workers at the completion of their contracts were moving to Honolulu, while others were moving to the mainland— where, they believed, life would be easier and their future brighter.

Encouraged by reports that Filipino laborers were hardworking and trainable, the HSPA appointed an attorney—A. F. Judd—as its representative, and sent him to the Philippines to recruit and bring back to Hawaii 300 families.

Judd left Honolulu on April 21, 1906. By July, he had obtained permission from U.S. officials in Manila to recruit laborers. Assisted by another American, George Wagner, Judd then started his recruiting efforts. Neither of them did very well; by the beginning of December, after having been in the Philippines for seven months, they had only recruited fifteen persons who had moved from the Ilocos region to Manila in order to look for work. Wagner then went to Ilocos, where he recruited ten more prospective immigrants.

However, since Judd wished to return to Hawaii before Christmas and the ten workers recruited by Wagner could not make their way to Manila in time, Judd sailed for Hawaii on the USS *Doric* with the fifteen Manila recruits. The group included a father and his four sons, and two sets of brothers. Four were newly married and were leaving their wives behind. The others, even though of marriageable age, were single. The ship arrived in Honolulu on December 20, 1906, and the fifteen were assigned to work on a plantation a few miles south of Hilo.

Under the terms of their contract, the workers were to receive $16 per month for a workday of ten hours and 26 workdays a month. The contract was valid for three years. Two dollars per month were deducted from the salary and set aside for the purchase of tickets to return to the Philippines once the contract had expired. If the employee failed to fulfill the contract terms, this deduction would be forfeited.

In 1907, 150 additional Filipinos sponsored by the HSPA arrived in Hawaii. A handful of women and children were part of the group.

The following year, because of the meager number of laborers coming from the Philippines and political opposition in Manila, the HSPA stopped recruiting. However, recruiting was started again in 1909, when Japanese plantation workers in Hawaii went on strike. This time, the recruiting efforts were more sustained; and 639 men, women, and children arrived in Hawaii from the Philippines during the year. Most of them were from the Ilocos province or the Visayan Islands—two regions that were overpopulated and where the land was not too fertile because of overexploitation. From 1909 to 1914, an average of 4,000 Filipinos per year arrived in Hawaii.

In 1915, the Filipino legislature passed a law that required the licensing of recruiters and provided for contracts to contain a clause guaranteeing a free return trip to the Philippines upon completion of 720 workdays. By then, the pay had risen to $20 per month.

The number of arrivals decreased somewhat between 1915 and 1920 to an average of 2,000 per year, but picked up again in the 1920s. By 1926, because of its success, the HSPA stopped paying the passage of Filipino immigrants to Hawaii; and many—still wishing to come—had to mortgage their land to accumulate the ship's fare, which was then approximately $70 for steerage passage.

During the 1920s, more than 65,000 men, 5,000 women, and 3,000 children came to Hawaii with contracts from the HSPA. Another 1,000 arrived in Hawaii on their own; and thousands more who were recruited by canners in Alaska and fruit farmers in California and Washington State headed directly for the U.S. mainland.

By the mid-1920s, Filipinos comprised 50% of all plantation workers in Hawaii; and by 1930, 75%. All in all, between 1909 and 1931, 112,820 Filipinos went to Hawaii to work. Of this number, 38,946 returned to the Philippines upon completion of their contract, and 18,607 moved to the mainland. Another 7,000 of the Filipinos remaining in Hawaii left the plantations and moved to Honolulu after completion of their contracts.[3] Still others had moved from the sugar plantation to the pineapple and coffee plantations, where salaries were higher.

The Great Depression curbed employment opportunities everywhere, including the plantations. In 1932, only 1,226 Filipinos were sponsored by the HSPA for entry into Hawaii; and 7,300 were repatriated to the Philippines, for lack of work. The numbers coming under sugar industry sponsorship dwindled further—with only 41 arriving in 1933 and 107 in 1934—and then stopped entirely. The last two sponsored groups of Filipino agricultural workers arrived in Hawaii in 1945/46, when the Pineapple Growers Association brought 6,000 male Ilocanos to work in that industry and the HSPA brought in 7,300 Filipinos for the sugar industry.

In the U.S. mainland during the entire period, the number of Filipinos was increasing. While the census of 1910 counted only 406 Filipinos outside of Hawaii, there were 5,603 by 1930. An overwhelming majority were residing in California, with sizable numbers also in Washington and Alaska. By 1930, the number in the U.S. mainland had increased to 45, 362; the total in Hawaii was then 63,052. By 1940, while the number of Filipinos in the mainland had remained stationary, the number in Hawaii had decreased by more than 10,000—mainly as a result of repatriation. In 1950, the number in the mainland and those in Hawaii were about equal, at a little over 61,000; since then, the number of Filipinos in the mainland has been much higher than those in Hawaii, with the preferred state of residence being California.

A Filipino in Hawaii faced a far different life from that at home. In Hawaii, he was a hired hand in a highly organized business and was bound by a myriad of company regulations. At home—while perhaps poorer—he had been a tenant farmer and, in most respects, had led a less regimented, more carefree and independent life. In Hawaii, he was kept separated from other immigrant groups, to prevent the formation of multi-ethnic labor unions; and, within his ethnic group, he tended to associate with those who were from his own province and spoke his dialect.

Family life presented another problem, due to the relative unavailability of Filipino women. In fact, of the 125,917 Filipinos who had been sponsored by the HSPA between 1909 and 1946, only 9,398 were women—less than one woman for each ten men; and Filipino women often became the cause of fights. Some Filipino men married women of other ethnic groups, such as Portuguese, Hawaiian, and Puerto Rican; but the majority remained single. Because of this problem, gambling, cockfights, and prostitution became the major recreational activities of Filipinos in Hawaii. Friendship with town "mates," province "mates," and reunions at baptisms, weddings, and funerals provided another acceptable avenue for social intercourse. During these occasions, the Filipinos' love for a "fiesta" readily came to the force.

Filipino immigrants to the mainland faced even more acute problems than those in Hawaii. As the last group of Asian immigrants to arrive in the United States, they became the victims of racist laws and discrimination. Signs stating "Filipinos and dogs not allowed" were hung in many restaurants and stores. The range of opportunities available to Filipinos in the Pacific rim states—where most settled—was very limited. Having little education and experiencing difficulty with the English language, most obtained employment as seasonal agricultural laborers.

During the winter, they stayed in the cities—working as domestics and gardeners; washing dishes in restaurants; and, in general, doing any menial task that others refused. During the summer, they moved back to the fields and harvested potatoes, strawberries, lettuce, sugar beets, and fruits.

In addition to those in California, other fairly large Filipino colonies of immigrants got started in the 1920s and the early 1930s in Chicago, New York, Philadelphia, and New Jersey.

One occupation in which Filipinos were employed in sizable numbers was in the Merchant Marine and the U.S. Navy. The Merchant Marine provided more than 5,000 jobs, while the U.S. Navy recruited about 4,000 Filipinos per year. In the Navy, however, Filipinos were only allowed to work as mess stewards. Most jobs in the Merchant Marine came to an end in 1936, when the Merchant Marine Act imposed the ruling that 90% of the crew on U.S. ships had to be U.S. citizens.[4]

Because of their mobility caused by seasonal employment, Filipinos in the mainland—unlike the Chinese and Japanese—failed to develop strong ethnic communities or neighborhoods. For most, the fragile American-Filipino neighborhood was a stopping place in periods of idleness and the place to go for entertainment: gambling, dancing, cockfighting. Famous in this respect were the dance halls in which young, single, Filipino males had the opportunity to mix with Caucasian girls. Such dance halls were the starting point of innumerable fights, and the source of friction and tension between whites and Filipinos.

The adversary attitudes of the majority of U.S. citizens against Filipino immigrants took many forms. Filipinos were characterized as unreliable, hot-tempered gigolos who loved to show off and have sexual relations with white women and who were prone to violence and crime.

Organized opposition to Filipinos was led by labor groups who claimed that this new group of immigrants engaged in unfair competition in the labor market by working for less money. Therefore, Filipinos were not welcome in established labor unions and formed their own labor organizations.

In Hawaii, the Filipino Federation of Labor was formed in 1911 by Pablo Manlapit, who tried to organize the sugarcane workers. By 1920, the union felt strong enough to call a strike for better pay and fewer hours of work. This strike was mainly a failure; after 165 days, the workers returned to the fields without having obtained any concessions. In April 1924 another strike—demanding a minimum wage of $2 a day for eight hours' work—turned violent and resulted in the death of 20: 16 Filipinos strikers and 4 policemen.

On the mainland, Filipinos did not fare any better. They organized the Filipino Federation of Labor in Los Angeles in 1927, and subsequently engaged in a number of strikes. Generally, however, they were not very successful and became the target of violence. For example, anti-Filipino riots took place in Yakima, Washington, in 1928 and in four places in California: Exeter, in 1929; Watsonville, in 1930; Salinas, in 1934; and Lake County, in 1939.

Labor and nativistic organizations clamored for a halt to Filipino immigration, and deportation of those already in the United States; but this was not legally possible: Filipinos were U.S. "nationals" and thus, until 1934, were not subject to immigration restrictions.

The Tydings-McDuffie Act of 1934, which limited Filipino immigration to the United States to 50 persons per year, practically ended immigration from the Philippines until after World War II. In any case, because of the impact of the Great Depression, shrinking economic opportunities, and the subsequent start of World War II in 1941, it seems likely that the number of Filipino immigrants would have dropped anyway.

No separate entry statistics for Filipinos were kept by the U.S. Immigration and Naturalization Service before 1950; from 1934 to 1940, Filipinos were included with those of immigrants from the other Pacific islands under U.S. administration. The total number given for the decade from 1930 to 1940—780—clearly shows the effect of the Tydings-McDuffie Act. In the following decade (1940-50), immigration statistics show 4,437 Pacific islanders admitted to the United States; it is likely that most of them were Filipinos who arrived in the United States after the end of the war.

In 1935, responding to the unabated anti-Filipino pressure from labor groups, Congress passed—the year after passage of the Tydings-McDuffie Act restricting immigration—the Repatriation Act, which provided free transportation for Filipinos returning home. For any who took advantage of that offer, subsequent reentry came under the annual quota of 50—making if extremely difficult, if not impossible, for them to return to the United States. However, only a very samll minority—a little more than 2,000— took advantage of free passage; some 5,000 others returned to the Philippines on their own—thus protecting their reentry rights, at least temporarily.

Prior to their country's independence in 1946, Filipino immigrants in the United States faced another serious legal problem. While considered nationals of the United States, they could not be naturalized as citizens, since legislation based on a 1790 statute that restricted naturalization to "free white persons" had been passed—barring the naturalization of any Asians.

Despite a number of court cases started by Filipinos seeking naturalization, the constitutionality of this law was upheld; and Filipinos in the United States thus remained in limbo: They were U.S. nationals, but were unable to become citizens. This statute restricted employment opportunities in the professions—since most states' licensing requirements included citizenship—and generally excluded Filipinos from obtaining most government jobs or benefits. Unable to become citizens, they also found it impossible to sponsor family relatives to join them from the Philippines; and, thus, a mostly male and aging immigrant group was perpetuated.

This problem was partially solved just prior to and during World War II. The Immigration and Nationality Act of 1940 allowed Filipinos who had entered as immigrants to apply for naturalization. However, this act did not apply to those who had entered the United States as nationals, prior to the Tydings-McDuffie Act of 1934; and, thus, the number of eligible immigrants was very small. Another act provided for persons who had served honorably in the U.S. Armed Forces for at least three years to apply for naturalization. Since thousands of Filipinos had served in the U.S. Navy, many were naturalized under this provision.

The act that definitely solved the problem, however, was the Nationality Act of 1946, signed by President Truman on July 2 of that year. It allowed all Asians who were permanent residents of the United States and met the other requirements to apply for naturalization. Many took advantage of the new law and became citizens. By doing so, they became able to petition for other members of their immediate families still in the Philippines to join them in the United States.

Meanwhile, with independence in 1946, the annual quota of Filipino immigrants was raised from 50 to 100 per year—the same as that of other independent Asian countries. But it was a negligible increase.

However, another factor produced a significant change in social conditions. The reestablishment of two large U.S. military bases in the Philippines—Subic Naval Base and Clark Air Force Base—led to numerous marriages of U.S. servicemen to Filipinos and to the latter's subsequent entry into the United States as nonquota immigrants.

Combined with the ability of newly naturalized Filipinos in the United States to petition successfully for nonquota relatives, this factor considerably raised the number of Filipinos entering the United States as immigrants. In the decade 1951-60, 19,307 Filipinos were admitted. Of this total, 70.9% were females and 93.5% were nonquota immigrants.[5]

The Immigration and Nationality Act of 1965, which placed citizens of all countries on an equal footing for immigration purposes and thus eliminated ethnic discrimination, provided the impetus for sustained immigration increases from the Philippines. The result is that Filipinos are now the second-largest national group coming to the United States—exceeded only by Mexicans—and the figure has continued to increase at a tremendous rate. The number of Filipinos in the United States doubled between 1960 and 1970—and more than doubled again, the following decade. By 1980, there were 774,652 Filipinos in the United States; of these, 501,440 were foreign-born.

The character of immigration following passage of the 1965 act has also changed. Whereas before, virtually all Filipino immigrants had been rural workers from Ilocos and the Visayas—with little education—the post-1965 immigrants included a significant number of highly educated professionals (such as doctors, engineers, teachers, and nurses) and a substantial proportion of urban dwellers.

These new immigrants are a world apart from the former immigrants. As a result, Filipino communities in the United States now appear to be fractured along more lines than they ever were. In addition to provincial and language groups, the different educational and socioeconomic characteristics of the new immigrants provide another source of friction. While the old-timers are mostly uneducated, clannish, and concentrated in low-paying occupations, the new arrivals are educated, cosmopolitan, and aggressive.

These frictions have somewhat diluted the incipient political power that Filipinos might have gained in Hawaii and California, because of their number. However, with the steady flow of new immigrants, this problem will tend to diminish in time, as more and more of the new Filipino immigrants take their rightful place in U.S. society—participating fully in all its endeavors and contributing their fair share to U.S. progress.

The overall growth of the Filipino population in the United States is shown in Table 3.1. The census of 1920 found a little more than 26,000 Filipinos in the United States—all but 21% residing in Hawaii. By 1930, the total had quadrupled to more than 108,000; the majority—58%—still resided in Hawaii. By 1940—as a result of the Great Depression, the Tydings-McDuffie Act, and the Repatriation Act—the number had dwindled to approximately 99,000. By then, however, a substantial number—more than 31,000, or 32%—lived in California. The 1950 census found that the number of Filipinos had risen to close to 123,000 and that they were almost equally divided between the continental United States and Hawaii. Of those in the continental United States, two-thirds were making their home in California. By 1960, the number of Filipinos had increased to more than 176,000: 39% in Hawaii; 37% in California; and the balance scattered in all states of the union, but principally in New Jersey, New York, Washington, Texas, and Illinois.

Following passage of the 1965 Immigration and Nationality Act, the number of Filipino immigrants coming to the United States mushroomed.

Table 3.1
Filipinos in the United States: Selected Years and States

	Total	Mainland	Hawaii	California	Illinois
1920	26,634	5,603	21,031	NA	NA
1930	108,424	45,372	63,052	NA	NA
1940	98,535	45,876	52,659	31,408	NA
1950	122,707	61,645	61,062	40,424	NA
1960	176,310	107,669	68,641	64,459	3,587
1970	343,060	247,308	95,680	135,248	12,355
1980	774,942	640,712	133,940	357,432	43,857

Source: U.S. Bureau of the Census, *Census of the Population* (Washington, D.C.: Government Printing Office, selected years).

Table 3.2
Filipino Immigration to the United States: Selected Years

1951–1960	19,307
1961–1965	15,290
1965–1970	83,086
1971–1980	354,987
1981–1983	130,420

Sources: U.S. Department of Justice, *1983 Statistical Yearbook of the U.S. Immigration and Naturalization Service* (Washington, D.C.: Government Printing Office, 1984); U.S. Bureau of the Census, *Historical Statistics of the United States* (Washington, D.C.: Government Printing Office, September 1975), part 1, series C83-119.

The census of 1970 found that, compared with the previous census, the number of Filipinos had doubled to 343,000. By now, California was the preferred state of residence, and more than one-third of all Filipinos lived there. By 1980, the Filipino population had again more than doubled, and California status as the preferred state of residence was confirmed. Hawaii trailed, with 17%; and Illinois—mainly in the Chicago area—was third, with 6%.

Table 3.2 shows the importance of the 1965 act for the rise of the number of Filipino immigrants and, consequently, the increase in the total number of Filipinos residing in the United States.

While in the decade 1951-60, the average number of Filipinos entering the United States was less than 2,000 per year—and in the period 1961-65, approximately 3,000 per year—in the period 1965-70, it had risen to close to 17,000 per year. The following decade—1971-80—saw this rate double; more than 35,000 Filipinos per year being admitted to the United States as permanent residents. The average during the last three years for which data is available—1981-83—was 43,000 per year. This high number is likely to continue for the foreseeable future.

4

Current Emigration Trends and Problems in the Philippines

The Philippines—with a burgeoning population, a relatively low standard of living, and a highly educated and skilled population—is a country of emigration. Legally or illegally, with tourist or immigrant visas or on temporary work permits, Filipinos who have left their country are found throughout the world.

Most of them—unable to obtain immigrant visas and leave permanently with their families—go overseas on the basis of work contracts, which lead to the issuance of temporary work visas. The largest number—around the million mark—are working in the Middle East; Saudi Arabia, Kuwait, Iraq, and Iran are the major employing countries. Filipinos hold all types of jobs in those countries; from manual laborers engaged in construction, to engineers, doctors, and nurses. Jobs in the Middle East are much sought after, since they pay on the average 5–10 times what the same job would pay in the Philippines. Workers generally go on a 1–3 year contract and return to the Philippines on vacation every year. By law, 75% of their salary must be sent back to the Philippines through official channels. While not all the workers comply with this law, remittances from temporary workers overseas are close to $1 billion a year, and provide a steady and valuable source of foreign exchange for the economy of the Philippines.

Other sizable numbers of Filipinos on temporary work contracts are found in Hong Kong, Japan, and Singapore. However, these workers are engaged mostly as domestic servants or entertainers. Large groups of

Filipinos are also found in southern Europe, particularly in Spain and Italy; approximately 50,000 (mostly females engaged as domestic servants) are found in each of these two countries, which most of them have entered as tourists—remaining illegally. An estimated 20,000 are also employed as seamen on ships throughout the world. Their salary—an average of $800 per month—is about ten times what they would get in the Philippines, were they able to locate employment there.

However, the United States is the preferred destination of all—whether for tourism, on a temporary work contract, or as immigrants. More than 100,000 applicants attempt to obtain tourist visas in Manila every year, with a success rate of 65-75%. Of those who obtain tourist visas and travel to the United States, 15-20% do not return home, but remain in the United States permanently. Going on a temporary work visa is preferable, however, since one can be employed legally and then eventually apply for adjustment of status to permanent resident.

Since there has been a shortage of nurses in the United States for the past ten years, Filipino nurses are the prime beneficiaries of temporary work petitions; every year, about 3,000 are successful in obtaining such visas, and come to the United States to practice their profession. Clearly, the main attraction for nurses moving to the United States is guaranteed employment and a decent salary. The Philippines currently have 146,000 registered nurses, and the nursing schools graduate an additional 15,000 each year. Salaries for nurses range from about $60 to $105 per month there, and employment is rather difficult to obtain.

Because of these factors, 89,000 of the 146,000 registered Philippine nurses are employed abroad. Of these, the overwhelming majority—an estimated 50,000—are in the United States, where salaries for registered nurses start at about $2,000 per month—about 20 times their salary in the Philippines.

An estimated 20,000 Filipino nurses are employed in New York; and sizable numbers are found in Chicago, Houston, Los Angeles, and San Francisco.[1] The overwhelming majority of these nurses remain in the United States permanently; after a few years of residence on a temporary work basis, they apply for adjustment of status as permanent residents.

Every year, another 40–50,000 Filipinos apply to enter the United States as immigrants on the basis that they are immediate relatives of U.S. citizens (who are exempt from numerical limitations) or are in one of the preference categories. Approximately 35,000 of them obtain such visas in Manila, and permanently move to the United States.

Since immigrant visa applications are processed by the U.S. Embassy in Manila in the order in which petitions (within each one of the various preference categories) are received, the waiting time before one can apply for the visa ranges from a matter of weeks to longer than 15 years. Spouses, children, and parents of U.S. citizens may apply at their convenience, since there are no numerical restrictions. On the other hand, brothers and sisters (and their spouses and children) may have to wait for as long as 15 years before their turn to apply is reached. The reason for this is that—within the limit of 20,000 immigrants per country per year as dictated by the Immigration and Nationality Act of 1965, and the percentage allocated to each preference category—an insufficient number of visas is available to accommodate all demands every year.

Furthermore, there is a multiplier effect in the number of intending immigrants newly entitled to apply: For each immigrant visa issued, two to three new applicants become qualified from petitions filed by their U.S. relatives. Thus, the number of registered quota applicants on the Philippines waiting list increases every year. Table 4.1 gives an indication of the magnitude of the numbers for selected years for which data is available at the U.S. Embassy in Manila.

If all Filipino applicants were able to make their applications and obtain visas on a first-come, first-served basis—given the 20,000 limitation per year—it would be 19 years before all who are currently registered could go to the United States. In actuality, it does not take that long for most applicants, because of two factors: (1) the preference categories and the percentages allocated to each of these out of the total number of available visas;

Table 4.1
Registered Quota Applicants on Immigration Waiting Lists in Manila: 1978–85

		Active	Inactive *1	Total *2
Jan. 1,	1978	NA	NA	150,238
	1979	NA	NA	210,217
	1980	NA	NA	243,061
	1981	217,887	37,340	255,827
	1982	260,755	41,395	302,150
	1983	258,839	36,790	295,629
	1984	326,174	42,711	368,885
	1985	336,284	45,837	382,121

[1]Inactive applicants are those who have failed for over a year to take any embassy-requested action to further their applications.
[2]The figures include a small number of non-Filipinos registered in Manila.
Source: U.S. Embassy in Manila, unpublished reports.

and (2) the fact that a number of registered applicants die, marry and form their own families, no longer wish to immigrate, and so forth.

With reference to the preference categories, the following numbers of active quota immigrants were registered in Manila as of January 1, 1985:

First Preference (unmarried sons and daughters of U.S. citizens)—2,050

Second Preference (spouses, and unmarried sons and daughters of permanent residents of the United States)—79,094

Third Preference (professionals whose services are required in the United States)—18,974

Fourth Preference (married sons and daughters of U.S. citizens)—29,929

Fifth Preference (brothers and sisters of U.S. citizens, their spouses, and minor children)—199,794

Sixth Preference (workers whose services are required by an employer in the United States)—5,874

Non-Preference (other registered immigrants not fitting into the above categories)—569

Comparing the above numbers of waiting applicants with the following numbers of available visas that were issued to qualified applicants by preference category in fiscal year 1984 (October 1, 1983–September 30, 1984) illustrates the magnitude of the problem:

First Preference—2,449

Second Preference—6,189

Third Preference—1,833

Fourth Preference—1,985

Fifth Preference—4,732

Sixth Preference—1,209

Non-Preference—0 (no visas were available)

Because of the law and the mechanics for the allocations of visas within the preference categories, applicants in the first preference were able to obtain visas right away; those in the second preference had waited about four years; those in the third preference, more than ten years; those in the fourth preference about five years; those in the fifth preference, more than ten years; and those in the sixth preference category, approximately three years.

An unintended effect of the law was that third preference applicants—professionals such as accountants, lawyers, architects, professors, and nurses—must wait longer than other prospective workers with lower skill levels, before they may apply for immigrant visas. This quirk has resulted from the large number of Filipino professionals who are seeking to obtain immigrant visas and move to the United States because of their inability to secure decent pay and employment in their own country.

Of the registered third-preference applicants, approximately 50% of the principals (not family members) are medical doctors who, although they originally qualified for immigration, will now be unable to obtain visas unless they comply with the 1976 amendment that requires comprehensive knowledge of the English language and medical knowledge comparable to that of graduates of U.S. medical schools.

In addition to preference applicants, the U.S. Embassy in Manila has files on another 40–50,000 intending immigrants who, as immediate relatives of U.S. citizens (children, spouses, or parents), do not require visa numbers to emigrate. A significant number of them are issued visas yearly in Manila to join their sons and daughters who are U.S. citizens, or to join or accompany their spouses and parents who are U.S. citizens. Data on the issuance of non-quota visas, as compared with quota visas, are given in Table 4.2. We see that about 50% of all applicants are issued immigrant visas outside the preference categories. In a recent year—fiscal year 1984—the number of these applicants broke down as shown in Table 4.3.

Two factors are of interest in the above data: First, virtually all petitions for spouses and children (or, more often, stepchildren) of U.S. citizens are a

Table 4.2
Quota and Non-Quota Visas Issued in Manila: Selected Fiscal Years

	Non-Quota	Quota	Total
1977	15,907	17,120	33,027
1978	14,487	16,105	30,592
1979	17,854	16,559	34,413
1980	16,360	19,075	35,435
1981	17,566	17,800	35,366
1982	16,700	17,248	33,948
1983	15,284	16,627	31,911
1984	15,984	17,482	33,466

Sources: U.S. Embassy in Manila and the Visa Office of the U.S. Department of State, unpublished reports.

Table 4.3
Immediate Relatives of U.S. Citizens Issued Visas in Manila, FY 1984

	Total	Percentage
Spouses of U.S. citizens	4,980	31.1
Children or stepchildren of U.S. citizens	4,429	27.7
Adopted or to-be-adopted children of U.S. citizens	425	2.7
Parents of U.S. citizens	6,150	38.5
Total	15,984	100.0

Source: U.S. Embassy in Manila, unpublished reports.

direct result of the presence of U.S. military forces at the two large bases in the Philippines. Servicemen who are not already married are likely to do so while in the Philippines and to bring their wives and stepchildren to the United States at the completion of the tour of duty. How long these marriages last after the return of the servicemen to the United States is not known, but it is believed that the rate of failure and subsequent divorce is rather high.

The second factor pertains to the parents of U.S. citizens who obtain U.S. immigrant visas. In a large number of cases, the applicants do not intend to permanently reside in the United States; they enter and remain in the country for a period of time sufficient to file visa petitions for their other children in the Philippines—who then qualify under the second preference category, rather than under the fifth. In this manner, the waiting time before being able to apply for visas is reduced by approximately two-thirds.

In addition to obtaining immigrant visas at a U.S. embassy or consulate overseas, a number of prospective immigrants who are seeking adjustment of status from nonimmigrant to permanent resident apply to the U.S. Immigration and Nationalization Service within the United States. In fiscal year 1983, 8,913 Filipinos did so. Of this total, 1,542 were chargeable to the various preference categories; and 4,882 were exempt from numerical limitations or quotas, because they were immediate relatives of U.S. citizens. Most of these individuals had originally entered as tourists, while some may have been students or on temporary work visas.

Because of the economic pressures in emigrating and the inability to do so easily and quickly, a significant number of prospective Filipino immigrants engage in fradulent activities to be able to enter the United States and remain there. Visa fraud in Manila is prevalent and highly profitable, and a number of syndicates are in the business of providing applicants with fradulent documents (which may result in the issuance of genuine visas) or counterfeit visas.

The Manila embassy—like other embassies—maintains a visa and passport Anti-Fraud Unit, which is staffed by two U.S. officers, one secretary, and six Filipino investigators. This unit conducts several thousand investigations per year, at the request of consular officers. Fraud is proven in approximately 25% of all investigated cases; in the remaining 75%, either the evidence is inconclusive or no fraud at all is discovered. Equally important to its investigative role on individual cases, the Anti-Fraud Unit provides liaison with local law enforcement agencies, airport authorities, the anti-fraud unit of other embassies, and embassy security officers (in cases involving suspected employee malfeasance).

Fraud perpetrated to gain entry into the United States is highly sophisticated and varied. In the case of applicants for nonimmigrant visas, attempts may take the form of fraudulent documents such as bankbooks, certificates of deposit, birth and marriage certificates, or land and housing titles (to prove the existence of strong ties in the Philippines, which would indicate a probably return there after a short stay in the United States).

Sometimes, it also involves the use of paid actors and actresses to undergo the interview at the embassy—and, if the visa is issued, a subsequent switch of passport photographs. In some cases, passport pages containing the visa are substituted; in others, a spurious visa manufactured in some back room is stamped in the passport. In other instances, the same nonimmigrant visa has been used a number of times by different individuals: After entry into the United States by the original owner, the passport is either mailed or hand-carried back to the Philippines; the photo is substituted; and a new client is soon on the way. In still other cases, individuals are sent by the visa "fixer" to Mexico—whence they then attempt to make their way into the United States.

Most immigrant visa fraud involves phony marriages to U.S. citizens, or petitions filed by fiancés of U.S. citizens for marriages in the United States. Other instances of fraud involve the concealment of marriages to obtain immigrant visas as unmarried sons and daughters of citizens or permanent residents, and the addition on one's own application of nephews and nieces as one's own children.

Fraudulent activities extend also to determination of U.S. citizenship where "adopted children" are presented as the natural issue of U.S. citizens, and to the use of "lost" genuine U.S. passports where the photograph of the rightful holder has been detached and a new photograph affixed.

But although fraudulent activities for visa purposes are a serious concern in Manila, the majority of visa applicants obtain visas and enter the United States legally.

The Government of the Philippines—through its Commission on Filipinos Overseas—aims to maintain close ties between the home country and Filipino communities overseas, and to establish a data base to help in the formulation of Filipino manpower and immigration policies. While the commission was established in 1980, two previous government organizations under the Ministry of Labor had been collecting data on Filipino immigrants since 1975.

The data collected by the Filipino government show that, in a little more than ten years, 413,456 emigrants were registered as planning to permanently reside abroad. Eighty percent indicated that they were moving to the United States, 11% to Canada, 6% to Australia, and 3% to other countries. Of the total, 37% indicated that they had an occupation; of the balance, 63% were housewives, students, retirees, or infants. More than 13% of all emigrants listed their occupations as professional, managerial, or executive. However, when only the 37% who declared an occupation is taken as the base, professionals/managers/executives were 37% of the total number who gave an occupation.

Data collected beginning in January 1984 give an indication of the educational status of emigrants from the Philippines: While 11% had no formal education and 21% had only finished elementary school, 26% were high school graduates and 37% had completed college-level studies.[2]

Through information provided by Filipino consulates and embassies in the country of destination, the commission has also compiled a list of problems most frequently encountered by immigrants overseas. These range from difficulty in adjusting to a new environment and finding employment to marital problems, accreditation problems for professionals, and racial discrimination. Despite any problems encountered overseas, Filipinos are likely to continue emigrating in large numbers—primarily in an attempt to improve their economic standing.

5

Social and Demographic Characteristics of Filipino Immigrants: 1980

In 1984, the U.S. Bureau of the Census tabulated data on the foreign-born, collected during the 1980 census. This data—available for a number of variables—has been tabulated by year of immigration, and provides a useful tool for the analysis of the socioeconomic characteristics of Filipino immigrants in the United States. When compared with statistical data for the general U.S. population, it also provides a benchmark to ascertain their degree of adaptation and progress. By analyzing such data, this chapter will explore selected socioeconomic and demographic characteristics of Filipino-born immigrants residing in the United States in 1980.

NUMBERS OF FILIPINOS IN THE UNITED STATES

The general questionnaire used in the 1980 census included a question asking the respondent to identify his race. A total of 774,640 identified themselves as Filipino, one of the categories listed in the questionnaire.

Through a question on place of birth, the Census Bureau also identified 501,440 persons who claimed to have been born in the Philippines. Thus, it appears that 273,200 persons who identified themselves as Filipinos in the race question must have been born in the United States or in countries other than the Philippines.

While this analysis is mainly concerned with the foreign-born Filipinos, it should be noted that, between 1970 and 1980, the number of ethnic

Filipinos in the United States increased by 125.8%—from 343,060 to 774,640. This was the second largest increase of any racial group— surpassed only by Koreans, whose numbers in the same period rose 412.8%. These dramatic increases were the result of the liberalization of U.S. immigration laws in 1965. According to the Immigration and Naturalization Service, 354,987 Filipinos entered the United States during the 1970s—accounting for the overwhelming percentage of the increase for Filipinos, as noted above.

Among the 15 racial groups identified by the 1980 census, Filipinos placed sixth—after whites, blacks, American Indians, Chinese, and "others." They had been in seventh place in 1970, when the Japanese were also more numerous.

If only the Asian-American population is considered, Filipinos were the third-largest ethnic group in 1970—after the Japanese and Chinese; by 1980, they had moved to second place—after the Chinese. It has been estimated that, by 1990—barring changes in our immigration laws—Filipinos in the United States will number more than 1,400,000 and will be the country's leading Asian ethnic group.[1]

The impact of the 1965 change in immigration laws can also be seen in Table 5.1. We see that 63.6% of all foreign-born Filipinos arrived in the United States during the 1970s; 22.6% in the 1960s; and only 13.8%, before 1960. If one takes 1965 as a departure date, we notice that 80.7% of all foreign-born Filipinos counted in 1980 have arrived in the United States since then. Thus, in 1980, approximately four-fifths of all foreign-born Filipinos had been in the United States for 15 years or less.

Table 5.1
Foreign-Born Filipinos in the United States: 1980

Year of Immigration	Total	%
	501,440	100
1975–1980	172,721	34.4
1970–1974	146,318	29.2
1965–1970	85,469	17.1
1960–1964	27,617	5.5
1950–1959	27,318	5.4
Prior to 1950	41,997	8.4

Source: U.S. Bureau of the Census, "Foreign-Born Immigrants: Filipinos—Tabulations from the 1980 U.S. Census of the Population and Housing," mimeographed report, Washington, D.C., October 1984.

PLACE OF RESIDENCE

Filipinos—just like other Asian-Americans, and immigrants in general—tend to be highly urbanized. While, at the beginning of their immigration to the United States at the turn of the century, the vast majority lived up in rural areas because of their occupations, the situation has changed in more recent times. In fact, in 1980, the data collected by the U.S. Bureau of the Census indicates that, of the total 501,440 foreign-born Filipinos, only 37,316—or 7.4%—resided outside a standard statistical metropolitan area. A few states had more Filipinos residing outside the metropolitan area than in it, but the total number of Filipinos in those states was not significant. The only state where a significant proportion of the Filipino foreign-born population was residing in a rural area was found to be Hawaii, with a full 25% of foreign-born Filipinos residing outside the Honolulu metropolitan area. That most of these are "old" immigrants is reflected by the percentage of those who immigrated to Hawaii prior to 1960 and were residing in rural areas: a full 53.5%.

While foreign-born Filipinos are found in every state of the union, close to two-thirds are concentrated in the Pacific rim states, the area where the first Filipino immigrants who came to the mainland originally settled. The rest form significant concentrations in states where economic opportunity appears to be great and the chance of finding employment at better than average salaries is enhanced.

Table 5.2 gives data on the Filipino foreign-born population in the ten states where most Filipinos live. The correlation between the percentages of all Filipinos and those born overseas indicates that, like other immigrants, Filipinos also tend to settle where Filipino communities are already established—provided that economic opportunities are still bright in that area.

Between 1970 and 1980—primarily due to immigration—the Filipino-born population of the United States increased 125.8% nationwide (as cited above) and grew fastest in Texas, New Jersey, Illinois, and Michigan. In the first two of these states, it more than tripled; in the other two, more than doubled. One of the lowest rates of increase was in Hawaii: only 42.6%, about one-third of the nationwide rate. Given the character of the new immigration, professional opportunities available to these immigrants in Hawaii would have been rather limited; and, thus, most of the new immigrants opted for the mainland and better economic opportunities, rather than the more balmy weather of Hawaii and the relative proximity to their country of origin for an occasional vacation or business trip.

AGE AND SEX COMPOSITION OF FILIPINO IMMIGRANTS IN THE UNITED STATES

Of the total 501,440 foreign-born Filipinos counted in the U.S. census of 1980, 232,385 were males and 269,055 females—with a ratio of 86.4 males

Table 5.2
Ten Preferred States of Residence for Filipinos: 1980

State	Foreign-Born Filipinos	% of Total	All Filipinos	% of Total
California	237,713	47.4	357,514	46.2
Hawaii	58,510	11.7	133,964	17.3
Illinois	34,299	6.8	43,839	5.7
New York	27,493	5.5	33,956	4.4
New Jersey	18,207	3.6	24,377	3.1
Washington	15,726	3.1	24,363	3.1
Virginia	12,672	2.5	18,901	2.4
Texas	11,553	2.3	15,096	1.9
Florida	10,258	2.0	14,212	1.8
Pennsylvania	5,987	1.2	8,267	1.1
Totals	432,418	86.1	674,489	87.0

Sources: U.S Bureau of the Census, *1980 Census of the Population* (Washington, D.C.: Government Printing Office, 1981) and "Foreign-Born Immigrants: Filipinos—Tabulations from the 1980 U.S. Census of the Population and Housing," mimeographed report, Washington, D.C., October, 1984.

for every 100 females. This ratio compares with a ratio of 94.5% for the entire U.S. population. However, the apparent imbalance is deceptive, since a noticeable number of female Filipinos marry male U.S. citizens every year—both in the Philippines and in the United States. Consequently, if one excludes interracial marriages, the ratio of males to females may be approximately even.

The age distribution of foreign-born Filipinos—as shown in Table 5.3—indicates that, when compared with the U.S. population, Filipinos had a much smaller proportion in the under-14 age bracket, but were overrepresented in the productive years—the 15–64 age group. In fact, while 66.1% of the U.S. population at large was in this age bracket, 78.3% of the foreign-born Filipinos were.

Filipinos males were overrepresented in the over-65 group—with

Table 5.3

Age Distribution of Foreign-Born Filipinos and Total U.S. Population: 1980 (in percentages)

Age	Both Sexes U.S. Pop.	Both Sexes Filipino Born	Males Total U.S. Pop.	Males Filipino Born	Females Total U.S. Pop.	Females Filipino Born
0–14	22.6	11.3	23.8	12.5	21.5	10.2
15–44	46.5	60.8	47.6	55.5	45.4	65.2
45–64	19.6	17.5	19.2	16.7	20.1	18.3
65 and over	11.3	10.4	9.4	15.3	13.0	6.3

Sources: U.S. Bureau of the Census, *1980 Census of the Population, U.S. Summary* (Washington, D.C.: Government Printing Office, 1981) and Filipinos—Tabulations from the 1980 U.S. Census of the Population and Housing," mimeographed report, Washington, D.C., October 1984.

15.3%—because, no doubt, most Filipinos who came to the United States prior to 1946 were males who did not immigrate with their families. The female foreign-born Filipino population was underrepresented in this age group: Only 6.3% were over 65, as compared with 13% for the U.S. population at large. On the other hand, 65.2% of female Filipino immigrants were in the reproductive age bracket—15–44—as compared with 45.4% of U.S. females in general. This factor points to a potential increase in the U.S.-born Filipino population, even though the Filipino fertility rates were similar to those of the U.S. female general population in the reproductive age group.

FERTILITY

In the Philippines, large families are the rule, rather than the exception; and families with six or more children are very common. This situation is due to several factors.

Religion—in particular, Catholicism—is one. Another factor is that children are considered assets for the parents' old age and do, indeed, provide assistance to their elders. Still another factor is that, in a developing society, both the pressures and the opportunities for multivaried forms of leisure as known in a developed society are lacking; and, therefore, the opportunity for and frequency of sexual relations leading to pregnancies and childbearing is more prevalent than in the United States.

However, in the United States, Filipino women—even those recently arrived—tend to have lower fertility rates than the U.S. population of childbearing age at large. Table 5.4 shows such rates for the U.S. female population, for all Asian immigrant women between the ages of 15 and 44, and for the same age group of Filipino women who came to the United States between 1970 and 1980.

The lower fertility rates of Filipino women may be explained partly by the higher educational achievements of recent Filipino women immigrants, and partly by their efforts in adapting to the new environment and in climbing the socioeconomic scale. The data also indicate that, while young Filipino women are more prolific than all Asian women who immigrated during the decade, their rate of fertility declines when they are past the age of 24, in comparison with both of the other two groups.

Another indication of the low fertility rate of Filipino-born immigrants can be gathered in a different context. The special 1980 census tabulations on foreign-born counted 205,416 households where the head of household or spouse was a native Filipino. Of these households, 39.4% had no children, 20.1% had one child, 21.8% had two, 12% had three, and only 6.7% had four or more. Thus, we can see that a total of 81.3% of foreign-born Filipino households had two children or less, and only 18.7% had three or more.[2]

MARITAL STATUS

The special tabulations of foreign-born of the 1980 census counted 444,725 Filipinos over the age of 15: 203,292 males and 241,433 females. Statistical data on their marital status are given in Table 5.5.

The evidence indicates that Filipino-born immigrants residing in the United States are more likely to be married and less likely to be separated

Table 5.4
Children Born to U.S. Women and to Asian and Filipino Women Who Immigrated between 1970 and 1980, as of 1980 (per 1,000 women)

Age	All U.S. Women	Immigrant Asian Women	Filipino-born Women
15–24	317	271	306
25–34	1,476	1,262	1,143
35–44	2,639	2,285	2,011

Source: U.S. Bureau of the Census, 1980 Census of the Population, U.S. Summary (Washington, D.C.: Government Printing Office, 1981).

Table 5.5

Marital Status of U.S. Population and Foreign-Born Filipinos over Age 15: 1980 (in percentages)

	U.S. Population		Filipinos	
	Males	Females	Males	Females
Over age 15	100%	100%	100%	100%
Single	29.7	22.8	23.9	21.7
Married	60.6	55.2	69.7	66.9
Separated	1.9	2.6	1.3	1.8
Widowed	2.5	12.3	2.3	6.7
Divorced	5.3	7.1	2.8	2.9

Sources: U.S. Census Bureau, *1980 Census of the Population, U.S. Summary* (Washington, D.C.: Government Printing Office, 1981) and "Foreign Born Immigrants: Filipinos— Tabulations from the 1980 U.S. Census of the Population and Housing," mimeo- graphed report, Washington, D.C., October 1984.

or divorced than the U.S. population at large. In fact, the percentage of divorced persons is about half that of the U.S. population, while the per- centage of those married is higher than the U.S. norm.

This condition can be attributed to the Filipinos' religious convictions (Catholicism); to the fact that divorce is not legally possible in the Philip- pines; and to strong family traditions, which are carried over to the new land of residence. As can be expected, length of residence in the United States and the subsequent acculturation of immigrants in U.S. society af- fected the percentage of those who are divorced. Such rates, by periods of immigration, are shown in Table 5.6.

Table 5.6

Divorce Rate of Filipino Immigrants, as of 1980

	1975–80	1970–74	1965–1969	1960–64	Before 1960
Males	1.3	2.2	2.1	2.5	4.9
Females	1.5	3.0	3.1	4.1	6.6

Source: U.S. Bureau of the Census, "Foreign-Born Immigrants: Filipinos—Tabulations from the 1980 U.S. Census of the Population and Housing," mimeographed report, Washington, D.C., October 1984.

From Tables 5.5 and 5.6, it can be seen that Filipino immigrants who have been in the United States for more than 20 years have divorce rates that approach those of the U.S. population at large.

FILIPINO IMMIGRANT HOUSEHOLD TYPE AND SIZE

The household patterns of Filipinos who immigrated between 1970 and 1980 mirrors both their background and their life-style in adapting to U.S. society.

Generally, such households are larger than U.S. households and tend to include relatives and acquaintances who not only provide assistance with domestic chores, but also may contribute financially to the welfare of the household through employment. This situation is not unusual in Filipino immigrant families, who carry on their traditional kinship system and have households that include parents, brothers and sisters, cousins, nephews and nieces, and even newly arrived "province mates."

The strength of the family bond and kinship can be seen by comparing the percentage of persons who are relatives (other than spouses and children) in U.S. households with that of Filipino-headed households where the householder immigrated to the United States in the period 1970-80. For the U.S. population at large, it is 4.2%; for Filipino households, 18.5%. Similarly, the percentage of nonrelatives living in the household is 2.7% of the total U.S. population and 4.2% of the above-mentioned Filipino households.[3] Thus, persons other than nuclear family members residing in the household tend to raise the average number of persons per household: Where the norm for the United States is 2.74 persons per household, the figure is 3.63 for Filipino households where the householder immigrated between 1970 and 1980.

EDUCATION

Educational attainment is one of the characteristics distinguishing Filipinos—as well as Asian immigrants, in general—from other immigrants who have come to the United States in the past and those currently coming from other parts of the world.

Data collected by the U.S. Bureau of the Census allow us to draw a fairly accurate picture of the educational achievements of Filipino immigrants in the United States, as shown in Table 5.7.

For Filipino immigrants over the age of 20 who came to the United States prior to 1959 and were still in residence when the 1980 census was taken, the educational achievement was not particularly noteworthy. Those who had not completed a fifth-grade education numbered 18.4%; 42.5% were high school graduates; and only 14.6% had completed college.

In contrast with this, immigrants who came in the period 1965-69 after

Table 5.7

Years of Schooling Completed by Filipino Immigrants over Age 20, as of 1980 (in percentages)

Years of School Completed	Year of Immigration			
	All Immigrants	1959 or earlier	1965–69	1975–1980
Elementary				
0–4	7.0%	18.4%	3.1%	6.6%
5–8	10.2	18.8	6.1	11.5
High School				
1–3	7.9	10.4	6.5	8.6
4	15.5	19.0	15.0	14.5
College				
1–3	20.1	18.8	20.0	19.4
4 or more	39.3	14.6	49.3	39.4

Source: U.S. Bureau of the Census, "Foreign-Born Immigrants: Filipinos—Tabulations from the 1980 U.S. Census of the Population and Housing," mimeographed report, Washington, D.C., October 1984.

passage of the Immigration and Nationality Act and who were over the age of 20 in 1980 were found to have a high level of educational achievement: Only 3.1% had less than a fifth-grade education. On the other hand, 84.3% were high school graduates and 49.3% had a college education.

The percentages for more recent immigrants—those who arrived between 1975 and 1980 and who, in 1980, were over the age of 20—turns out to be 6.6% with less than fifth-grade education, 73.0% with a high school education, and 39.4% with four or more years of college.

When we include all native Filipinos over the age of 20 (regardless of the year of immigration), we find that 7% have less than five years of education, 74.9% are high school graduates, and 39.3% are college graduates. The percentages for high school and college graduates are even higher if the cutoff age used is 25, the age a person is more likely to have completed college education. We then find that 87.3% are high school graduates and 47% have completed four or more years of college. Comparable figures for all Filipinos immigrating between 1970 and 1980 are 77.1% for high school and 47.9% for college.

For 1980, these educational achievements stack up very favorably with the educational achievements of the total U.S. population and those of all foreign-born over the age of 25 in 1980. In fact, the percentage of high school graduates was 66.5 for the U.S. population and 56.9 for all foreign-born. The figures for those with four or more years of college education were 16.2% for the U.S. population and 22.2% for all foreign-born.

When the variable of sex is introduced, native Filipino women over the age of 20 have a higher proportion of college graduates than males. Where 43.4% of females were college graduates, only 34.4% of males had four or more years of college. This difference may be due to the large number of female nurses who come to the United States each year with work permits and eventually acquire immigrant status.

Another indication of the drive for high educational achievement is evident from the number of Filipino-born over the age of 16 who are employed and who, at the same time, were attending school in 1980: 34,837. A very high proportion of these—59.4% were doing undergraduate work in college, while another 22.6% were enrolled in postgraduate courses.

Some available evidence indicates that most Filipino immigrants obtained their education in the Philippines prior to coming to the United States. According to a statistical analysis presented by Gardner, Robey, and Smith in their recent report on Asian-Americans, comparison of data from the 1980 census of the Philippines with the 1980 U.S. census shows that 84.9% of Filipinos who immigrated to the United States in the period 1975-80 at the age of 20-39 were high school graduates. Similarly, out of 32,521 Filipino immigrants who came during that period and who were in the 30–39 age group in 1980, 18,868—or 58%—had four or more years of college education.[4]

Since comparable figures for all Filipinos residing in their own country are much lower, it is evident that immigration to the United States is taking the "cream of the crop" produced by the educational system in the Philippines and that the complaint of "brain drain" has some validity. According to Immigration and Naturalization Service statistics for 1983, 42.7% of all Filipino immigrants who declared an occupation when entering the United States were in the professional, technical, or executive category.[5]

From time to time, the exodus of educated people is decried in the Philippines, both in the press and in academia. Dr. Rene Mendoza, a professor of Philippines Studies at the University of the Philippines, has indicated that the emigrants' "contribution to the economic well-being of the American society could have been a substantial contribution to a developing country's economic well-being."[6]

Abad and Eviota are even more vehement on the deleterious effects of emigration of highly skilled professionals and technical workers from the Philippines. They argue that the Philippines, with an overdeveloped educational system and an underdeveloped economy, pays for the cost of educating these emigrants without deriving any benefits and that their remittances to the home country do not go into productive endeavors. The skill drain also diminishes the economic base of the sending country and reinforces development inequalities between the two countries.[7]

However, emigration of skilled persons has been rationalized as a safety valve in relieving unemployment pressures on the educated classes of the sending country—a group with the potential to become politically active and to foster instability in the Philippines. Further, it has been argued that skilled workers who emigrate contribute to the nation's foreign exchange needs and also enhance the good name of the Philippines abroad.

In any case, the problem with the brain drain—as far as the individual immigrant is concerned—appears to be academic. Given the opportunity, he would rather make a salary 10–20 times as much in the United States as in his country; and, therefore, the exodus—barring unforeseen circumstances—is most likely to continue.

FILIPINO IMMIGRANTS AT WORK

Labor Force Participation

One indicator of the contribution of a group to the economic life of the nation is the degree of participation in the labor force by those over the age of 16. It is measured by the ratio of those employed or seeking work to the total number of those over 16.

As shown in Table 5.8, out of the 437,564 foreign-born Filipinos over the age of 16 who were in the United States in April 1980, 317,756—or 72.6%—were in the labor force. For males, the rate of labor force participation was 77.6%; for women, it was 68.7%. These rates were higher than those of both the U.S. population at large and other ethnic groups. In comparison, the rate of labor force participation for all races in the United States in 1980 was 62%. For white males, it was 76%; and for white females, 49%.

As shown in Table 5.9, the rate of participation is influenced by the length of time that Filipino immigrants have been in the United States. For

Table 5.8
Labor Force Participation of Filipino Immigrants over Age 16: 1980

	Total Immigrants	In Labor Force	%
Total over age 16	437,564	317,756	72.6
Males over age 16	199,781	154,292	77.2
Females over age 16	237,783	163,464	68.7

Source: U.S. Bureau of the Census, "Foreign-Born Immigrants: Filipinos—Tabulations from the 1980 U.S. Census of the Population and Housing," mimeographed report, Washington, D.C., October 1984.

Table 5.9
Labor Force Participation of Filipino Immigrants over Age 16, by Year of
Immigration: 1980 (in percentages)

| | Year of Immigration | | | | |
	1975–80	1970–74	1965–69	1960–64	1959 and earlier
Both sexes	67.2	80.0	83.2	81.2	54.6
Males	78.3	88.2	88.8	90.1	52.3
Females	59.9	75.2	78.1	73.6	59.7

Source: U.S. Bureau of the Census, "Foreign-Born Immigrants: Filipinos—Tabulations from the 1980 U.S. Census of the Population and Housing," mimeographed report, Washington, D.C., October 1984.

males, it tends to rise with length of stay—dropping off only for immigrants who came prior to 1960, since very close to half of this group are already retired and no longer in the labor force.

A different trend is observed for women. While the rate of labor force participation generally goes up with length of stay in the United States, it drops off for those who came to the United States before 1965. In any case, even after dropping off, the rate of labor participation for Filipino female immigrants is still considerably higher than that of the total U.S. white female population.

Employment and Unemployment

Of the 317,756 Filipino immigrants in the labor force, 298,463—or 93.9%—were in the civilian labor force; the balance (19,293) were in the military, mostly with the U.S. Navy.

In April 1980, the overwhelming majority of these immigrants in the civilian labor force were employed, and their rate of unemployment was lower than that of the U.S. work force at large. Actually, as shown in Table 5.10, while the rate of unemployment for all races in April 1980 was 6.5%— and for all foreign-born in the United States, 7.2%—the rate for Filipino immigrants was 4.5%. Even in the case of the newest arrivals—those who arrived between 1975 and 1980—the 6% rate of unemployment was lower than that of the U.S. labor force as a whole.

The rate of unemployment varied with the length of time that the immigrant had been in the United States. It was as low as 2.9% for female im-

Table 5.10
Employment and Unemployment Rates of Filipino Immigrants in the Civilian Labor Force: 1980 (in percentages)

	All	1975–80	1970–74	1965–69	1960–64	1959 and previous
Both Sexes						
Employed	35.5	94.0	96.4	96.8	95.3	94.7
Unemployed	4.5	6.0	3.6	3.1	4.7	5.3
Males						
Employed	95.4	94.0	96.7	95.6	95.0	94.1
Unemployed	4.6	6.0	3.3	4.1	5.0	5.9
Females						
Employed	95.6	94.0	96.2	97.1	95.5	96.1
Unemployed	4.4	6.0	3.8	2.9	4.5	3.9

Source: U.S. Bureau of the Census, "Foreign-Born Immigrants: Filipinos—Tabulations from the 1980 U.S. Census of the Population and Housing," mimeographed report, Washington, D.C., October 1984.

migrants who had arrived in the United States between 1965 and 1969 and for male immigrants who had come between 1970 and 1974. In general, unemployment rates were lower for women than for men.

One additional insight into the unemployment and employment experience of the Filipino-born labor force is gleaned by examining their work experience during 1979, in comparison with that of the U.S. work force at large and that of all foreign-born in the work force. Data presented in Table 5.11 show that, while Filipinos were more likely to have been unemployed during 1979, their periods of unemployment were shorter than those of the U.S. labor force at large and that of the total foreign-born work force. This indicates an ability—when unemployed—to locate employment faster than their counterparts, perhaps because of their willingness to accept employment in occupations other than their own. No noticeable differences are found when the variables of sex and length of stay in the United States are examined in relation to the average number of weeks of unemployment.

In fact, the number of weeks of unemployment in 1979 averaged lower for the more recent Filipino immigrant arrivals, for both males and females. Male immigrants who arrived between 1975 and 1980 and were unemployed during 1979 had an average 12.1 weeks of unemployment. Females in the same group time frame had 12.0 weeks of unemployment. The males who arrived between 1960 and 1964 had 13.9 weeks of unemployment; and females, 12.7. This last variation is probably attributable to the lower skill levels of education possessed by the immigrants who came to the

Table 5.11
Work Experience of Filipino Immigrants in the U.S. Labor Force: 1979
(in percentages)

	All U.S. Workers	All Foreign- Born Workers	All Filipino- Born Workers
% Worked during 1979	98.2	97.5	97.9
% Worked full time 50–52 weeks	52.2	50.6	51.7
% Worked 40–49 weeks	13.2	15.9	20.1
% Worked 27–39 weeks	8.3	8.3	7.0
% Worked 1–26 weeks	18.0	17.0	15.1
% Unemployed in 1979	18.6	20.8	19.7
% Unemployed 15 weeks or longer	6.2	7.5	5.9
Average weeks of unemployment per unemployed worker	14.1	14.5	12.7

Sources: U.S. Bureau of the Census, *1980 Census of the Population, U.S. Summary* (Washington, D.C.: Government Printing Office, 1981) and "Foreign-Born Immigrants: Filipinos—Tabulations from the 1980 U.S. Census of the Population and Housing," mimeographed report, Washington, D.C., October 1984.

United States prior to 1965—resulting in their likelihood of longer periods of unemployment and additional difficulty in finding work.

Occupations

Foreign-born Filipinos in the United States enjoy a much higher occupational status than that of the U.S. population at large: 20.1% of all foreign-born Filipinos over the age of 16 who were employed in 1980 were professionals, as compared with 12.3% of the U.S. population over age 16.

In comparison with the general population, Filipinos were also overrepresented as technicians (6.6% versus 3.1%), in clerical jobs (21% versus 17.2%), and in the services field (16.2% versus 12.9%).

Underrepresentation occurred in the skilled production and repair crafts (7.3% versus 12.9%); in sales jobs (5% versus 10%); and in the machine operator, transportation worker, and laborer occupations.

The picture that emerges from a review of the data presented in Table 5.12 would appear to indicate that Filipinos prefer white-collar jobs and, in general, tend to shun occupations involving labor intensive, repetitive tasks.

Table 5.12
Occupational Distribution of Filipino Immigrants among the U.S. Employed: 1980 (in percentages)

Occupation	By percentages U.S. Labor Force	Filipino Born Labor Force
1. Executive, Administrative & Managerial	10.4	7.9
Professional Specialty	12.3	20.1
Technicians & Related Support	3.1	6.6
Sales	10.0	5.0
Administrative Support, involving clerical	17.2	21.0
Private Household Services	.6	.6
Protective Services	1.5	.8
Other Services	10.8	14.8
Farming, Forestry, and Fishing	2.9	2.7
Precision Production Craft & Repair	12.9	7.3
Machine Operators and Assemblers	9.3	8.9
Transportation & Material Moving	4.5	1.4
Handlers, Helpers & Laborers	4.5	2.9

Sources: U.S. Bureau of the Census, *1980 Census of the Population, U.S. Summary,* (Washington, D.C.: Government Printing Office, 1981) and "Foreign Born: Filipinos—Tabulations from the U.S. Census of the Population and Housing," mimeographed report, Washington, D.C., October 1984.

Taking one occupational category—the professionals—an analysis of the data collected by the U.S. Bureau of the Census in 1980 indicates that, when correlated with the year of immigration, the percentage of Filipinos employed in this category has decreased, after reaching a peak with those who came here in 1965-69 shortly after passage of the new U.S. immigration law. According to the year of immigration, the percentage of those employed who were engaged in the professions in 1980 turns out to be as follows: for older immigrants (those who immigrated in 1959 or earlier), 13.9%; for those who came between 1960 and 1964, 26.4%; for immigrants from the period 1965–69, 27.2%; for those coming between 1970 and 1974, 22%; and for the latest groups (the ones who arrived between 1975 and 1980), 14.4%.

However, the lower percentage of employed professionals does not indicate that the more recent Filipino immigrants are less likely to be professionals and to be eventually so employed. It is, rather, a reflection of other factors—such as difficulty in obtaining professional licenses, the need to quickly obtain employment in any occupation upon arrival, and lack of knowledge concerning the social and economic mores of the United States.

Furthermore, no doubt, some vestiges of discrimination influence the above data. This hypothesis is borne out by looking at the percentage of college graduates among Filipino-born immigrants versus their percentages of professionals, by year of immigration. The data for these two factors are presented in Table 5.13—which shows that length of stay in the United States has, indeed, a high correlation with whether or not immigrants are able to put education and skills to good use. While 39.4% of all immigrants arriving between 1975 and 1980 had four or more years of college by 1980, only 14.4% were working in the professions. Conversely, while only 14.6% of those who immigrated prior to 1960 had that level of education, 13.9% were employed as professionals. Thus, it becomes evident that, at the beginning of their new life in the United States, a substantial number of immigrants start their employment in occupations that do not reflect their skills and education.

Another characteristic of Filipino-born workers was their low rate of self-employment: Only 2.3% of the total number employed were self-employed. The comparable rate for the U.S. population at large is 6.3%—considerably higher. Most Filipinos were working for private companies (79.9%); and a substantial number (17.0%), for the various levels of government. Only an insignificant number—0.2%—were employed without pay in family businesses.

Income

In comparison with the population at large or other Asian immigrant groups, Filipino immigrants in the United States have done very well.

Table 5.13

Filipino Immigrants with Higher Education and in Professional Occupations: 1980 (in percentages)

	Year of Immigration				
	Before 1960	1960–64	1965–69	1970–74	1975–80
4 or more yrs. of college	14.6	32.9	49.3	49.5	39.4
Employed as Professionals	13.9	26.4	27.2	22.0	14.4

Source: U.S. Bureau of the Census, "Foreign Born: Filipinos—Tabulations from the 1980 Census of the Population and Housing," mimeographed report, Washington, D.C., October 1984.

While the median income of a Filipino full-time worker was less than that of a white worker ($12,715 versus $15,572), it was higher than that of blacks, Hispanics, and any other Asian immigrant group except Indians ($13,138). However, the median household income where one of the householders was Filipino-born was higher than that of all U.S. households: $22,787 versus $16,841. This higher household income may be attributable to the fact that the mean number of persons who are employed in a household where the householder was a Filipino is higher than the mean number for all U.S. households.

More extensive information is available on families whose head or spouse was a Filipino and whose immigration to the United States occurred between 1970 and 1979. In such families, the median income was $24,480, which compares favorably with the median family income for all U.S. families ($19,917) and was even higher than that of white families ($20,800). However, without a doubt, this was also due to the fact that the average number of workers per family was higher for Filipino immigrants: 2.1 versus 1.6 for all U.S. families.

Thus, we see that the higher labor-force participation—and a willingness to arrange their life-style and living conditions to maximize income—account for the higher income level of Filipino families. The importance of more workers per family unit in raising income level is seen by comparing all U.S. families with Filipino-headed families who immigrated to the United States between 1970 and 1979, both in terms of median income and workers per family (Table 5.14).

The household income distribution for the same group of Filipino immigrants is another way of showing their income standing in relation to the

Table 5.14
Workers per U.S. and Filipino Immigrant Family and Median
Family Income: 1979

No. of Workers	U.S. Families	Income	Filipino-Headed Fam. Immigrated 1970-79	Income
No worker	12.8	7,791	2.7	3,112
1 worker	33.0	16,181	19.3	12,432
2 workers	41.6	23,058	55.7	25,340
3 or more workers	12.6	31,880	22.3	35,043

Source: U.S. Bureau of the Census, *1980 Census of the Population, U.S. Summary,* (Washington, D.C.: Government Printing Office, 1981).

general population in the United States. Table 5.15 shows that 16.1% of Filipino-headed households had an income below $10,000, versus 29.2% for all U.S. households. At the opposite end of the scale, while 43.8% of Filipino households had an income over $25,000, that was true for only 29.8% of U.S. households.

Again, the higher income of Filipino immigrant households is primarily due to three factors: They are more likely to be families than U.S. households, the size of the household is on the average larger than the average U.S. household (4.04 persons per household versus 3.63), and more numbers of the household are likely to be employed.

The indicated level of income has kept most Filipino families above the poverty line. In fact, while the percentage of all U.S. families with incomes below the poverty level in 1979 was 9.6%, it was only 5.3% for all families headed by a Filipino or with a Filipino spouse. As might be expected, the percentages of families with income below the poverty level were greatest for families whose arrival was more recent—8.8% for those who immigrated between 1975 and 1980—and lowest for those who came between 1965 and 1969—3.6%.

In terms of individuals whose income was below the poverty level, the differences between the entire U.S. population, other groups, and Filipinos who arrived in the United States between 1970 and 1980 are even more drastic. The percentages were 6.8 for Filipinos, 12.4 for the entire U.S. pop-

Table 5.15
Household Income Distribution of Filipinos Who Immigrated between 1970 and 1979 versus All U.S. Households: 1979 (in percentages)

Income	U.S. Households	Immigrant Filipino Households
Less than $5,000	13.3	5.9
$5,000 - $7,499	8.0	4.1
$7,500 - $9,999	7.9	6.1
$10,000 - $14,999	15.3	13.1
$15,000 - $19,999	14.1	13.5
$20,000 - $24,999	12.5	13.4
$25,000 - $34,999	15.7	22.0
$35,000 to $49,999	8.6	15.1
$50,000 or more	4.6	6.7

Source: U.S. Bureau of the Census, *1980 Census of the Population, U.S. Summary,* (Washington, D.C.: Government Printing Office, 1981).

ulation, 23 for all immigrants who arrived between 1970 and 1980, 10.7 for all foreign-born who came before 1970, and 12.2 for all U.S.-born.

Within the Asian immigrant group, Filipino immigrants appeared to have the lowest percentage of persons with an income below the poverty level.

Occupations and Income

While, in general, educational achievement and a longer period of residence in the United States translate into higher earnings for the individual, families, and households, there is evidence available from recent studies that Filipinos have only recently attained economic parity with the native white U.S. population.

In a study completed in June 1984, Goza—taking into account such variables as education, years of job experience, weeks worked, language skills, and length of residence in the United States—discovered that Filipino immigrant workers were earning less in 1959 and 1969 than their white counterparts, and that Filipino immigrant workers earned less in both years than U.S.-born Filipinos. By 1979, however, foreign-born Filipinos were earning substantially more than Filipinos born in the United States, and were better educated than the latter. By 1980, foreign-born Filipinos received more income than whites, in relation to skills offered. This did not hold for U.S.-born Filipinos. The differences in earnings between foreign and U.S.-born Filipinos (when all other variables remain equal) was attributed by Goza to socioeconomic discrimination.[8]

Wong, in a previous study published in 1982, discovered that, while the average annual earnings of Filipinos were considerably less in 1960 and 1970 than those of whites, the gap had been greatly reduced by 1976; and Filipinos, while still earning less than whites, were receiving greater rates of return when the variables of education, generation status, and occupation were taken into account.[9]

Thus, we can conclude that, while Filipinos in the past encountered significant socioeconomic discrimination, this factor has been overcome in recent years, for the most part.

ACCULTURATION

Data on the ability to speak English and on naturalization as U.S. citizens—two factors that point to the degree of acculturation of Filipino immigrants in the United States—are available from the special tabulations on the foreign-born made by the U.S. Bureau of the Census in 1980.

In 1980, 44.7% of all native Filipinos were found to be naturalized U.S. citizens—a high percentage, exceeded only by immigrants of a few Asian countries. Since five years of permanent residence are required before applying for naturalization, this percentage becomes even higher if one excludes the immigrants who arrived in the period 1975-80 and who, thus, may not have been eligible for naturalization: By 1980, 62.9% of all Filipino immigrants who arrived prior to 1975 were U.S. citizens.

The increase (by year of immigration) in the percentage of Filipino immigrants who became U.S. citizens is given in Table 5.16. We note by looking at the data in this table that, by 1980, more than 56% of those immigrants who had been in the United States for 5–10 years were naturalized; of those who had been in the United States for 10–15 years, more than two-thirds were U.S. citizens; and of those who had been in the United States for 15–20 years, four-fifths had become U.S. citizens by 1980.

In the case of Filipinos, knowledge of the English language is not the best indicator of acculturation, because most Filipinos have some knowledge of the language. Still, for a good percentage of Filipino immigrants, language must be a major stumbling block in integrating with U.S. society, since most Filipinos speak their own dialect first and English second. Therefore, a look at the English-language proficiency of Filipino immigrants may be useful.

Table 5.16
Naturalization of Filipino Immigrants, as of 1980

Years of Immigration	Total	Naturalized	% Naturalized
All periods	501,440	223,995	44.7
1975–1980	173,721	17,204	10.0
1970–1974	146,318	67,519	46.1
1964–1969	85,469	58,853	68.9
1960–1964	27,617	22,242	80.5
1959 & earlier	69,315	58,177	83.9

Source: U.S. Bureau of the Census, "Foreign-Born Immigrants: Filipinos—Tabulations from the 1980 U.S. Census of the Population and Housing," mimeographed report, Washington, D.C., October 1984.

In 1980, there were 483,762 Filipino immigrants over the age of five residing in the United States as household members. Only a small percentage—13.2—lived in households where only the English language was spoken. The balance resided in households where one of the Filipino dialects was spoken at home. Of these, 50% also spoke English very well, 29% spoke it well, 7% spoke it poorly, and 0.8% did not speak English at all (Table 5.17).

By looking at the period of immigration and proficiency in speaking the English language, one can obtain a limited insight into this component of the acculturation process. While other factors (such as education received in the Philippines and urbanization) affect language proficiency, the ability to speak English well—however acquired—is still one of the means to obtain a more rapid entry into U.S. society.

In general, the exclusive use of the English language at home—as might be expected—increased with length of time in the United States; and conversely, the percentage of those who spoke one of the Filipino dialects at home decreased. The percentage of those who spoke another language at home and also spoke English well or very well also went up with increased length of residence, except for immigrants who had arrived prior to 1965— probably due to the fact that this group had a lower educational achievement.

The immigrants who came prior to 1960 present a more varied picture. While more than one-fifth spoke only English at home, one-tenth spoke English poorly. Again, these data reflect their lower educational achieve-

Table 5.17
Ability to Speak English among Filipino Immigrants over Age 5: 1980
(in percentages)

	All	Year of Immigration				1959 and Previous
		1975–80	1970–74	1965–69	1960–64	
1. Speak only English at Home	13.2	7.0	13.8	14.6	19.3	22.5
2. Speak Language other than English at home	86.8	93.0	86.2	85.4	80.7	77.5
A. Speak English very well	50.0	43.4	56.2	59.1	55.6	39.2
B. Speak English well	29.0	36.7	25.7	22.9	22.2	27.6
C. Speak English not well	7.0	11.4	3.8	3.1	2.7	10.1
D. Do not speak any English	.8	1.5	.5	.3	.2	.6

Source: U.S. Bureau of the Census, "Foreign-Born Immigrants: Filipinos—Tabulations from the 1980 U.S. Census of the Population and Housing," mimeographed report, Washington, D.C., October 1984.

ments; rural background; and probably the fact that these immigrants have continued to live in ethnic neighborhoods, where it is possible to conduct their daily affairs and socialize even if their knowledge of the English language is not the best.

6

Conclusions and Prospects for the Future

Filipinos in the United States make up a sizable ethnic minority, in which 35.3% were U.S. born and 64.7% are natives of Philippines. Because of continuous, heavy immigration of more than 40,000 Filipinos for permanent residence each year, their number in the United States will continue to increase, and they will displace the Chinese as the largest Asian group.

In 1980, Filipino immigrants were a highly urbanized group, with 92.6% of the total residing in metropolitan areas. A little more than 50% were concentrated in two West Coast states: California and Washington.

Since a sizable number of immigrants are female spouses of U.S. citizens, female native Filipinos in the United States are in the majority—with a ratio of 86.4 males to 100 females. As to age, a larger percentage of foreign-born Filipinos than the U.S. population at large are in the productive age brackets, 15-64. In fact, native Filipinos in this age group comprise 78.3% of the total number of foreign-born in their ethnic group, versus 66% for the U.S. population.

Contrary to their previous experience in the Philippines, Filipino-born women in the United States have lower fertility rates than American women, despite the fact that they are more likely to be married. Similarly, divorce rates for foreign-born Filipinos are lower than those of the overall U.S. population—a reflection of family cohesiveness and stability.

The households of native Filipinos tend to be larger than the average for U.S. households, and frequently include relatives other than nuclear family members. While such relatives make up only 4.2% of the number of persons residing in U.S. households, they account for 18.5% of persons residing in the households of Filipino immigrants.

On the average, Filipino immigrants are more highly educated than Americans. In fact, a total of 47% of those over age 25 had attended college for four years or more, as compared with 16.2% for the U.S. population. Similarly, 87.3% were high school graduates, versus 66.5% in the U.S. population.

In the work place, Filipino immigrants had a higher rate of participation in the labor force than Americans—72.6% compared to 62%. This tended to be true even for the newest immigrants, those who had arrived between 1975 and 1980. Similarly, the percentage of unemployed Filipino immigrants in the U.S. work force was lower than that of the total U.S. population—regardless of sex and date of arrival. In comparison with the U.S. work force, Filipino immigrants were overrepresented in the professions, technical occupations, clerical jobs, and the service area. They were underrepresented in the skilled production area and in the blue-collar occupations. A significant number—17%—worked for the various levels of government, and only a meager 2.9% were self-employed. From these occupational characteristics, it may be concluded that Filipino immigrants generally fail to exercise entrepreneurial skills and prefer white-collar occupations—even though these may pay lower salaries—to risk-taking and more hard-labor occupations.

These work characteristics have had the effect of dragging down the median income of full-time Filipino-born workers. However, the median household income in a Filipino immigrant household was considerably higher than that of U.S. households in general—$22,787 versus $16,841. Median family income of Filipino immigrants who arrived in the United States between 1970 and 1979 was also higher than that of all U.S. families as a whole, and even higher than that of white families—by 23% and 18%, respectively.

The household income distribution analysis also yielded results favorable to Filipino immigrant households. While 29.2% of U.S. households had incomes of less than $10,000 in 1979, only 16% of the 1970-80 Filipino immigrant households were in this income range. At the other end of the scale, 43.8% of the 1970-80 Filipino immigrant households enjoyed an income of $25,000 or more, as compared with 28.9% of all U.S. households. Because the median income of a full-time native Filipino worker in 1980 was lower than that for a comparable American worker, the higher household and family income of Filipino immigrants can only be attributed to the fact that Filipino households and families both had more employed persons per unit. Among immigrant Filipino families who came between 1970 and 1979, 78% had two or more workers; the comparable share for all U.S. families was 54.2%.

In 1980, about half of all foreign-born Filipinos in the United States were U.S. citizens; this percentage increased with length of residence. In fact, more than four-fifths of those who had arrived in the United States prior to 1965 were U.S. citizens by 1980.

While only 13.2% of the Filipino immigrants spoke English at home, an additional 79% also spoke English well or very well—with the number who did not speak English at all being less than 1%.

By 1980, in comparison with the U.S. population at large, Filipino immigrants appeared to be doing very well educationally, economically, in terms of family stability, and in their absorption into the mainstream of U.S. society.

Barring unforeseen circumstances (such as changes in U.S. immigration laws and internal changes in the Philippines in the post-Marcos period), the steady stream of immigrants from that country is likely to continue unabated; and, by the turn of the century, the number of Filipinos in the United States may be close to the 2 million mark.

KOREA

7

A Short History of Korean Immigration to the United States

The emigration of Koreans to foreign countries dates from the turn of this century. During the previous two centuries of isolation—in which Korea acquired the nickname "The Hermit Kingdom"—it was forbidden by law to leave the country, under penalty of death.

Following the extension of Japanese influence in Korea and the eventual annexation of the country to Japan in 1910, several million Koreans emigrated to China and Russia. During the Japanese period (1910-45), many either emigrated or were forcibly brought to Japan to provide manpower for the Japanese war machine. Substantial remnants of these immigrants are still present in those countries: In 1961, there were 1.25 million Koreans in Manchuria, 300,000 in Siberia, and 600,000 in Japan.[1]

Immigration to the United States started in 1885, with the arrival of three Koreans who claimed to be political refugees. Five more, who came in 1899, were believed to be Chinese and were counted as such. In January 1900, two more entered Hawaii to remain as immigrants. During the period 1890–1905, 64 more Koreans arrived in Hawaii to become students in Christian mission schools; most members of this group eventually returned home to Korea.

Sustained immigration to the United States started in 1902: The Korean government set up an immigration office in Seoul where a Hawaiian plantation manager named D.W. Keshler, who was helped by Protestant missionaries, was given permission by the Korean government to open a recruiting office.

Just as in the case of Filipino immigrants, the Hawaiian connection was the need for "cheap" labor to work on the booming sugar plantations. Because of the chaotic political and economic conditions in Korea at this time, Keshler was able to recruit a sizable number of immigrants; and, by December 1902, 121 Koreans embarked on the U.S.S. *Gaelic* bound for Hawaii. Of that number, 19 failed a required medical exam when the ship stopped in Japan, and were sent back to Korea. The balance—comprising 56 men, 21 women, and 25 children—arrived in Honolulu on January 13, 1903. This first group was followed by others; and, by May 1905, more than 7,000 Koreans—mostly males—had arrived in Hawaii to work in the sugar plantations.

In November 1905, the Korean government stopped immigration, because of complaints concerning the treatment of its nationals in the United States. The number of immigrants then dwindled from more than 2,500 arrivals in 1905 to 8 in 1906.

On Hawaii's plantations, Koreans lived in camps separated from other racial and ethnic groups, and quickly developed group unity—setting up their own rules of behavior and social intercourse, in line with Confucian principles. Generally, the oldest male (with the help of the camp council) became the spokesman for the group, settled all internal disputes, and provided leadership in dealing with the employers and the outside world.

These early Korean immigrants remained in the plantations until the 1920s, when they drifted to Honolulu and obtained employment in the pineapple canneries, worked at the docks, or engaged in cabinetmaking or tailoring. By 1932, only 442 Koreans remained on the plantations—as compared with 34,915 Filipinos and 9,395 Japanese.[2]

Additionally, between 1905 and 1916, a number of these immigrants returned to Korea. Some moved to the mainland—to Salt Lake City and Seattle—and others settled in Montana, where they engaged in farming.

The early immigrants came to the United States for a variety of reasons: to escape crop failures and famine, rampant inflation, and exploitation by the government. Most were not peasants but laborers, ex-soldiers, students, and political refugees who were fleeing both the Korean government and the growing influence of the Japanese over Korea.

For all intents and purposes, the early Korean immigration stopped in 1907 when the U.S. government refused to recognize Korean passports, which had been issued against the wishes of the Japanese occupiers. The Japanese demanded that everyone leaving Korea do so with a Japanese passport, and subsequently forbade immigration completely. However, by the terms of the gentleman's agreement between the United States and Japan, Korean "picture brides"—like Japanese female immigrants—continued to be admitted to the United States. These were women who contracted marriage to immigrants of their ethnic group in the United States on the basis of an exchange of correspondence and photographs. Since most of the early Korean immigrants had been men, this practice flourished. Between 1910 and 1924, more than 1,000 Korean "picture brides" were admitted—most of them to join their spouses in Hawaii.

After Korea was annexed by Japan in 1910, young Korean political activists started making their way to the United States. By 1924 (when the new immigration laws severely restricted the entry of Orientals), 541 Koreans claiming to be political refugees had entered the United States.

From 1924 to the end of World War II when Korea was liberated from the Japanese, practically no Korean immigrants came to this country. Several hundred students were admitted; but eventually, at the completion of their studies, virtually all left the United States and returned to Korea.

Korean immigrants—both those who stayed in Hawaii and those who moved on to the mainland—shared several common characteristics in addition to their nationality, customs, and language.

First, the great majority were Christians—generally, Protestants. Second, the Koreans tried to preserve their own culture and attempted to become literate at least in their own language. Third, they continued to take an active part and interest in the political affairs of their country of origin.

No sooner had the first group of immigrants arrived in Hawaii than they organized their own churches, where they regularly held services. Generally, a church was opened in each work camp: The church served a dual purpose, since it was used during the week as a school to teach the Korean language. The teachers in the church also taught the history and culture of the mother country.

Three of the earliest Korean immigrants to the United States became influential political figures who aimed to regain Korean independence from the Japanese occupiers. One of them, Ahn Chang Ho, started to organize students and other Koreans in 1903—believing that publicity and subsequent pressure from the world powers would convince the Japanese to leave Korea. He eventually returned to Asia, but was captured by the Japanese and died in a Japanese prison in 1938.

The second, Pak Yong-Man, started a Korean military organization in 1910—dedicated to the liberation of Korea. In 1912—leaving this enterprise to others—he went to Hawaii, where he published a Korean newspaper; and, in 1916, he moved on to China to organize efforts to free the homeland from there. In 1928, he was assassinated in China, by a Korean.

The third and most famous of these three Koreans was Syngman Rhee, who came to the United States as a student and obtained a doctorate from Princeton University in 1910. He then returned to Korea to organize opposition to the Japanese. To escape capture, however, he soon came back to the United States, where he remained until 1945—returning to Korea after the Japanese defeat.

During his residence here, Rhee was a tireless political organizer and dominated the Korean independence movement, which he had founded. In 1948, he became the first president of the Republic of Korea; he retained that post for 12 years until 1960, when he was forced to resign and go into exile.

Korean immigrants—both in Hawaii and on the mainland—did not engage in agricultural work for long, since only a small percentage were farmers by trade. Eventually, they drifted into the cities and took up other jobs. Some went into business for themselves and engaged in the restaurant trade, operated vegetable stands or small stores, or took up carpentry or tailoring.

Because—as Asians—they were ineligible to apply for U.S. citizenship, Koreans found it difficult to engage in any of the professions that required citizenship for licensing. Thus, they found themselves restricted to occupations that provided low salaries and only slim opportunities for social and economic progress. During and following World War II, with the liberalization of U.S. laws concerning citizenship (and despite a degree of social discrimination), Koreans started to enter the professions—particularly medicine, dentistry, architecture, and the scientific fields.

The large-scale movement of Korean immigrants to the United States began only after passage of the U.S. Immigration and Nationality Act of 1965. Consequently, major Korean immigration is a recent phenomenon. While a notable number of Korean women entered the United States as wives of U.S. citizens after World War II, the total number of immigrants who came in the 1950s was 6,231—about 600 per year. In the following decade, the number increased fivefold to 34,526; and, in the 1970s, it increased again by nearly 800%—to 267,638. For the last several years, this number has averaged more than 30,000 per year, and—barring a change in U.S. law—this trend is expected to continue.

A number of factors have influenced these spectacular increases and determined the composition of the immigrant stock arriving from Korea. By and large, post–World War II Korean immigrants have tended to be females, both because of their skills and because they married U.S. citizens. In fact, during the period 1950-75, 28,205 Koreans entered the United States as spouses of U.S. citizens, and another 7,000 came on the basis of their skill as nurses.[3]

Furthermore, more than three-fourths of the immigrants were under the age of 40; a majority came from the urban middle class of Korean society and included a large number of educated, college-trained professionals. About half were Christians.[4]

U.S. culture and policies have also had a significant effect—along with Korean factors—in both the number and composition of Korean immigrants. Since the end of the Korean War in 1953, Korea has experienced a tremendous population growth accompanied by industrialization and rapid urbanization. These factors have created pressures that forced the Korean government into undertaking policies to mitigate and control population increases. While the major efforts have been focused on family planning, emigration policies have also been liberalized.

The large number of U.S. servicemen stationed in Korea during and since the end of the Korean War has also affected emigration—not only because of the servicemen's marriage to Korean women, but also because of the adoption of Korean children by U.S. citizens, as well as the impact of U.S. mass culture in depicting the United States as a land of opportunity and freedom. Finally, news gathered from the kinship network, the fear of internal political problems in South Korea, the specter of a new conflict with North Korea, and the ease with which Korean children are able to pursue higher education in the United States, all have played a major role in the mushrooming of Korean emigration.

The Korean government's attitude toward emigration has also evolved—making emigration legally possible and easier. Following the founding of the Republic of Korea in 1948, emigration was discouraged and basically forbidden (except in special cases) on the basis that the nation required its population both for economic development and for defense against the communist north. This policy continued with minor changes until 1962, when an office of emigration was established in the Ministry of Health. Since then, emigration policies have gradually been relaxed, and a modest level of emigration has been encouraged.[5]

The increase in the number of Koreans in the United States since 1910 is shown in Table 7.1. These data clearly show that the greatest increase in numbers occurred in the 1970s—primarily because of immigration, rather than natural increase. In fact, 81.8% of all Koreans in the United States in 1980 were foreign born; 42.4% had arrived between 1975 and 1980; and an additional 25.7%, between 1970 and 1974. Therefore, more than two-thirds of all Koreans living in the United States in 1980 had been in residence for less than ten years.

While the early Korean immigrants tended to concentrate heavily in Hawaii and California, recent immigrants have tended to reside in a number of states. By 1970, California had the largest number—followed by Hawaii, New York, Illinois, Pennsylvania, and Washington. In 1980, while a little less than a third resided in California, other states held significant concentrations. More than 33,000 were in New York; close to 25,000, in Illinois; 17,000, in Hawaii; and nearly 15,000, in Maryland. Texas, Washington, Virginia, and New Jersey also had more than 10,000 Koreans each.

Most of the Koreans in California—an estimated 100,000—resided in Los Angeles, where they had settled west of downtown and had revitalized a neighborhood that was turning into a slum only a few years before.

New Korean immigrants have formed and are active in a large number of ethnic and religious organizations; and, despite all types of social dis-

Table 7.1
Koreans in the United States: Selected Years

Year	Numbers	Percentage of increase over Previous Years
1910	4,994	--
1920	6,627	32.7
1930	8,321	25.6
1940	8,562	2.8
1950*	8,176	--
1960*	14,331	--
1970	70,598	--
1980	354,329	401.9

*Only foreign-born Koreans included in total; complete data not available.

Source: U.S. Bureau of the Census, *Census of the Population* (Washington, D.C.: Government Printing Office, selected years)

cord within these organizations, they generally present a united front to outsiders.

One of the distinguishing features of Korean immigrants is the fact that a sizable number have engaged in business enterprises. Most of these are small operations located in large metropolitan areas—serving a clientele that has been neglected or abandoned by U.S. businessmen: the blacks, Chicanos, and Puerto Ricans. Because of their willingness to work hard, utilize ethnic financial resources, and employ family members, most of these businesses are successful.

A survey done in 1977 by Hyung Gi Jin revealed that an astounding 32% of Korean households in the United States were engaged in businesses and that an additional 28% were thinking of opening a business.[6]

According to a study made by Kwang Chung Kim and Won Moo Hurth on Korean-owned businesses in Chicago, most Korean businesses are concentrated in the retail and service sectors. Fruit and vegetable stands, grocery stores, service stations, and liquor stores are some of the favorite retail activities. Accounting, real estate, building maintenance, and repair services are the most popular service activities. Kim and Hurth also found that most Korean businesses are not located in areas that serve other Koreans, but do business with the underprivileged and minorities. A majority of the new

Korean businessmen had started their enterprises within three years of arrival in the United States and had had no previous business experience in Korea.[7]

The rate of success for such businesses appears to be quite high. A survey conducted by Pyong Gap Min and Charles Jaret in Atlanta indicates that only 8% were not successful. Success was ascribed to long working hours, frugality, and the employment of family members and relatives in the enterprise.[8]

Korean immigrants and their children—with their love of learning, drive for achievement and mobility, and strict adherence to the work ethic—appear to be one of the most successful of the ethnic groups that have recently immigrated to the United States. However, Koreans maintain a distinct ethnic identity that does not appear to be affected by length of residence, socioeconomic status, and cultural and social assimilation rates. The old habits and culture are retained and the new culture super-added.[9]

Whether this is a pattern likely to continue or whether it is due to the fact that most Korean immigrants have not been in the United States very long, remains to be seen. This judgment will have to wait until a large number of Koreans are born here, and the "old country" and its customs become less important in their lives than they appear to be now.

8

Current Emigration Trends and Problems in Korea

The rapidly rising population level in South Korea, its urbanization and rapid industrialization, the connection through the political/military alliance with the United States, and the stationing of large number of U.S. military personnel in the country, all have created conditions conducive to both permanent and temporary emigration.

Korea started to keep statistical data on permanent emigration in 1962, when the Office of Emigration was formed within the Ministry of Health. From that year to 1983, 516,078 Koreans applied for and received approval and passports for permanent emigration. In 1980, 69.1% of emigrants from Korea were leaving to join relatives overseas; 3% were emigrating on the basis of their occupation; 16.6% were the spouses of foreign citizens; and 11.1% were children adopted by foreigners. The data indicate that the number emigrating on the basis of their occupation was highest between 1970 and 1975, and that the percentage of emigrants joining relatives abroad reached its peak in 1980 and has since been declining. In 1983, emigrants joining relatives abroad made up about 50% of the total.[1]

The overwhelming majority of Koreans approved for emigration from 1962 to 1983—80.7%—reported the United States as their destination. During the same period, Canada was the given destination of 4.5% of the total. In a recent year (1980), 37,510 emigrants received permission to leave Korea; 33,638—or 89.7% of the total—indicated that they were going to the United States.[2]

Temporary emigration from Korea on the basis of labor contracts is more important and larger, and has recently been 4–5 times larger than permanent emigration. For the most part, temporary emigration is directed to the Middle East, although sizable numbers of Koreans also work on foreign ships as seamen. In 1980, 120,535 Koreans left the country for employment in the Middle East, and an additional 21,649 were employed as seamen on foreign-flag vessels. The main reason for acceptance of employment abroad is the higher wages that these workers can earn—partially because of overtime and other fringe benefits, which bring the overall salary to approximately twice what they would have earned in Korea. Remittances to relatives back in Korea passed the $1 billion mark in 1979 and were close to $2 billion in 1982—constituting more than one-fourth of the invisible trade receipts and, in 1982, 8% of the foreign exchange used by Korea for imports.[3]

As we have seen, the United States is by far the most popular destination for Korean immigrants. Because of the system of preferences and the processing of applications on a first-come, first-served basis within each preference, a backlog of qualified applicants has developed. The total number of applicants (in all preference categories) for which data are available from the U.S. Embassy in Seoul is given in Table 8.1.

In May 1985, the embassy was authorized to actively process the applications of registered intending immigrants with the following priority

Table 8.1
Registered Quota Applicants on Immigration Waiting Lists in Seoul: Selected Years

	Active	Inactive *	Total **
January 1981	84,737	60,427	145,164
1982	105,432	67,472	172,904
1983	120,806	74,594	195,400
1984	107,630	28,449	136,079
1985	121,425	33,978	155,403

*Inactive applicants are those who have not taken any embassy-requested action to further processing of their application.

**Numbers include a small number of non-Koreans registered in Seoul as intending immigrants.

Source: U.S. Embassy in Seoul, unpublished reports.

dates: first Preference—all applicants; second Preference—prior to June 1, 1984; third Preference—prior to July 8, 1984; fourth Preference—all applicants; fifth Preference—prior to March 15, 1980; sixth Preference—prior to July 1, 1983; non-preference—none, since no visas were available in this category.[4]

We see from the data that the intent of U.S. law to put priority in reuniting families is working fairly well with reference to Korean applicants and that the only such applicants who face very long delays before being able to apply for U.S. immigrant visas are the brothers and sisters of U.S. citizens and their dependents.

By preference categories, the number of Korean applicants who were registered in Seoul on January 1, 1984 and issued immigrant visas in fiscal year 1984 (October 1, 1983–September 30, 1984) is given in Table 8.2.

Worthy of note is the fact that, of the applicants who were issued visas in fiscal year 1984, only 92 secured them on the basis of their professional qualifications; while additional professionals undoubtedly obtained visas under the family reunification preferences, it appears that independent emigration of professionals has slowed down considerably from its heyday in the 1970s.

In addition to those in the preference categories, 11,802 Koreans were issued immigrant visas in Seoul in fiscal year 1984 as the immediate relatives of U.S. citizens. Data on these immigrants are given in Table 8.3. These figures indicate that the adoption or prospective adoption of Korean children by U.S. citizens is exceptionally strong—accounting for close to

Table 8.2
Applicants Registered for Immigration and Issued Visas in Seoul: FY 1984

Preferences	Registered Applicants	Issued Visas FY 1984
1st Preference	64	78
2nd Preference	9,503	7,498
3rd Preference	543	312
4th Preference	474	568
5th Preference	107,805	7,309
6th Preference	1,788	1,385
Non-Preference	555	0

Source: U.S. Embassy in Seoul, unpublished reports.

Table 8.3
Immediate Relatives of U.S. Citizens Issued Visas in Seoul: FY 1984

	Number	Percentage
Spouses of U.S. Citizens	3,235	27.4
Children or Stepchildren of U.S. Citizens	650	5.5
Adopted or to be Adopted Children of U.S. Citizens	5,245	44.5
Parents of U.S. Citizens	2,672	22.6

Source: U.S. Embassy in Seoul, unpublished reports.

50% of all immigrant visas that were issued in Korea to immediate relatives.

While obtaining an immigrant visa in Korea is the prevalent procedure for intending immigrants to acquire permanent residence, U.S. law also provides for applications for adjustment of status from nonimmigrant to immigrant to be made within the United States.

In fiscal year 1983 (October 1, 1982–September 30, 1983), 4,320 Koreans had such applications approved by the Immigration and Naturalization Service within the United States. This number included 1,475 persons who had entered as tourists, 510 who were temporarily residing in the United States as investors or international traders, and 419 students. Of the total, 1,937 were preference immigrants and, thus, chargeable to the overall 20,000 visas per country per year; and the balance (2,385) were exempt from such limitations—most of them as the immediate relatives of U.S. citizens.

Every year, the U.S. Embassy in Seoul also issues more than 50,000 non-immigrant visas to Koreans who are coming temporarily to the United States for various reasons. In fiscal year 1983, while 55,493 nonimmigrant visas were issued in Seoul, 96,293 Koreans were temporarily admitted by the U.S. Immigration and Naturalization Service. Thus, we see that the percentages of adjustment of status on the nonimmigrant visas issued in Seoul and the entry of Koreans into the United States in fiscal year 1983 were 7.8% and 4.5%, respectively.

While the overall situation is not desperate for qualifed prospective immigrants who are endeavoring to obtain immigrant visas within a reasonable time, other Koreans who have no relatives in the United States—and no skills entitling them to qualify on the basis of a job offer—frequently resort to fraudulent activities in their attempts to enter the United States. Fraud continues to present a major challenge to the consular personnel in the U.S. Embassy in Seoul; and the embassy is devoting substantial resources to stop it or, at least, to decrease its incidence. As a ranking consular officer in Seoul is quoted to have recently said, "It is a battle of wits. We can't check everything; they can't forge everything."

Korean fraud in securing visas or illegally entering the United States takes many forms: from counterfeit immigrant and nonimmigrant visas and the entire range of documents used to support visa applications, to entry into countries bordering the United States and subsequent illegal entry, to fraudulent marriages to U.S. citizens, and to the insertion of fraudulent visa petitions into the embassy files.

By focusing its efforts on ringleaders and "visa brokers" and by using computerized data, the embassy—with the cooperation of Korean authorities—is having some success, as evidenced by the increased number of mala fide applicants who attempt to enter Mexico and then make their way into the United States. Of the 3,327 cases referred by consular officers to the embassy investigative unit, 2,329 were investigated—which, in 342 instances, resulted in the refusal of sought benefits, generally a visa. While fraud is indeed a serious problem, the majority of Korean visa applicants are honest and enter the United States legally.

9

Social and Demographic Characteristics of Korean Immigrants: 1980

KOREANS IN THE UNITED STATES

Koreans are the ethnic group that, between 1970 and 1980, increased faster than any other group identified by the U.S. Bureau of the Census in its census question on race. In fact, while 70,598 persons identified themselves as Koreans in 1970, 354,529 did so in the 1980 census—an increase of 401.9%.

Of all racial/ethnic groups identified, Koreans were eighth in number. Among the Asian-American population, they were in fifth place—after the Chinese, Filipinos, Japanese, and Asian Indians. Bouvier and Agresta have estimated that—barring unforeseen changes in current trends—Koreans in the United States will number more than 800,000 by 1990, and more than a million by the year 2000.[1]

In 1980, the overwhelming majority of Koreans in the United States were foreign born: 81.8%—or 289,885—indicated birth in a foreign country. The dramatic change in the total number and the high percentage of foreign-born are primarily the result of the 1965 U.S. Immigration and Nationality Act, which liberalized U.S. immigration laws and—for immigration purposes—placed all foreign countries on an equal footage. The importance of this law in influencing the growth of Korean immigrants in the United States can be ascertained from Table 9.1. The data clearly show the impact of the change in immigration laws, since 83.9% of all Korean-Americans arrived in the United States in the decade from 1970 to 1980.

Table 9.1
Foreign-Born Koreans in the United States: 1980

Year of Emigration	Percentage
1975–1980	52.3
1970–1974	31.6
1960–1969	13.0
1959 or earlier	3.1

Sources: U.S. Bureau of the Census, "Foreign-Born Immigrants—Tabulations from the 1980 U.S. Census of the Population and Housing," mimeographed report, Washington, D.C., October 1984.

PLACE OF RESIDENCE

As with other Asian-Americans and most immigrants in general, Koreans prefer to reside in large urban settings, for a number of reasons. Most of them came from urban areas, their skills can best be employed in an urban environment, and—of equal importance—an urban residence provides proximity to others of the same race or ethnic group who can give tangible material and psychological support during the initial period of adjustment to life in the new country.

Of the total number of Koreans in the United States in 1980—both those born in this country and those born in Korea—92.5% preferred to reside within standard statistical metropolitan areas, as defined by the U.S. Bureau of the Census. Although Koreans live in every state of the union, there are a little more than one-third dwelling in the Pacific rim states—particularly, California. Data on the ten states containing the largest number of Koreans are given in Table 9.2.

The Korean population distribution in these ten states indicates that Korean immigrants generally tend to settle where other groups of their countrymen already are—a normal pattern. In this matter, however, Koreans appear to be more unconventional than other ethnic groups. The greatest changes between 1970 and 1980, when their total number increased by 401.9%, did not occur in the traditional states of residence— California and Hawaii—but in the states of Washington, Virginia, and Maryland (to name the top three). Conversely, the state where the Korean population increased the least was Hawaii, where the change was 107.3%— approximately one-fourth of the national norm.

Table 9.2
Ten Preferred States of Residence for Koreans: 1980

State	All Koreans	% of Total	Foreign-Born	% of Total Foreign-Born
California	103,981	29.3	83,180	28.7
New York	34,157	9.6	27,104	9.4
Illinois	23,980	6.8	19,383	6.7
Hawaii	17,948	5.1	9,060	3.1
Maryland	15,087	4.3	12,444	4.3
Texas	13,997	3.9	11,562	4.0
Washington	13,077	3.7	11,389	3.9
New Jersey	12,845	3.6	10,679	3.7
Virginia	12,550	3.5	10,816	3.7
Pennsylvania	12,503	3.5	10,497	3.6

Sources: U.S. Bureau of the Census, *1980 Census of the Population, Supplementary Reports* (Washington, D.C.: Government Printing Office, July 1981) and "Foreign-Born Immigrants: Koreans—Tabulations from the 1980 U.S. Census of the Population and Housing," mimeographed report, Washington, D.C., October 1984.

AGE AND SEX DISTRIBUTION

Of the 289,885 Korean natives identified in the special foreign-born census tabulations prepared from 1980 census data, 116,292 were males and 173,623 were females—a ratio of 67.0 males per 100 females. The ratio for the entire U.S. population is 94.5 males per 100 females; and that of all Koreans—both native and foreign-born—residing in the United States, 72.2 males per 100 females. These ratios indicate that immigration from Korea has been a predominantly female phenomenon—partially because of the high number of marriages of U.S. male citizens who are stationed in Korea with the military, and partially because of the higher proportion of Korean female children being brought here for adoption by U.S. citizens.

With reference to age distribution—as indicated in Table 9.3—Koreans in the United States have a very young profile. Both in the under-14 group and in the 14-44 group Koreans are overrepresented, in comparison with the total population.

The foreign-born, in particular, have a much higher percentage in the 15-64 age group—the productive period of life. In fact, while the proportion of

Table 9.3
Age Distribution of Koreans and Total U.S. Population: 1980 (in percentages)

Age	U.S. Population	All Koreans	Foreign-Born Koreans
0-14	22.6	32.3	24.2
15-44	46.5	54.8	62.0
45-64	19.6	10.5	11.2
65 & over	11.3	2.4	3.6

Source: U.S. Bureau of the Census, "Foreign-Born Immigrants: Koreans—Tabulations from the 1980 U.S. Census of the Population and Housing," mimeographed report, Washington, D.C., October 1984.

the total U.S. population in this age bracket is 66.1%, it is 73.2% for foreign-born Koreans.

Both in toto and for the foreign-born, Koreans are vastly underrepresented in the over-65 age bracket. While 11.3% of the total U.S. population are over the age of 65, only 2.4% of all Koreans and 2.6% of the foreign-born Koreans fall in this age group.

FERTILITY

The young age profile of the Korean population residing in the United States and the fact that most of them are comparatively recent immigrants would appear to indicate that their fertility rates are high. Yet, this is not the case at all. The birth rate in Korea has been dropping considerably, and apparently this trend has continued after the immigrants' entry into the United States.

Lower fertility rates in comparison with the U.S. population at large may also be accounted for by the higher educational level of Koreans coming to the United States, by the fact that their background in Korea is urban rather than rural, and because the pressures of living in a new environment and the striving to move up the socioeconomic ladder tend to have a negative impact on the number of children that women have.

Fertility rates for various age groups, as reflected in the number of all children born to Korean women, are shown in Table 9.4.

Another indication of the lower fertility rates of Korean natives is seen in the data of the special 1980 census tabulation on the foreign-born. Of 109,033 Korean households, 33.6% had no children, 23.5% had one child, 27.5% had two children, 12.3% had three children, and only 3.1% had four

Table 9.4
Number of Children Born to U.S. Women and to Asian and Korean Women
Who Immigrated between 1970 and 1980, as of 1980 (per 1,000 women)

Age	Total U.S. Women	Asian Women Who Immigrated 1970–80	All Korean Women in U.S.	Korean Women Who Immigrated 1970–1980
15–24	317	271	236	245
25–34	1,476	1,262	1,244	1,234
35–44	2,639	2,285	2,045	2,097

Source: U.S. Bureau of the Census, *1980 Census of the Population, U.S. Summary* (Washington, D.C.: Government Printing Office, 1981).

or more children. Thus, we see that a total of 84.6% of these households had two children or less, and only 15.4% had three or more children. It is clear that recent Korean female immigrants—contrary to the experience of immigrant women in the nation's past—have low fertility rates.

MARITAL STATUS

The special census tabulations indicate that 219,790 foreign-born Koreans over the age of 15 were living in the United States in 1980. Of these, 84,885 were males and 134,905 were females. Data on their marital status are given in Table 9.5.

The data show that Korean immigrants are more likely to be married and less likely to be divorced or separated than the general U.S. population. The percentage of divorced males is less than one-third that of the U.S. male population at large; and that of females, a little more than half the rate for females. The higher female divorce rate is probably attributable to the number of marriages contracted by U.S. servicemen who subsequently ended the marriage by divorce some time after returning home with their wives.

The effect of length of residence on divorce rates of Korean natives is explored in Table 9.6. While the divorce rate for males is only marginally affected by length of residence in the United States and is far below that of the U.S. population (even after a residence of 20 years or longer), the rate for females increases proportionately to their length of residence—and for those who have been in the United States for more than 20 years, surpasses the rate for the total U.S. population.

Table 9.5
Marital Status of U.S. Population and Foreign-Born Koreans over Age 15: 1980
(in percentages)

	U.S. Population		Korean-Born	
	Males	Females	Males	Females
Single	29.7	22.8	28.3	17.5
Married	60.6	5.2	68.3	70.0
Separated	1.9	2.6	1.2	2.0
Widowed	2.5	13.3	.6	6.2
Divorced	5.3	7.1	1.6	4.3

Sources: U.S. Bureau of the Census, *1980 Census of the Population, U.S. Summary* (Washington, D.C.: Government Printing Office, 1981) and "Foreign-Born Immigrants: Koreans—Tabulations from the 1980 U.S. Census of the Population and Housing," mimeographed report, Washington, D.C., October 1984.

HOUSEHOLD COMPOSITION AND SIZE

Data available from the 1980 census for all Koreans and for those who immigrated to the United States between 1970 and 1980 reflect the family and kinship bonds prevalent in Korean society and the fact that Korean families very often include relatives in a proportion higher than that of U.S. households in general. Of all Koreans living in households, 6.2% are not primary family members, but relatives. For Koreans who immigrated between 1970 and 1980, the proportion is 7.6%. The comparable rate for U.S. households in general is 4.2%.

However, Korean households are less likely to include nonrelatives than

Table 9.6
Divorce Rates of Korean Immigrants over Age 15: 1980

	1975–80	1970–74	1965–69	1960–64	Before 1960
Males	1.4	1.5	1.6	2.7	3.4
Females	2.8	4.9	6.4	6.7	7.3

Source: U.S. Bureau of the Census, "Foreign-Born Immigrants: Koreans—Tabulations from the 1980 U.S. Census of the Population and Housing," mimeographed report, Washington, D.C., October 1984.

U.S. households in general. While nonrelatives make up 2.7% of persons living in U.S. households, they make up only 2.2% of the members of Korean households and only 1.9% of those residing in households of Korean immigrants who arrived between 1970 and 1980.

The average number of persons in either a household or a family is higher for Koreans — both as a whole and for the recent immigrants — compared with that of U.S. households and families, in general. For all Korean households, the average size is 3.40 persons; and for all Korean families, 3.81 persons. Korean immigrant households and families who came to the United States between 1970 and 1980 are slightly larger: 3.48 persons per household and 3.85 per family. The comparable figures for the entire U.S. population are 2.74 per household and 3.27 per family.

EDUCATION

Two of the major factors impelling Koreans to immigrate are the relative lack of educational opportunities for study at the university level in their country, and the relative lack of opportunities to advance in the socio-economic ladder by exploiting educational achievements. When those factors are combined with family cohesiveness, pride in achievement, and a strong work ethic, it is not surprising that both the Korean immigrants themselves and their offspring in the United States rate exceedingly well in educational achievements.

To Koreans, education represents the road to economic freedom and independence. One has only to talk to teachers or professors, to understand the commitment and drive that this relatively new immigrant group has brought to the nation's classrooms. Very strong parental support and pressure—along with single-mindedness and discipline—appear to be the main reasons for the high levels of achievement.

Statistical data collected during the 1980 census for both all ethnic Koreans and those born overseas bear out the above conclusions. While, in 1980, the proportion of persons over the age of 25 who graduated from high school in the U.S. population at large was 66.5%, that of Koreans (whether born in the United States or in Korea) was 78.1%. Similarly, the percentage of those over age 25 with four or more years of college education was 16.2 for the U.S. population at large and more than double that figure for all Koreans—33.7%. When only foreign-born Koreans are taken into account, we find that 77.8% of those over the age of 25 were high school graduates and 34.2% had completed four or more years of college.

Because their society and traditions are still male dominated, Koreans place a higher emphasis on the education of males. Consequently, while 90% of all Korean males over the age of 25 in the United States are high school graduates and 52.4% had four or more years of college education, the figures for Korean women in the same age group are 70.6% for high school graduates and 22% for the college-educated: higher than the U.S. norm, but still considerably lower than the male percentage—particularly at the university level, where (as we have seen above), the rate for males is more than double that of females.

The special census tabulation, by year of immigration, provides a clearer picture of the educational status and achievements of Korean immigrants residing in the United States in 1980. Since such data were tabulated for all foreign-born Koreans over the age of 20, the percentages for those who graduated from high school are accurate, but those for college graduates are lower than they would be if the cutoff age had been 25. In fact, at age 20, the majority of students have not yet completed their college studies. This proviso must be kept in mind when examining the data in Table 9.7.

In all time periods, the percentage of persons with either a high school diploma or four-or-more years of college is consistently higher than the U.S. norm. While, no doubt, a significant number of these immigrants (particularly those who have been in residence for more than ten years) may have acquired part of their education in the United States, a high proportion were already high school or college graduates when they arrived.

A recent study by Gardner, Robey, and Smith reports that, in 1980, 93.6% of male Koreans between the ages of 20 and 29 who immigrated to the United States in the period 1975-80 were high school graduates. The percentage for women in the same age group was 70.6%. Comparable figures for Koreans residing in Korea in 1980 were 53.7% for males and 36.1% for females.[2]

Table 9.7
Years of Schooling Completed by Korean Immigrants over Age 20, as of 1980 (in percentages)

Educational Level	All Periods	Year of Immigration				
		1975– 1980	1970– 1974	1965– 1969	1960– 1964	1950 & Earlier
Less than five years' elementary education	3.7	4.1	3.4	3.4	3.2	2.8
High-school graduates	78.8	77.1	79.9	81.3	78.4	83.8
Four or more years of college	30.5	25.7	31.6	44.0	36.2	37.4

Source: U.S. Bureau of the Census, "Foreign-Born Population: Koreans—Tabulations from the 1980 U.S. Census of the Population and Housing," mimeographed report, Washington, D.C., October 1984.

Thus, it becomes evident that—at least as far as their high school education is concerned—the overwhelming majority of Korean immigrants of the period in question were educated in Korea and that they were much better educated than the general population there.

An additional indication of the love for learning and of the achievement aspiration of Korean immigrants can be observed by looking at another factor: the number of native Koreans over the age of 16 who were in the labor force in 1980 and attended school at the same time. Out of a total of 137,355 Koreans over that age, 18,140—or 13.2%—were attending achool in addition to working. Of these, 76.3% were attending college—with 18.3% pursuing graduate studies.

Culture, traditions, discipline, and self-confidence—together with kin pressure and support for high educational achievement—distinguish Koreans from the U.S. population at large and from other groups of non-Asian immigrants. Unless Koreans are discriminated against in college admission policies because of their visibility, educational success guarantees that a good proportion of the future teachers, engineers, and scientists in the United States will be Korean-Americans.

KOREAN IMMIGRANTS AT WORK

Labor Participation Rate

Labor force participation—one of the leading indicators of the work ethic, self-sufficiency, and drive of a population—is the ratio of those who are 16 years of age or older and are employed or looking for work, to the entire population in that age group.

Korean immigrants in the United States in 1980 had a high labor-participation rate. For the total U.S. population aged 16 or older, the rate was 62.0%: 75.1% for males and 49.9% for females. For Korean immigrants, it was 63.8% for both sexes: 78.2% for males and 54.8% for females.

Labor force participation—as can be seen in Table 9.8—is directly related to length of stay in the United States (with one minor exception). The longer Korean immigrants have been in residence, the more likely they are to be participants in the labor force. For male Koreans who arrived between 1975 and 1980, the rate was lower than that of white U.S. males. For male Korean immigrants who have been in the country for longer than five years, the rate was significantly higher, and reached a participation rate close to 90% for male immigrants who have resided in the United States for 20 or more years.

Rates of labor-force participation for Korean females are higher than those for U.S. females—with more than half of the Korean female population over age 16 in the labor force, regardless of year of immigration.

Table 9.8
Labor-Force Participation of Korean Immigrants over Age 16: 1980

		Year of Immigration				
Sex	All Periods	1975-80	1970-74	1965-69	1960-64	1959 and Earlier
Both	63.8	59.4	66.7	68.6	70.2	70.6
Males	78.2	73.4	80.6	85.2	85.5	89.7
Females	54.8	50.3	58.1	58.8	62.7	58.0

Source: U.S. Bureau of the Census, "Foreign-Born Immigrants: Koreans—Tabulations from the 1980 U.S. Census of the Population and Housing," mimeographed report, Washington, D.C., October, 1984.

Employment and Unemployment

In 1980, the total number of Korean immigrants over the age of 16 in the labor force was 137,355. Of these, 135,675 were in civilian employment. The balance (1,680) were in the U.S. military.

In April 1980, the large majority of these immigrants were employed, and their unemployment rate of 6.5% was equal to that of the U.S. labor force at large. However, it was lower than that of all foreign-born in the United States—which was then 7.2%.

The rate of unemployment varied by sex and length of residence. Table 9.9 shows that it was invariably higher for women than for men—perhaps because women in Korean society are not so highly educated as men and, therefore, do not possess the same degree of marketable skills.

Length of residence was generally inversely proportional to unemployment rates. The longer an individual had resided in the United States, the less likely he or she was to be unemployed.

Men were less likely to be unemployed than the U.S. labor force at large—even among the recent arrivals who came between 1975 and 1980 and would be more likely to be unemployed, because of their unfamiliarity with the labor market, the language, and U.S. society in general.

A comparison of the work experience of Korean immigrants with that of all U.S. workers and all foreign-born workers during 1979 sheds further light on the subject of employment and unemployment, because of an additional variable. While the preceding analysis was static, in that it considered only employment status at a particular point in time (the month of April 1980), the following analysis explores work experience during the entire preceding year (1979), and considers the length of both employment and unemployment during that year.

Table 9.9

Employment and Unemployment Rates of Korean Immigrants in the Civilian Labor Force: 1980 (in percentages)

	All Periods	1975–80	1970–74	1965–69	1960–64	1959 and Earlier
			Year of Immigration			
Both Sexes						
Employed	93.5	93.0	95.1	95.6	94.9	96.2
Unemployed	6.5	7.0	4.9	4.4	5.1	3.8
Males						
Employed	95.8	94.9	96.5	97.7	96.9	96.6
Unemployed	4.2	5.1	3.5	2.3	3.1	3.4
Females						
Employed	92.7	91.2	93.8	93.8	93.5	95.3
Unemployed	7.3	8.8	6.2	6.2	6.5	4.7

Source: U.S. Bureau of the Census, "Foreign-Born Immigrants: Koreans—Tabulations from the 1980 U.S. Census of the Population and Housing," mimeographed report, Washington, D.C., October 1984.

The data shown on Table 9.10 indicate that Korean immigrants in 1979 were more likely to have been unemployed than the general U.S. labor population and foreign-born workers as a whole: More than one-fourth of the Korean labor force did in fact have some unemployment during the year—compared with less than one-fifth of the entire U.S. labor force and a little more than one-fifth of all foreign-born in the work force. However, the average number of weeks of unemployment per unemployed Korean worker was smaller than that of the other two groups—indicating an ability to find employment sooner (perhaps by accepting any type of employment available, rather than restricting themselves to the field in which they had been trained). This factor held true even for the immigrants who arrived between 1975 and 1980. In such cases, the average length of unemployment per unemployed worker was 13.5 weeks, which was still less than the national average of 14.1 weeks.

Occupations

The occupational status of Korean natives in the United States is shown in Table 9.11. In comparison with the general population, Koreans were overrepresented in the professional category; in the sales field; in services such as food, health, and building services; and as machine operators. They were underrepresented in the clerical area; in precision production; in crafts; and in the lower skill end of the blue-collar factory worker.

Table 9.10
Work Experience of Korean Immigrants in the U.S. Labor Force: 1979
(in percentages)

	All U.S. Workers	All Foreign-Born Workers	Korean-Born Workers
Worked during 1979	98.2	97.5	96.8
Worked 50–52 weeks	52.2	50.6	48.4
Worked 40–49 weeks	13.2	15.9	17.6
Worked 27–39 weeks	8.3	8.3	9.2
Worked 1–26 weeks	18.0	17.0	21.7
Had some unemployment in 1979	18.6	20.8	26.0
Unemployed 15 weeks or longer	6.2	7.5	7.9
Average weeks of unemployment per unemployed worker	14.1	.14.5	12.8

Sources: U.S. Bureau of the Census, *1980 Census of the Population, U.S. Summary* (Washington, D.C.: Government Printing Office, 1981) and "Foreign-Born Immigrants: Koreans—Tabulations from the 1980 U.S. Census of the Population and Housing," mimeographed report, Washington, D.C., October 1984.

The large percentages employed in services and sales may be a function of the entrepreneurial spirit of Korean immigrants. They appear to favor working independently and, according to several studies, run a large number of small stores and service operations in the large metropolitan areas. In the Los Angeles area, the number of such businesses is reputed to be more than 6,000; in the New York City area, about 1,000.

Analyzing those in the professional category, we see in Table 9.12 that the number of Korean immigrants employed in the field (correlated with the year of immigration) appears to be decreasing, after reaching a high level for those who immigrated in 1965-69—when a flood of professionals entered the country following passage of the 1965 Immigration and Nationality Act.

The percentage of professionals in 1980 was 27.2 for those who had im-

Table 9.11

Occupational Distribution of Korean Immigrants among the U.S. Employed: 1980 (in percentages)

Occupation	U.S. Labor Force	Korean Born Labor Force
1. Executive, administrative and Managerial	10.4	9.8
2. Professional	12.3	14.6
3. Technicians and related support	3.1	3.7
4. Sales	10.0	13.8
5. Administrative support including clerical	17.2	9.4
6. Private household services	.6	.3
7. Protective services	1.5	.2
8. Other services	10.8	16.6
9. Farming, forestry and fishing	2.9	.8
10. Precision production craft and repair	12.9	9.6
11. Machine operators and assemblers	9.3	17.2
12. Transportation and material moving	4.5	.9
13. Handlers, helpers and laborers	4.5	3.1

Sources: U.S. Bureau of the Census *1980 Census of the Population, U.S. Summary* (Washington, D.C.: Government Printing Office, 1981) and "Foreign-Born Immigrants: Koreans— Tabulations from the 1980 U.S. Census of the Population and Housing," mimeographed report, Washington, D.C., October 1984.

migrated prior to 1960, and 26.1 for those who came betweeen 1965 and 1969. However, this figure was only 16% for those who had entered the United States between 1970 and 1974, and 8.6% for the latest arrivals (the immigrants who came between 1975 and 1980).

The table also indicates, by year of immigration, the percentage of

Table 9.12
Korean Immigrants over Age 20 with Higher Education and in Professional Occupations: 1980 (in percentages)

	Year of Immigration				
	1975–80	1970–74	1965–69	1960–64	1959 and earlier
A. 4 or more yrs. of college	25.7	31.7	44.0	36.2	37.4
B. Professional employment	8.6	16.0	26.1	21.5	27.2
Ratio (A/B)	3.0	2.0	1.7	1.7	1.4

Source: U.S. Bureau of the Census, "Foreign-Born Immigrants: Koreans—Tabulations from the 1980 U.S. Census of the Population and Housing," mimeographed report, Washington, D.C., October 1984.

Korean immigrants over age 20 in the United States in 1980 who had completed four or more years of college, as compared with the percentage of those engaged in the professions.

The data in this table lead to two conclusions: (1) The percentage of highly educated immigrants from Korea—taking into account the fact that some of the earlier immigrants may have been educated in the United States—appears to be declining. (2) The percentage of those with four or more years of college who practice one of the professions is also declining and is directly related to length of residence.

This situation is due, no doubt, to a number of factors that make it difficult for Korean immigrants who have not been in the United States very long to practice in the professions. Limited knowledge of the English language, problems in obtaining required professional licenses, and lack of the "economic cushion" that allows one to look for and engage in appropriate employment may be some of these factors.

The high incidence of self-employment in businesses not directly related to the individual's academic training may also be an important factor. In fact, 12.2% of all employed Koreans work in their own businesses (close to double the rate of 6.3% for the U.S. employed labor force), and an additional 1.7% work in family businesses without financial remuneration. This spirit of entrepreneurship in starting businesses is one of the distinguishing and most obvious features of the Korean immigrant work force. The high visibility of such businesses, which are generally located in an urban environment where other racial minorities reside, is a factor that may also lead to increasing social conflict between the Korean shopkeepers and their black, Puerto Rican, or Chicano customers.

Income and Poverty

In comparison with other immigrant groups, Koreans appear to fare poorly in some respects. While the median income for full-time white workers in 1979 was $15,572, it was only $9,589 for the native Koreans—lower than that of Indians, Filipinos, Chinese, and Japanese; and only barely higher than that of Vietnamese full-time workers, which is the major ethnic group in the bottom rung of the income ladder. However, when household median income is taken as a measure of economic success, Korean immigrants fared much better. Their median household income in 1979 was $18,085—higher than that of U.S. households as a whole ($16,841), U.S. native-born households ($17,010), and all households headed by foreign-born ($14,588).

In terms of median household income within the major Asian immigrant groups, Koreans placed behind Indians, Filipinos, and Chinese; but they were ahead of the Japanese, Thais, and Vietnamese.

The census of 1980 provides more detailed information on Korean families who came to the United States between 1970 and 1979. Their median income was $18,342, which was about 8% lower than that of U.S. families in general and 12% lower than that of white U.S. families.

In some respects related to income, Korean-headed families show some of the same characteristics of U.S. families in general. For example, the median number of workers per U.S. famlily is 1.6, as compared with 1.7 for Korean immigrant families—only marginally higher. Furthermore, the percentage of Korean families with two, three, or more persons employed is only marginally higher than that of U.S. families, but their earnings are substantially lower. Data on this variable as it affects family income are shown in Table 9.13.

Table 9.13
Workers per U.S. and Korean Immigrant Family and Median Family Income: 1979

Number of Workers Per Family	U.S. Families	Median Income	Korean Families Who Immigrated 1970-79	Median Income
No workers	12.8 %	$ 7,791	6.5 %	$ 2,500
1 worker	33.0	16,181	33.0	13,082
2 workers	41.6	23,058	46.5	21,016
3 or more workers	12.6	31,880	13.9	26,432

Source: U.S. Bureau of the Census, *1980 Census of the Population, U.S. Summary* (Washington, D.C.: Government Printing Office, 1981).

The relative income of Koreans who immigrated between 1970 and 1979 in comparison with all U.S. households is another gauge of their economic progress. Table 9.14 shows that, for the lowest income levels (less than $10,000), the percentage of such Korean households was approximately the same as that of all U.S. households. This also holds true for households with incomes over the $25,000 mark: 28.9% of all U.S. households were in this income group, as compared with 27.5% of Korean households.

However, Korean immigrant families—as reflected in the percentage of families and individuals whose 1980 income was below the poverty line—did not fare too well. While that percentage was 9.6% for all U.S. families, it was 10.4% for all Korean immigrant families and 16.1% for those families who had arrived in the United States between 1975 and 1980. If individuals (rather than families) are taken into account, the percentage of Korean immigrants with incomes below the poverty level is marginally higher than that of the U.S. population at large: 13.1% versus 12.4%.

ACCULTURATION

The special census tabulation on foreign-born living in the United States in 1980 provides some data that give an indication of the degree and pace of

Table 9.14
Household Income Distribution of Koreans Who Immigrated between 1970 and 1979 versus All U.S. Households: 1979 (in percentages)

Income	U.S. Households	Korean Immigrant Households
Less than $5,000	13.3	14.8
$5,000–7,499	8.0	7.8
$7,500–9,999	7.9	7.3
$10,000–14,999	15.3	15.7
$15,000–19,999	14.1	13.5
$20,000–24,999	12.5	13.4
$25,000–34,999	15.7	15.0
$35,000–49,999	8.6	7.7
$50,000 or more	4.6	4.8

Source: U.S. Bureau of the Census, *1980 Census of the Population, U.S. Summary* (Washington, D.C.: Government Printing Office, 1981).

acculturation of Korean immigrants into U.S. society. Two factors that exhibit the degree of acculturation are English language ability and naturalization as U.S. citizens.

Data on the percentage of Korean immigrants who were U.S. citizens in
1980, by year of immigration, are shown in Table 9.15. While the number of
all Korean immigrants who have become U.S. citizens—34.6%—appears to
be rather low, this figure is deceptive, since the vast majority of these
immigrants—52.3%—arrived in the United States between 1975 and 1980;
and thus, by 1980, most of them could not have met one of the requirements for naturalization: five years of permanent residence. However,
if we exclude this group of immigrants, the proportion of pre-1975 Korean
immigrants who were naturalized as U.S. citizens by 1980 jumps to
61.7%—a clear indication that close to two-thirds of all Korean immigrants
who met the residency requirement for naturalization had chosen to do so
and to participate actively in both the benefits and duties that citizenship entails.

As could be expected, length of residence in the United States affected
the naturalization rate positively: By 1980, more than 80% of the pre-1970
immigrants were U.S. citizens.

As an indicator of the reach and progress of acculturation, the ability to
speak English is even more important than naturalization; it affects educational achievements, the availability of employment opportunities, and
full participation in U.S. social and economic life.

In this respect, Koreans have been doing extremely well, as shown in
Table 9.16. The exclusive use of English at home has consistently risen with

Table 9.15
Naturalization of Korean Immigrants, as of 1980

Year of Immigration	Number of Immigrants	Number Naturalized	% Naturalized
All periods	289,885	100,198	34.6
1975–1980	151,587	16,796	11.1
1970–1974	91,712	44,098	48.1
1965–1969	25,154	22,318	88.7
1960–1964	12,500	10,947	87.5
1959 and earlier	8,932	8,059	90.2

Source: U.S. Bureau of the Census, "Foreign-Born Immigrants: Koreans—Tabulations from
the 1980 U.S. Census of the Population and Housing," mimeographed report,
Washington, D.C., October 1984.

Table 9.16
Ability to Speak English among Korean Immigrants over Age 5: 1980
(in percentages)

| | All | Year of Immigration | | | | |
		1975–1980	1970–1974	1965–1969	1960–1964	1959 and Earlier
1. Speak only English at home	14.8	8.7	16.4	23.2	37.9	41.1
2. Speak language other than English at home	85.2	91.3	83.6	76.8	62.1	58.9
A. Speak English very well	25.0	17.4	30.7	37.7	33.1	34.5
B. Speak English well	33.5	34.3	35.7	31.5	23.5	16.7
C. Speak English not well	22.0	31.9	15.2	6.6	4.8	6.3
D. Do not speak any English	4.7	7.7	2.0	1.0	.7	1.4

Source: U.S. Bureau of the Census, "Foreign-Born Immigrants: Koreans—Tabulations from the 1980 U.S. Census of the Population and Housing," mimeographed report, Washington, D.C., October 1984.

length of residence—going from a low of 8.7% for those who arrived between 1975 and 1980 to a high of 41.1% for the pre-1960 immigrants. Similarly, the number of those immigrants who speak a language other than English at home but also speak English well or very well, is very high, ranging from 51.2% for those who came prior to 1960 to 69.2% for those who arrived between 1965 and 1969 — probably the most highly educated group of Korean immigrants. The newest immigrants (1975-80), while they had the highest percentage of persons who spoke Korean at home and the highest percentage pf persons who did not speak English at all, also had a large percentage of bilingual persons who spoke English well or very well—51.7%.

If we consider citizenship and language to be two of the important indicators of acculturation and integration in U.S. society, we can conclude that Korean immigrants are on their way to full participation in the national life.

10

Conclusions and Prospects for the Future

If the recent past can be taken as a predictor for future trends, the Korean ethnic community in the United States will continue to increase at a rapid pace. Bouvier and Agresta have estimated that, by 1990, the number of Koreans in the United States—principally through immigration, but also through natural increases—will more than double to 800,000 or more, and may reach the 1.3 million mark by the year 2000.[1]

Of course, sustained emigration from Korea to the United States may be affected by changes in our immigration laws, foreign relations between the United States and Korea, and the prospects for peace and reunification between North and South Korea.

Unlike other ethnic immigrant groups, Koreans in the United States will continue to spread out and take up residence in a number of states where their total number may be relatively small—but the potential economic opportunities, brighter.

Foreign-born Koreans have a distinct demographic profile, which (in comparison with U.S. norms) includes a young active population, high marriage rates, few divorces, and low fertility rates. However, both household and family size are slightly larger than the U.S. norm.

One distinguishing feature of Korean immigrants is their high level of educational achievements. In 1980, close to one-third of all foreign-born Koreans residing in the United States had attended college for four or more years.

In the employment area, Korean immigrants had a high rate of labor force participation. However, their unemployment rate was the same as that of the U.S. labor force, and they were more likely to have been unemployed in 1979—albeit for shorter periods of time than the U.S. unemployed work force. In comparison with the U.S. work force, Koreans were overrepresented in the professional, sales, and services occupations and underrepresented in the clerical and craft occupations. Significantly, 12.2% of all employed Korean immigrants were self-employed—double the U.S. norm.

While the median household income of Korean immigrants was higher than the median income of all U.S. households, both median family income and median income for a full-time worker were lower than the U.S. norm. The percentage of both families and individuals with incomes below the poverty levels were marginally higher than the U.S. norm, despite the fact that the number of workers per family was higher than the U.S. norm. The comparison indicates that Korean immigrants had not been able to translate educational achievement and entrepreneurial spirit into income to the degree that might have been expected.

Korean immigrants had high rates of naturalization as U.S. citizens: in fact, by 1980, about half of those who had been in the country for 6–10 years and more than four-fifths of those who had been in the United States for 16–20 years were U.S. citizens. Similarly, more than 60% of the latest Korean immigrant arrivals (1975-80) spoke English well or very well, with the rate of English language proficiency rising directly with the length of residence.

The Korean immigrants' tenacity, distinct work ethic, commitment to educational achievement, and entrepreneurial spirit should bode well for their future in the United States. As more and more of the immigrants' children work their way through the U.S. educational system and enter the labor market, their employment status and income attainments should also rise substantially.

Outwardly, it appears that Korean immigrants are becoming rapidly assimilated in U.S. society: in education, employment, language usage, and citizenship. However, it also appears that, culturally, Korean immigrants will continue to maintain a strong attachment to their traditional ethnic heritage—just as have the Chinese in the United States. It remains to be seen whether, with the passage of time, these traditional cultural ties will be completely severed.

CHINA

11

A Short History of Chinese Immigration to the United States

In comparison with other Asian ethnic groups, Chinese immigration and settlement in the United States has a long history. Interest in China and Chinese art antedates Chinese immigration to the United States. For centuries following the return of Marco Polo and other travelers and missionaries, Europe was fascinated with China and things Chinese. This fascination reached its peak in the seventeenth century, and spread from Europe to the New World. Indeed, as Stamford M. Lyman states, "Several magnificent houses were built in 'Chinese style' in Colonial America, and Chinese tapestries adorned many a wall" in the New World.[1] According to the same author, one of the economic reasons for the American Revolution was the wish of many American traders to engage in direct trade with China, rather than through the British; and, shortly after independence in 1786, the United States appointed its first consul to Canton.[2]

Trade between China and the Philippines—and subsequent shipment of the goods to Mexico via the Manila Galleon Trade—afforded Chinese sailors the opportunity to travel to the New World; and a Chinese colony was established in Mexico City in 1635. By the time of U.S. independence, Chinese sailors were familiar figures on western ships engaged in the China trade; and a few Chinese remained in the United States—generally as servants in the employ of a sea captain or a merchant.

One Chinese named Ah Nam went from Mexico to California in 1815 and was employed by the Spanish governor as a cook, until his death in

1817.[3] Starting in 1818 a total of five Chinese students attended a missionary school in Cornwall, Connecticut; but the experiment ended in failure, and the shool was closed a few years later.[4]

Sustained immigration to the United States started after 1848, when gold was discovered in California. Attracted by the promise of wealth, many Chinese—like thousands of others from all over the world—emigrated to California, with San Francisco as the major port of entry. Both San Francisco and California, in general, became known to Chinese immigrants as Gam Saan, the "Golden Mountain."

However, emigration to the United States represented a small part of the exodus from China that placed millions of Chinese in the Philippines, Vietnam, Thailand, Malaysia, Indonesia, South America, and the Caribbean. A combination of natural disasters, rebellions, revolutions, disastrous foreign wars, and pressures from the European powers inflicted great hardships on the Chinese masses. Political uncertainties—coupled with unstable social conditions, high taxes, and a concentration of land ownership in the hands of a few—forced a large number of Chinese males to emigrate. Between 1840 and 1900, an estimated 2.4 million workers left China in search of a better life elsewhere.[5]

The news of the discovery of gold in California traveled back to China via two sources, principally: through a few Chinese merchants who had settled in California or through the sea captains and shipping lines that realized the profits to be made in carrying passengers to the "Golden Mountain" in California.[6]

In addition to violating Chinese laws (which made it illegal to emigrate), Chinese going overseas also violated several tenets of Confucian doctrine, which prescribed that a man's duty was to stay with his family. However, the lure of gold and the harsh living conditions in their own land proved too much for some, who headed for California in the hope of striking it rich and returning home wealthy. The immigrants left their families behind—in most cases, as it tragically turned out, never to see them again. Most of the early immigrants were young, married men from the Toishan district in Kwangtung Province.

While many of the immigrants were able to purchase tickets for the trans-Pacific passage out of their own or family funds, many others were not. In such cases, the immigrants coming to the United States used the so-called "credit-ticket system," under which the prospective immigrant was advanced funds by fellow villagers, and he agreed to pay their emissaries in the United States once he found employment in the new land. On arrival in San Francisco, the emissaries met the immigrant at the docks, provided him with sleeping quarters and food, and acted as contractors in securing work for him. Funds to repay the debt were then deducted from his wages before the immigrant received them.

At first, the Chinese encountered no hostility; but then, invariably—

because of their skin color, language, clothing, and hair style—they were the victims of curiosity and racism.[7]

Both historical statistics compiled by the U.S. Immigration and Natural-ization Service and data from the U.S. Bureau of the Census give an idea of the number of Chinese who came to the United States temporarily and of those who remained. In 1820, only one Chinese was admitted; in the next decade, two came; and in the following decade, only eight arrived. Thirty-five were admitted from 1841 to 1850. However, it has been estimated that there were more than 4,000 Chinese in the United States by 1850. Data available from city records in San Francisco indicate that, out of an es-timated population of 100,000 in 1849, only 325 were Chinese. Therefore, most of the Chinese immigrants in California must have lived and worked outside the San Francisco city limits.

According to the Immigration and Naturalization Service, the period be-tween 1850 and 1860 saw 41,538 Chinese enter the country; 64,759 came the following decade; and the number nearly doubled to 123,201 in the 1870s. Yet by 1880, when a total of 229,045 Chinese had entered the United States, only 105,465 were enumerated by the U.S. Bureau of the Census in the decennial census.[8] These numbers indicate that most Chinese were in-deed "sojourners," who ultimately returned to China. This conclusion can be safely reached even if mortality and undercounting by the Census Bureau are taken into account.

At first, the Chinese—who were mostly located in San Francisco area—encountered no overt legal discrimination; but as soon as they fanned out to the gold fields to stake claims, they came into conflict with white miners, who often chased them away and cheated them out of their claims. As the number of Chinese grew, mining camps passed resolutions excluding them. The state legislature—which first (in 1850) passed a Foreign Miner's Tax Law that was specifically directed to Mexican miners, and then subse-quently repealed it—repassed such a law in 1852. This time, however, the Chinese were the target. According to Lyman, the Chinese "paid 50% of the total revenues obtained from it during the first four years and 98% during its final sixteen years of enforcement."[9]

Because of active opposition from white miners and the legal restrictions, Chinese were left to mine areas that had been abandoned by white miners, as being unproductive. When the gold fever abated after a few years, Chinese miners found ready employment when a decision was made to link the Pacific coast to the rest of the country via a transcontinental railroad. Since the labor was dangerous and backbreaking, few whites would accept the hardships involved. The Chinese responded to the call; and, from 1862 to 1869 when the Central Pacific section of the transcon-tinental railroad was completed, from 12,000 to 25,000 Chinese immigrants were employed in railroad building projects.[10]

Their subsequent period of unemployment was temporary. The completion of the railroads—the Union Pacific, Central Pacific, Southern Pacific, and Northern Pacific—encouraged general immigration to the west, and enabled California particularly—as a state blessed with many resources and excellent weather—to embark upon its agricultural and industrial development, a process in which Chinese immigrants played a major part. They cleared swamps in the valleys of central California and remained to plant, cultivate, and harvest the vegetable and fruit crops. By 1860, more than one-third of all truck gardening workers in California were Chinese. Their vast contributions in this field are best exemplified by the development of a new cherry, called "Bing" after Ah Bing, a Chinese who developed it while he was working in the orchards of Oregon in the 1870s.[11]

Chinese factory workers also played a major role in the industrial development of California after the Civil War. In the early 1870s, Chinese workers in San Francisco comprised about two-thirds of all garment industry workers and 90% of the cigar makers.[12] They also engaged in construction projects, and worked in the occupations that are generally associated with Chinese immigrants: restaurants, laundries, and domestic service. In California, Washington, Alaska, British Columbia, and Louisiana, many found employment in the fishing industry and canneries; others continued to work in the mining industry—digging coal and borax in Oregon, Utah, Wyoming, Nevada, and other states.

Being an enterprising thrifty people, some Chinese started their own businesses—concentrating in the labor-intensive garment and shoe manufacturing industries, in which they provided work for other Chinese.

Most Chinese immigrants were young males; and, although Chinese immigrants accounted for only about 10% of California's population between 1860 and 1880, they comprised close to a quarter of the state's work force. Other workers—mostly, whites—commenced to feel threatened by such numbers, and started to agitate against further immigration from China. Samuel Gompers, founder of the American Federation of Labor, declared that "racial differences between American whites and the Asiatics would never be overcome. The superior whites had to exclude the inferior—aided by law, or if necessary by force of arms."[13]

To his voice was added that of Dennis Kearney, a labor leader who organized the California Workingman's Party. Kearney always started his speeches by attacking the rich and powerful and the corporations, but he always ended with the cry "The Chinese must go!" He rationalized this by pointing to the fact that the Chinese accepted employment for lower wages, and thus deprived the whites of jobs.[14] Therefore—in the struggle between big business and large-scale farmers, on the one hand, and white workers, small businessmen, and small farmers, on the other—the Chinese immigrants became a pawn against whom frustrations could be safely vented without fear of consequences.

Economic problems in California and the nation at large were brought about by intensive stock market speculations in 1872 and by a severe drought in 1876. Coupled with the large number of white workers migrating to California from other states, the economic setbacks exacerbated the situation. The stage was set: first, for local and state legal restraints on the activities of Chinese immigrants; and, subsequently, for national legislation to prevent their entry into the nation.

In his book called *Brothers under the Skin,* Carey McWilliams has analyzed how one state of the union—California—could successfully impose its views on the immigration of Chinese upon the rest of the country. He concluded that a combination of factors made this possible: First, California—which supported the South in Congress in efforts to deny civil rights to the newly freed blacks—was able, in turn, to obtain support for its views on the Chinese; second, former southerners comprised a considerable portion of California's population and were thus, on principle, against granting legal equality to any but whites; and third, in the two decades following the Civil War—when the north was solidly Republican, and the South solidly Democratic—the West held the balance of power, which it skillfully used to its advantage.[15]

Locally, San Francisco passed laws that limited the activities of Chinese working in laundries, delivering food (accomplished by the use of poles for balancing loads), and living in boardinghouses, and that denied them fishing licenses because they were ineligible for citizenship. While most of these laws were struck down by the federal courts as unconstitutional, state courts were another matter. California Chief Justice Hugh C. Murray ruled that Chinese were of the same race as Indians and thus, under state laws, could not testify in court against a white person! The ruling remained in force until 1875.

Chinese children were also discriminated against: The state legislature gave to the state superintendent of education the power to deny admission to a public school to members of minorities if the school was attended primarily by whites.[16]

Following California's lead, other states passed similar discriminatory laws. Mob violence generally followed. Seventeen Chinese were killed in Los Angeles in 1871; one, in Denver in 1880 during a riot that destroyed the Chinese community; and 28, during rioting in Rock Springs, Wyoming, in 1885. Innumerable other incidents took place daily, often resulting in loss of property or—worse—injury or death to the Chinese immigrants.

The Chinese response to hostile legislation, discriminatory practices, and physical danger was twofold: First, they began to geographically disperse, by moving to the Northwest or to the East; and second, they grouped tightly together in ethnic neighborhoods, where protection was easier. In this manner were born the various Chinatowns throughout the United States: in San Francisco, Los Angeles, Seattle, Chicago, New York, and Boston.

Life in these ghettos provided other advantages besides physical se-curity. Ethnic food was always available; old customs could be freely followed; funds could be easily sent to family and relatives in China; and social intercourse was possible with persons who spoke the same language and did not consider one to be a stranger. Disadvantages in living in Chinatown were also evident. Exploitation in pay and unemployment were common; and gambling, prostitution, and opium smoking were prevalent among the majority of young men who were away from their families. Stranded in the United States and without family, Chinese immigrants faced a bleak future. Their conditions were well summed up in the saying "Not a Chinaman's chance," which was coined at that time.[17]

A major social problem facing Chinese immigrants was the shortage of women. In the United States in 1860, there were 1,858 Chinese males per 100 females; and the situation had worsened by 1890, when the ratio of males to females was 2,679 to 100. Not until the 1970s—about a century later—did the ratio of males to females approach parity. This situation led to the use of the few available women as prostitutes, and caused cries of im-morality in the white community. In turn, control of gambling and prostitu-tion led to gang wars—the so-called Tong wars—which resulted in many deaths, often of innocent persons within the Chinese community.

Various associations flourished within such communities and provided their inhabitants with charitable, social, and other services. The most im-portant of these was the "Huiguan"—or district association—composed of all immigrants from the same district in China. In San Francisco, the six ex-isting district associations united in 1882 under an umbrella organization called the Chinese Consolidated Benevolent Association. In its dealings with the outside world, this association represented all Chinese and helped the community to deal more effectively with the city's power structure.

Secret societies, which had their political origin in antigovernment ac-tivities in China, also flourished in the Chinese communites in the United States during the late nineteenth century. However, in the United States, most of these secret societies degenerated into criminal associations that fought for the control of vice and illegal activities in the area. The illicit ac-tivities of the secret societies were moderated after the turn of the century, as Chinatowns slowly became law-abiding neighborhoods—very often safer than the rest of the city.

In addition to discrimination from individuals and local and state governments, Chinese immigration eventually was forbidden by federal laws—starting with the Chinese Exclusion Act of 1882, which barred the entry of Chinese laborers for ten years and prohibited the naturalization of Chinese immigrants as U.S. citizens. In 1892, the Geary Act extended these provisions for a further ten years; and, in 1898, the act was extended to Chinese immigrants seeking to enter the Hawaiian Islands. Finally, in 1904, the Chinese Exclusion Act was extended indefinitely.

Because of these laws, the number of Chinese entering the United States fell from a high of 22,781 in 1876 to a low of 10 in 1887. Each year, however, a few thousand immigrants continued to enter—either as immediate relatives of U.S. citizens, or illegally. Others came with their families as traders, who were exempt from the restriction because of a treaty with China; and a comparatively large number entered as U.S. citizens, on the basis that they had acquired citizenship through their U.S.-born Chinese fathers or both parents. Between 1920 and 1940—according to H.M. Lai— 71,040 China-born U.S. citizens were admitted to the United States.[18]

Once the right of derivative citizenship had been established by court rulings, Chinese-Americans returning to the United States from China or coming for the first time as U.S. citizens born abroad would falsely claim children allegedly born in China and left behind—both for monetary reasons and to help reunite family members of relatives and friends. In this manner, they established future U.S. citizenship claims, or the right of an emigrant to be reunited with an immediate family member. This system of creating "paper families" became known to U.S. authorities fairly quickly; and rather than being allowed to disembark in San Francisco, Chinese immigrants were held on Angel Island in San Francisco Bay until their credentials and their legal right of entry could be established—as with European immigrants held on Ellis Island.

Economically, most Chinese immigrants continued to hold marginal jobs in the service sector and in industries where the work hours were long, and the pay poor—though a considerable number went into business for themselves. Capital to start such enterprises was acquired from a rotating credit association. Through this device (called a "Hui"), members would contribute funds to a common pool, and one of the association members would then use the entire amount to open a business. The process was restarted at regularly set times, and another member would use the funds collected— until all members had had a chance to take advantage of the "Hui" and open a business. Most businesses were located in Chinatown and were family operated, although some employed other Chinese in small manufacturing concerns (especially in the garment-making sector).

Slowly, with the passing away of the first generation, U.S.-born Chinese—although still facing discrimination—advanced both educationally and economically; and a few who had managed to acquire a higher education started to practice in the professions.

Even during the Depression, community cohesiveness among the Chinese remained high; and, to a very large extent, the Chinese continued to take care of their own through their associations and kinship ties. In Chicago in 1933, while 10% of the whites were on relief, only 4% of the Chinese were getting this form of assistance. In New York, comparative figures were even lower: 9% of the whites versus 1% of the Chinese.[19]

World War II was a catalyst in the upward development of the Chinese in the United States. Because of severe manpower shortages, opportunities opened in industry; the Chinese aggressively took advantage of the situation, by filling a variety of positions. At a time when the entire Chinese population of the United States was less than 80,000, and estimated 10% of this number served with the U.S. Armed Forces and, took advantage of benefits available to veterans for furthering their education after the war.[20]

As China was an ally of the United States in the struggle against Japan, the Chinese Exclusion Acts were repealed in 1943; and Chinese immigrants who were permanent residents of the United States were allowed to apply for naturalization. Although the immigration quota for China was set at 105 persons per year, many more entered under special legislation, in order to be reunited with their families. The majority of such immigrants were women, which alleviated the major social problem in the Chinese community: lack of women of the same ethnic group.

The Chinese also benefited from the general economic prosperity that followed World War II; and increasingly, they both entered the professions and started their own businesses.

In 1950, when the Chinese population in the United States was about 117,000, Chinese owned more than 16,000 small businesses—albeit most being laundries and restaurants.

Although Chinese immigration to the United States continued during the 1950s and 1960s, it was only after the Immigration Act amendments of 1965 that the numbers substantially increased—jumping from a total of 34,764 in the 1961–70 period to 124,326 in the following decade, and 42,475 in fiscal year 1983 alone.[21] If present trends continue, the decade of the 1980s will see close to 400,000 new Chinese immigrants in the United States. (See Table 11.1.)

In this respect, because of China's complex political status, Chinese benefit from more than the 20,000-visa limit for preference immigrants, as prescribed by U.S. law for natives of each country. The People's Republic of China has a limit of 20,000; Taiwan has a separate 20,000; and Hong Kong, as a dependency of Great Britain, has 600 slots under the limitation for British natives. Technically, in this manner, 40,600 quota immigrants can legally come from China each year (aside from immediate relatives of U.S. citizens, who are not counted under the limit).

The surge in Chinese immigration has brought new opportunities with it, as well as new problems. Chinatowns have been revitalized by the infusion of new blood and have become lively centers of commerce, social intercourse, and tourist attractions. However, immigration has also increased overcrowding, fostered unsanitary conditions, encouraged marginal employment at substandard wages, and contributed to an increase in the incidence of crime.

While Chinese immigrants in the past were mostly from the Canton region, post–1965 immigrants are less homogeneous—coming from every

Table 11.1
Chinese in the United States: 1860–1980

Year	Chinese Population	Total Chinese immigrants admitted in decade ending in year cited
1860	34,933	41,397
1870	63,199	64,301
1880	105,465	123,201
1890	107,488	61,711
1900	89,863	14,799
1910	71,531	20,605
1920	61,639	21,278
1930	74,954	29,907
1940	77,504	4,928
1950	117,629	16,709
1960	198,958	9,657
1970	383,023	34,764
1980	812,178	124,326

Sources: U.S. Immigration and Naturalization Service, *Annual Report, 1983* (Washington, D.C.: Government Printing Office, 1984; U.S. Bureau of the Census, *Census of the Population* (Washington, D.C.: Government Printing Office, 1860–1980).

part of mainland China, as well as Hong Kong and Taiwan. The overwhelming majority are better educated than the former immigrants, and most have an urban background. A significant number, having come from Hong Kong or Taiwan, are also westernized.

As both parents work in most Chinese families of recent immigrants, the absence of parental control has somewhat weakened the traditional family ties—increasing cultural and intergenerational conflicts.

Socially, the old Chinese associations have lost most of their power and influence. In their place, other groups that aim to assist immigrants in adjusting to U.S. society have arisen. Such groups—generally led by highly educated and competent Chinese-Americans—are funded by the various levels of government and by private means, and provide a number of social services to their constituency.

While, generally, the social and economic standing of the Chinese in U.S. society has enormously improved during the past 20 years, two groups appear to be less benefited by the general trend: the aged bachelors who still live in Chinatown; and most of the new immigrants, who—until they establish a foothold in the country—continue to live in substandard conditions, work for substandard wages, and be exploited often by members of their own ethnic groups who are the employers.

12

Current Emigration Trends and Problems in China

At the present time, references to China embrace three separate political entities: the People's Republic of China; Taiwan; and Hong Kong, a colony of Great Britain.

The United States has not had formal diplomatic relations with Taiwan since 1979. In that same year, Congress—in the Taiwan Relations Act—authorized establishment of the American Institute in Taiwan (AIT), a private, nonprofit corporation charged with implementing unofficial relations between the people of the United States and the people of Taiwan. AIT maintains offices in Taipei and Kaoksiung. Taiwan is within the consular district of the U.S. Consulate General at Hong Kong, which issues visas for residents of Taiwan.

Immigrant visa applications in the People's Republic of China are processed and issued at two posts: Beijing, the capital; and Guangzhou (Canton).

Immigrant visa applications are also accepted and processed in the British Colony of Hong Kong, where a large consulate handles applications of Hong Kong residents, Taiwan residents, and former residents of mainland China (the People's Republic).

Table 12.1 gives the number of immigrant visa applicants born in the above three political entities and registered for immigration to the United States at U.S. consular offices as of January 1, 1985.

Table 12.1
Chinese Quota Applicants Registered for Immigration to the United States:
January 1, 1985

Place of Birth	Active Case	Inactive Cases*	Total
China-Mainland	107,448	14,602	122,050
China – Taiwan	59,541	12,633	72,174
Hong Kong	31,953	2,359	34,312

*Inactive cases are those in which applicant has failed to take action requested by consular office and has not communicated with such office for a year or longer.

Source: Visa Office of the U.S. Department of State, unpublished reports.

In addition to these, some other applicants who are not subject to the numerical limitation prescribed by U.S. law are registered at consular offices. These include the spouses and children of U.S. citizens, adopted children or stepchildren of U.S. citizens, parents of U.S. citizens, and special immigrants (such as ministers of religion and certain former employees of the U.S. government). The number of registered applicants in these classifications is relatively small, as they may apply for and receive visas—if eligible—at their convenience. A continuous turnover is always in effect: As applicants receive their visas, new petitions are received—making this a fluid, fluctuating situation rather than a static one.

Most of the Chinese applicants who are subject to numerical limitations were so registered on the basis of relationship to a U.S. citizen or to a permanent resident of the United States. Table 12.2 gives the breakdown by preference category: Only active cases—the great bulk—are taken into account.

As can be seen, most applicants are registered on the basis of relationship to a U.S. citizen or to a permanent resident (first, second, fourth, and fifth preference categories). Relatively few have qualified for registration on the basis of their profession (third preference) or on the basis that their skills are needed by an employer in the United States (sixth preference). The overwhelming majority of applicants are registered in the fifth preference category—as brothers and sisters of U.S. citizens, and their spouses and children.

As of May 1985—since the number of applicants in many preferences was larger than the number of visas available (20,000 for China-Mainland, 20,000 for China-Taiwan, and 600 for Hong Kong)—only applicants whose registration dates as intending immigrants were earlier than the dates given in Table 12.3 were able to apply. The other applicants had to wait until their priority dates were reached in the strictly first-registered, first-to-apply sys-

Table 12.2
Chinese Preference* Applicants Registered for Immigration to the United States: January 1, 1985

| | January 1, 1985 | | |
Preferences	Born in Mainland China	Born in Taiwan	Born in Hong Kong
1st Pref.	97	44	111
2nd Pref.	6,205	5,924	5,825
3rd Pref.	251	820	253
4th Pref.	1,458	307	1,354
5th Pref.	95,382	49,569	23,707
6th Pref.	2,493	2,731	541
Non-Pref.	1,562	146	162

*The various preferences are explained in Chapter 4.

Source: Visa Office of the United States Department of State, unpublished report, February 1985.

tem. From Table 12.3 it becomes evident that many applicants—particularly those born in Hong Kong—will have to wait a number of years before they can apply for U.S. immigrant visas.

After 1997, when Hong Kong reverts back to China—in accordance with the recent agreement between the People's Republic and Great Britain—all registered immigrant visa applicants born in Hong Kong will be subject to the numerical limitations for mainland China, under current U.S. laws. Since most of the Hong Kong–born applicants have earlier priority dates than those born on the mainland, it is possible under the present system that, for several years after 1997, most of the applicants obtaining immigrant visas in China will be the Hong Kong natives. To resolve this potential problem, in 1985 legislation was introduced in the U.S. Congress to increase the yearly numerical limit for Hong Kong natives from the current 600 to several thousand. This legislation became law in November 1986; thus the current application backlog may be resolved during the next ten years.

During a recent year—fiscal year 1983 (October 1, 1982–September 30, 1983)—25,777 applicants born in mainland China were admitted to the United States as permanent residents. Of these, 19,116 were subject to the numerical limitations of 20,000; and 6,651 were not—being special immigrants or immediate relatives of U.S. citizens. Of the total, 19,520 were new arrivals from overseas, while 6,257 who were already in the United

Table 12.3
Chinese Immigrant Visas Processing Dates, as of May 1985

Preferences	Born in Mainland China	Born in Taiwan	Born in Hong Kong
1st Pref.	All dates	All dates	Prior to 4-30-84
2nd Pref.	Prior to 6-1-84	Prior to 6-1-84	Prior to 10-20-78
3rd Pref.	Prior to 7-8-84	Prior to 7-8-84	Prior to 6-2-79
4th Pref.	All dates	All dates	Prior to 9-1-79
5th Pref.	Prior to 8-2-79	Prior to 3-22-81	Prior to 6-21-73
6th Pref.	Prior to 3-15-83	Prior to 7-1-83	Prior to 5-23-79
Non-Pref.	None	None	None

Source: Visa Office of the U.S. Department of State, Immigrant Visa Numbers for May 1985, Number 69, Volume V.

States on temporary visas adjusted their status to permanent residents without leaving the country. About one-third of those who adjusted their status were in the United States as tourists; and more than one-sixth, as students.

Comparable figures for Taiwan-born immigrants reveal that a total of 16,698 were admitted as permanent residents in fiscal year 1983. Of these, 14,843 were subject to numerical limitations; 1,855 were not; and 3,772 adjusted status within the United States. Close to half of those who adjusted status had been in the country as students; and about one-fifth, as tourists.

In the case of Hong Kong natives, 5,948 persons were admitted for permanent residence in fiscal year 1983. Of these, 4,364 were subject to numerical limitations, while 1,584 were special immigrants or immediate relatives of U.S. citizens: 4,501 were new arrivals; and 1,447, adjusted status. The number of Hong Kong–born quota immigrants who were admitted was larger than the 600 per year limit that is prescribed by law, because of a technical legal device called alternate chargeability. Thus, for the purpose of keeping members of a nuclear family together, all its members applying for a visa may be charged to the quota for the country of either parent or spouse, as the case may be. About one-third of those adjusting status were tourists, and another fourth were in the United States as students.

For all three areas of birth, female immigrants were slightly more numerous than male immigrants.

It is unlikely that, under present circumstances, the number of Chinese immigrating to the United States will decrease. We can therefore expect that, each year, 40,000 to 50,000 additional Chinese will obtain immigrant visas or adjust their status to permanent residents within the United States.

13

Social and Demographic Characteristics of Chinese Immigrants: 1980

CHINESE IN THE UNITED STATES

In 1980, Chinese comprised the largest ethnic Asian-American group—numbering 812,178 persons, an increase of 85.3% over the number counted in the 1970 census (441,853). Of the total, 54.4% named mainland China, Taiwan, and Hong Kong as their countries of birth. As other persons who ethnically identified themselves as Chinese may have been born in other nations of the world (especially other Asian countries), it seems probable that the actual percentage of all foreign-born ethnic Chinese who were counted in the 1980 census was closer to 60% than to 54%.

Of the former group, 64.8% were born in mainland China; 17%, in Taiwan; and 18.2%, in Hong Kong. About one-fourth of those born on the mainland had been in the United States longer than 20 years, and close to half had arrived in the 1970s. Conversely, 80% of the natives of Taiwan had arrived during the 1970-80 period, and less than 2% had been in the United States earlier than 1960. The same seems to apply—to a degree—to natives of Hong Kong: While two-thirds of those counted in 1980 had arrived during the preceding decade, only 6.6% had been in the country more than 20 years.

Again, we see the importance that the 1965 Immigration and Nationality Act amendments have played in the flow of immigrants to the United States. It has been estimated that the Chinese ethnic population in the

United States will reach the 1.25 million mark by 1990 and grow close to 1.7 million by the year 2000, principally because of immigration.

PLACE OF RESIDENCE

As with other Asian immigrants and—for that matter—immigrants in general, the Chinese tend to settle in urban areas and—more frequently than not—in the various Chinatowns located in the major cities of the United States. There they are able to easily find work (even without adequate language skills), find ingredients for preparing favorite foods, and generally engage in social intercourse with people who speak the same language and have the same customs and traditions.

While 96.1% of the Chinese ethnic population—both foreign- and U.S.-born—reside within a standard statistical metropolitan area, 96.5% of the foreign-born fall into this category. The slightly higher percentage of foreign-born is natural, since U.S.-born Chinese are more likely—because of their more favorable economic circumstances—to be dispersed, rather than concentrated in an urban area.

Although the Chinese population started to disperse throughout the country beginning in the late 1800s, significant concentrations still exist in certain states—such as New York, California, Illinois, and Hawaii.

Table 13.1 gives data on the ten states where the largest number of Chinese—both total and foreign-born—reside. As can be seen, California is still their preferred place of residence, with New York being a strong second. In fact, New York seems to be a particularly preferred place of residence for the foreign-born Chinese, since the percentage of those residing there is several points higher than that of the total Chinese ethnic community in the state. On the contrary, Hawaii—where a considerable number of the "old" Chinese immigrants settled between 1852 and 1898—does not appear to be a preferred place of residence for the new immigrants. While 6.9% of all ethnic Chinese resided there in 1980, only 2.3% of the foreign-born Chinese had chosen to make Hawaii their home.

AGE AND SEX DISTRIBUTION

As we have seen, a lopsided, overwhelming distribution of males in the Chinese ethnic community was—until recently—the source of the greatest social problem within the community and a contributor to the reputation that Chinatowns were dens of prostitution, gambling, and opium smoking. As late as 1960, the ratio of males to females was 133 males to 100 females. In 1970, it was reduced to 112 males for 100 females; and in 1980, to 102 males per 100 females. These favorable changes have occurred because of a predominantly female immigration from Taiwan, and apparently also because the majority of U.S.-born Chinese have been females. Data on the

Table 13.1
Ten Preferred States of Residence for Chinese: 1980

State	All Chinese	% of Total	Foreign- Born Chinese	% of total Foreign-Born
1. California	325,882	40.1	174,421	39.5
2. New York	147,250	18.1	96,135	21.8
3. Hawaii	55,916	6.9	10,183	2.3
4. Illinois	28,847	3.6	16,772	3.8
5. Texas	26,714	3.3	16,486	3.7
6. Massachusetts	24,882	3.1	14,650	3.3
7. New Jersey	23,432	2.9	13,591	3.1
8. Washington	17,984	2.2	9,716	2.2
9. Maryland	15,037	1.9	8,617	1.9
10. Pennsylvania	13,769	1.7	7,939	1.8
Total	679,773	83.7	368,520	83.4

Source: U.S. Bureau of the Census, *1980 Census of the Population, Supplementary Reports* (Washington, D.C.: Government Printing Office, July 1981) and "Foreign-Born Immigrants: Chinese—Tabulations from the 1980 U.S. Census of the Population and Housing," mimeographed report, Washington, D.C., October 1984.

sex of foreign-born Chinese counted in the 1980 census appear in Table 13.2. We see that the sex ratio for Chinese immigrants works out as follows: for those born on the mainland, 102 males per 100 females; for those born in Taiwan, 85.5 males per 100 females; and for those born in Hong Kong, 101.9 males per 100 females.

As for the age distribution of immigrants (when compared with that of the entire U.S. population in 1980), Table 13.3 shows that most immigrants fall in the productive age bracket—15–64—and that (apart from those born on the mainland) only a minute percentage are over the age of 64. In fact, mainland Chinese over the age of 64 represent 14.8% of all immigrants in this group—higher than the 11.3% of the entire U.S. population in this age bracket, and ten times as high as the comparable percentage of Taiwan and Hong Kong natives.

Why are the differences between these three groups so pronounced? The answer lies in the fact that, out of 286,120 mainland-born Chinese, 72,092—or 25.2%—had arrived in the United States prior to 1960. In comparison, only 1.9% of the Taiwan natives and 6.6% of the Hong Kong

Table 13.2
Sex Distribution of Chinese Immigrants: 1980

	Born in Mainland China	Born in Taiwan	Born in Hong Kong
Males	144,507	34,721	40,570
Females	141,613	40,632	39,810

Source: U.S. Bureau of the Census, "Foreign-Born Immigrants: Chinese—Tabulations from the 1980 U.S. Census of the Population and Housing," mimeographed report, Washington, D.C., October 1984.

natives had come before 1960. Thus, we see that, while the mainland-born population contained a high percentage of persons in the productive age bracket, it also encompassed an abnormally higher percentage of retired persons and, conversely, a relatively small number of persons under the age of 15.

FERTILITY

The fact that the great majority of Chinese immigrants are in the reproductive age would appear to point to high fertility rates and comparatively large families; yet, this is not the case. Data on the fertility of Chinese women are available both in the general 1980 census reports and in the special tabulations on the foreign-born. Unfortunately, these data are not

Table 13.3
Age Distribution of U.S. Population, Total Ethnic Chinese Population, and Foreign-Born Chinese Residents: 1980 (in percentages)

Age	U.S. Population	Total Ethnic Chinese Pop.	Born in Mainland China	Born in Taiwan	Born in Kong Kong
0–14	22.6	21.1	3.8	13.9	15.8
15–44	46.5	53.9	48.8	77.1	76.1
45–64	19.6	18.1	32.6	7.5	6.7
Over 64	11.3	6.5	14.8	1.5	1.4

Source: U.S. Census Bureau; (Washington, D.C.: Government Printing Office, 1981) and "Foreign-Born Immigrants: Chinese—Tabulations for the 1980 U.S. Census of the Population and Housing," mimeographed report, Washington, D.C., October 1984.

comparable: Data on the foreign-born do not give fertility rates, but only the number of children per household.

Table 13.4 shows that the fertility rate for all Chinese women in this country—both U.S.-born and foreign-born—is considerably lower than that of the U.S. female population on the whole. In fact, for the youngest group (age 15-24), it is one-fourth that of the total U.S. female population. For ages 25-34, it is less than two-thirds that of the U.S. female population; and for ages 35-44, only four-fifths that of the comparable U.S. female population. While the fertility rate of Chinese women who immigrated to the United States between 1970 and 1980 is higher than that of female Chinese immigrants as a whole, it is still lower than that of the entire U.S. female population.

The special tabulation on foreign-born done by the U.S. Bureau of the Census gives an indication of the fertility rates of immigrant women in a different manner: by indicating the number of children per Chinese household (Table 13.5).

As is evident, close to half of the households in the case of both the mainland- and Taiwan-born—and more than 60% in the case of those born in Hong Kong—have no children. When this percentage is combined with those for households with one or two children, we find that 86.7% of the households of mainlanders, 89.8% of the households of Taiwanese, and 91.7% of the households of those born in Hong Kong have two or fewer children. This characteristic—despite the fact that the percentage of Chinese female immigrants in the prime reproductive age group (15-44) is much higher than that of the U.S. population at large—indicates that Chinese immigrants may be less likely to have children than other population groups in the United States.

Table 13.4
Number of Children Born to U.S. Women, to All Chinese Women in the United States, and to Asian and Chinese Women Who Immigrated between 1970 and 1980, as of 1980 (per 1,000 women)

Age	Total U.S. Women	Asian Women Who Immigrated 1970–80	All Chinese Women in U.S.	Foreign-Born Chinese Women Who Immigrated 1970–1980
15–24	317	271	82	150
25–34	1,476	1,262	939	1,111
35–44	2,639	2,285	2,233	2,393

Source: U.S. Bureau of the Census, *1980 Census of the Population, U.S. Summary* (Washington, D.C.: Government Printing Office, 1981).

Table 13.5
Number of Children in Chinese Immigrant Households: 1980 (in percentages)

Number of Children	Mother China-Born	Mother Taiwan-Born	Mother Hong Kong Born
None	49.6	43.7	60.6
1	17.5	20.6	16.4
2	19.6	25.5	14.7
3	9.3	8.5	6.3
4 or more	4.0	1.7	2.0

Source: U.S. Bureau of the Census, Foreign-Born Immigrants: Chinese—Tabulations from the 1980 U.S. Census of the Population and Housing," mimeographed report, Washington, D.C., October 1984.

MARITAL STATUS

The special census tabulations of the foreign-born counted in the United States in 1980 show that Chinese over the age of 15 totaled 407,744 in this country. Of these, 201,698 were males; and 206,046, females. Data on marital status are given in Table 13.6.

Several facts can be observed in the data. While mainland and Taiwan Chinese are more likely to be married than the U.S. population at large—

Table 13.6
Marital Status of U.S. Population and Foreign-Born Chinese over Age 15: 1980 (in percentages)

Status	U.S. Native Male	Female	Mainland Male	Female	Taiwan Male	Female	Hong Kong Male	Female
Single	29.7	22.8	17.1	10.4	36.2	26.3	63.6	47.3
Married	60.6	55.2	76.9	71.9	62.1	68.1	34.5	47.9
Separated	1.9	2.6	1.2	1.3	.4	.9	.5	.6
Widowed	2.5	13.3	2.7	13.7	.4	2.6	.4	2.4
Divorced	5.3	7.1	2.1	2.6	.9	2.1	1.0	1.8

Sources: U.S. Bureau of the Census, *1980 Census of the Population, U.S. Summary* (Washington, D.C.: Government Printing Office, 1981) and "Foreign-Born Immigrants: Chinese—Tabulations from the 1980 U.S. Census of the Population and Housing," mimeographed report, Washington, D.C., October 1984.

both males and females—the percentage of those born in Hong Kong who are married is considerably lower. Conversely, the percentage of Hong Kong Chinese over the age of 15 who are single is higher than that of the other three groups analyzed: Close to two-thirds of the Hong Kong Chinese males and half of the females are single. No explanation is available for this fact, since the percentage of Hong Kong immigrants in the age group 15–44 is much higher than that of mainland-born and only marginally lower than that of Taiwanese in the same age bracket.

The divorce rates for all three Chinese groups, as might be expected (given the traditional closeness and stability of Chinese families), are much lower than those of the U.S. population at large. Yet, while it could be thought that this rate would be higher for Taiwan and Hong Kong natives— who are more westernized and come from a much more mobile society— than for mainland Chinese, the reverse is true: The divorce rates for these two groups are lower than those for the mainland Chinese.

HOUSEHOLD COMPOSITION AND SIZE

As the special 1980 census tabulations on the foreign-born do not describe household size or composition, this demographic factor cannot be analyzed by place of birth (the mainland, Taiwan, and Hong Kong). However, we can look at available data for all Chinese (whether born in the United States or in China) to compare the figure for those immigrants who came to the United States between 1970 and 1980 and on whom data are available from other reports of U.S. Bureau of the Census.

The average number of persons in a U.S. household is 2.74 persons; in a U.S. family, 3.27. Both average household and family size are larger for the Chinese. The average for all Chinese households is 3.11 persons; that of Chinese immigrants who arrived in the United States between 1970 and 1980 is 3.47. The average Chinese family is composed of 3.64 persons; and that of Chinese immigrants who came between 1970 and 1980, 3.86 persons.

The composition of Chinese households also reflects the strong family traditions and obligations for taking care of relatives and, in some cases, friends. In fact—while only 4.2% of persons living in an average U.S. household are not primary family members (spouses and children), but simply relatives—the comparable percentage for all Chinese households is 7.7%. The proportion is even higher for households of Chinese immigrants who came to the United States in the period 1970-80: 14.6%.

Similarly, while nonrelatives residing in U.S. households in general make up 2.7% of household members, this figure is 3.6% for all Chinese households and 3.8% for the Chinese households of immigrants who came in 1970-80.

EDUCATION

Like other Asian-American ethnic groups and Asian immigrants, Chinese residing in the United States exhibit a high level of educational achievement. Most Chinese students are spurred to excel in education by a tradition of respect for learning, parental support, and the view that education in a highly mobile society such as the United States is the avenue to economic achievement and the "good life."

While the proportion of high school graduates in the U.S. population at large over the age of 25 is 66.5%, it is 75.2% for all Chinese—both immigrants and U.S.-born. Moreover, young Chinese are more likely to stay in school longer, at both the high school and the college level; in fact, while 89% of the white U.S. population aged 16-17 are enrolled in school, the figure for Chinese in the same age group is 96%. Furthermore, by the college years, the gap widens: 23.9% of the whites aged 20-24 are enrolled in school, as compared with 59.8% of the Chinese who are attending college. As a result, 47.8% of Chinese-Americans over age 25 are college graduates, versus 16.2% of the general U.S. population.

Data available on the foreign-born Chinese reveal the same pattern, with minor exceptions. For all three foreign-born Chinese groups, the percentage of college graduates is higher than that of the U.S. population over the age of 20. Likewise, 67.2% of the Chinese born in Taiwan who came to the United States between 1965 and 1969 are college graduates, as compared with 16.2% for the U.S. population; the lowest number of Chinese college graduates—20.6%—is that of Hong Kong natives who immigrated between 1975 and 1980. Still, this is more than four percentage points higher than that of the U.S. population.

Another salient feature—with respect to college education—is the fact that, generally, length of time in the United States is directly proportional to the percentage of college graduates. The longer the immigrants have been in the United States, the more they are likely to have had a higher education (the only major exceptions are the older immigrants from mainland China and Taiwan who came to the United States before 1960). This may be the result of two factors: the fact that more educational opportunity and the economic means to pursue it are available in the United States, and the possibility that the 1965-75 immigrants were better educated to begin with than those who preceded or followed them. (See Table 13.7).

In contrast to the figure for Taiwan-born immigrants, the percentage of high school graduates among all immigrants born in Hong Kong and mainland China—regardless of year of immigration—is lower than that for Americans in general. Similarly, for mainland Chinese immigrants over age 20, the percentage of those with less than five years of schooling is much higher than the general U.S. average. For those born in Hong Kong or Taiwan, this percentage is higher only for those immigrants who came to the United States before 1960.

Table 13.7

Years of Schooling Completed by Chinese Immigrants over Age 20, as of 1980 (in percentages)

| Place of Birth | Educational Level | All Periods | Year of Immigration | | | | |
			1975– 1980	1970– 1974	1965– 1969	1960– 1964	1959 & Earlier
Mainland China	Less than 5 years	15.7	15.6	14.2	13.6	13.3	19.3
	High-School Graduate	47.7	44.9	49.5	51.2	54.0	44.0
	4 or more years college	28.9	22.9	31.0	34.3	37.0	25.9
Taiwan	Less than 5 years	1.8	1.9	1.8	1.1	1.8	4.3
	High School Graduate	71.0	69.9	68.9	78.1	84.9	69.7
	4 or more years college	56.0	54.2	53.3	67.2	64.4	48.4
Hong Kong	Less than 5 years	3.5	3.7	3.1	2.8	2.9	6.7
	High-School Graduate	53.3	54.2	55.5	56.6	58.2	60.4
	4 or more years college	33.6	20.6	37.6	38.3	40.8	42.5

Source: U.S. Bureau of the Census, "Foreign-Born Immigrants: Chinese—Tabulations from the 1980 U.S. Census of the Population and Housing," mimeographed report, Washington, D.C., October 1984.

Of additional interest is the fact that a remarkable number of Chinese immigrants over the age of 16 who are in the labor force are also students: For the Taiwanese, it is about 14.8%. An overwhelming majority of these—91.8%—are pursuing university-level studies, with 53.6% studying for advanced degrees. The percentage of labor-force students born in Hong Kong is even higher: 20.7%. Of these, 59.3% are pursuing undergraduate degrees; and 20.6%, graduate degrees. Immigrants born in mainland China have the lowest percentage of those in the labor force who also attend school: 5.5%. Of these, 50.1% are undergraduates; and 38.9%, graduate students.

It is clear that Chinese residents of the United States—both the native and the foreign-born—are educational high-achievers who will make their influence in the professional world felt more and more, in the future.

CHINESE IMMIGRANTS AT WORK

Labor Force Participation

One of the major indicators of the self-reliance of a population group—its work ethic and its drive and energy—is its labor participation rate, the percentage of those over the age of 16 who are employed or actively seeking employment.

In 1980, the rate of labor participation for the entire U.S. population over the age of 16 was 62.0%: 75.1% for males and 49.9% for females. For the total Chinese-American population over the age ot 16, the overall labor participation rate was 66.4%; the rate breaks down to 74.3% for males and 58.3% for females—substantially higher than for that of the U.S. population at large.

The same was substantially true of Chinese immigrants (Table 13.8). With few exceptions, the rates of labor force participation were higher than those for the U.S. population at large—reaching 90.8% for Taiwanese who immigrated to the United States prior to 1965. Similarly, females born in Hong Kong who came to the United States before 1960 have a labor force participation rate of 68.3%. Only when we consider the most recent arrivals (Chinese immigrants who came between 1975 and 1980) do we find labor participation rates lower than U.S. averages.

Generally, the rate increases with length of stay in the United States. The pattern is broken only by mainland-born Chinese who arrived prior to 1960. This is no surprise and—in fact—is to be expected, since 29.6% of this group are over the age of 65 and, thus, likely to be retired. This percentage is double that of the total mainland-born population over the age of 16.

Employment and Unemployment

In 1980, the foreign-born Chinese labor force in the United States was composed of 262,862 persons, of whom 262,153 were in the civilian labor force. The balance (709) were presumably in the U.S. military.

When the U.S. census was taken in 1980, the unemployment rate in the United States for both male and female workers was 6.5%. The rate for Chinese immigrants was about half that of all U.S. workers—3.7% for both sexes: 3.0% for males and 4.6% for females.

Some variations were found in the unemployment rate, depending on the immigrant's sex and place of birth. However, in no case was the unemployment rate higher than 5.4%, which is still lower than the U.S. average. The data are given in Table 13.9.

Unemployment was lower than the 6.5% rate for the U.S. work force—even for the latest Chinese immigrant arrivals (those who came to the United States between 1975 and 1980). In fact, it stood at 4.9% for the

Table 13.8

Labor Force Participation of Chinese Immigrants over Age 16: 1980 (in percentages)

Place of Birth	All Periods	1975–1980	Year of Immigration 1970–1974	1965–1969	1960–1964	1959 & Earlier
Mainland China						
Both Sexes	66.5	58.5	73.6	74.4	74.7	60.2
Males	77.0	68.8	85.6	88.4	88.7	67.5
Females	56.0	48.8	61.7	62.2	62.6	50.6
Taiwan						
Both Sexes	59.6	50.3	66.2	73.7	74.8	75.6
Males	72.0	61.1	82.1	87.5	90.8	90.8
Females	49.0	41.4	56.3	59.5	58.3	64.6
Hong Kong						
Both Sexes	65.1	54.7	68.1	68.4	71.9	76.7
Males	68.3	55.5	71.5	71.7	76.3	85.5
Females	62.0	53.9	64.7	65.0	67.6	68.3

Source: U.S. Bureau of the Census, "Foreign-Born Immigrants: Chinese—Tabulations from the 1980 U.S. Census of the Population and Housing," mimeographed report, Washington, D.C., October 1984.

Table 13.9

Unemployment Rates of Chinese Immigrants in the Civilian Labor Force: 1980 (in percentages)

Place of Birth	Unemployment Rate Both Sexes	Males	Females
Mainland China	3.7	3.0	4.6
Taiwan	3.6	2.1	5.4
Hong Kong	3.9	3.8	4.0

Source: U.S. Bureau of the Census, "Foreign-Born Immigrants: Chinese—Tabulations from the 1980 U.S. Census of the Population and Housing," mimeographed report, Washington, D.C., October 1984.

Taiwanese; 5.3%, for those from Hong Kong; and 5.5%, for natives of mainland China.

Another facet of the employment experience of Chinese immigrants can be observed by looking at their periods of employment and, conversely, unemployment during the year preceding the census (1979), and by comparing this data with those of the U.S. work force and that of all foreign-born residents of the United States.

In Table 13.10, we see that Chinese immigrants—except those from the mainland—were less likely to have worked the full year than the U.S. work force or the entire foreign-born work force. Invariably, the percentage in all three groups of Chinese immigrants who had some period of unemployment during 1979 was higher than that of the U.S. or total foreign-born work force. However, the average number of weeks of unemployment for the mainland-born unemployed worker was only slightly higher than that of the U.S. work force; and for unemployed workers from both Taiwan and Hong Kong, was lower. The same pattern held true even for those who immigrated in the period 1975-80: The average weeks of unemployment were 14.7 for the unemployed mainland-born worker, 12.7 for the Taiwanese, and 13.1 for those born in Hong Kong.

Table 13.10
Work Experience of Chinese Immigrants in the U.S. Labor Force: 1979 (in percentages)

	U.S. Work Force	All Foreign-Born Work Force	Mainland Chinese Natives	Taiwanese Natives	Hong Kong Natives
Worked during 1979	98.2	97.5	97.8	97.2	97.9
Worked 50–52 weeks	52.2	50.6	59.6	49.8	47.9
Worked 40–49 weeks	13.2	15.9	16.7	14.5	16.2
Worked 27–39 weeks	8.3	8.3	7.4	9.5	9.0
Worked 1–26 weeks	18.0	17.0	14.0	23.5	24.8
Had some unemployment in 1979	18.6	20.8	19.4	21.4	21.6
Unemployed 15 weeks or longer	6.2	7.5	6.7	6.3	6.1
Average weeks of unemployment per unemployed worker	14.1	14.5	14.5	12.7	12.0

Sources: U.S. Bureau of the Census, *1980 Census of the Population, U.S. Summary* (Washington, D.C.: Government Printing Office, 1981) and "Foreign-Born Immigrants: Chinese—Tabulations from the 1980 Census of the Population and Housing," mimeographed report, Washington, D.C., October 1984.

Occupations

Compared with the U.S. work force, the Chinese—whether U.S.-born or immigrants—display an impressive degree of occupational achievements. In fact, as can be seen in Table 13.11, the percentage of Chinese in the professional and executive/managerial occupations is higher than that of the U.S. employed population at large. While the percentage is 22.7 for the U.S. labor force, it is 32.5 for Chinese-Americans, 29.6 for immigrants from the mainland, 44.7 for Taiwanese, and 30.8 for those from Hong Kong.

The Chinese are likewise overrepresented in the technical occupations—which include such jobs as medical technologists, engineering and scientific workers, computer programmers, airplane pilots, and broadcast specialists.

While—apart from the natives of Hong Kong—Chinese are underrepresented in the administrative support and clerical occupations, all groups (in relation to the employed U.S. work force), are overrepresented in the service occupations—which include many low-paying, limited-skill jobs in food service, cleaning, and personal services.

Chinese immigrants born in mainland China also have a high percentage working as machine operators—most likely working in the apparel industry.

One fact that stands out in Table 13.11 is that 30.4% of the employed immigrants born in Taiwan are engaged in the professions. This is likely a result of the large number of students who come to the United States every year to pursue graduate studies and who, eventually—rather than returning to Taiwan—decide to stay and apply for adjustment of legal status to permanent residents. Estimates indicate that the number of such students remaining in the United States after completing their graduate degree work is higher than 90%. In a typical year (1983), Taiwanese students adjusting their status to permanent residents of the United States constituted 44.7% of all such adjustments by Taiwanese. When their dependents were added, this rose to 57.2%. Thus, we see that Chinese immigrants in the work force are concentrated in two occupational clusters: the professional/administrative/managerial groups, and the service occupations. Because of this, they encompass two extremes: individuals and families with excellent incomes, and others who lead most of their lives in substandard conditions on minimal salaries.

Income and Poverty

Working Chinese-Americans—if the native and foreign-born are taken as a group—were reported by the U.S. Census Bureau through data collected in 1980 to be doing well. In fact, the median income of a full-time Chinese-American worker in 1979 was $15,753. Among all major Asian-

Table 13.11
Occupational Distribution of Chinese Immigrants among the U.S. Employed: 1980 (in percentages)

Occupation	U.S. Labor Force	Chinese Labor Force	Mainland Immigrants	Taiwan Immigrants	Hong Kong Immigrants
1. Executive, administrative, managerial	10.4	12.9	12.8	14.3	11.7
2. Professionals	12.3	19.6	16.8	30.4	19.1
3. Technical & related support	3.1	6.3	5.1	11.4	6.6
4. Sales	10.0	8.6	7.1	8.4	8.2
5. Administrative support, including clerical	17.2	15.2	9.8	11.9	20.7
6. Private household services	.6	.5	.8	.4	.3
7. Protective services	1.5	.4	.2	.1	.2
8. Other services	10.8	17.6	23.5	13.3	18.0
9. Farming, forestry, and fishing	2.9	.5	.5	.4	.2
10. Precision production craft & repair	12.9	5.6	5.8	3.1	3.8
11. Machine operators and assemblers	9.3	9.9	15.2	4.8	8.0
12. Transportation & material-moving	4.5	1.0	.8	.4	1.1
13. Handlers, helpers, and laborers	4.5	1.9	1.6	1.0	2.1

Sources: U.S. Bureau of the Census, *1980 Census of the Population, U.S. Summary* (Washington, D.C.: Government Printing Office, 1981) and "Foreign-Born Immigrants: Chinese—Tabulations from the U.S. Census of the Population and Housing," mimeographed report, Washington, D.C., October 1984.

American ethnic groups, this sum was exceeded only by Asian Indians ($18,707) and Japanese ($16,829), and was higher than that of Filipinos, Koreans, and Vietnamese. This median income was also marginally higher than that of a full-time white worker ($15,572) and considerably higher than that of Hispanic and black workers.

Both the household and family median incomes of Chinese-Americans were also higher than those of the total U.S. population at large. The median household income of Chinese-Americans was $19,561, versus $18,841 for U.S. households; and the median family income was $22,559, as compared with $19,917 for U.S. families.

The median income for foreign-born Chinese full-time workers varied with the place of birth: In 1979, it was $10,794 for those born on the mainland, $11,818 for natives of Taiwan, and $11,790 for those born in Hong Kong. These figures were lower than those for most ethnic groups, both native and immigrant. Among the foreign-born Asian groups, however, Chinese exceeded the median income of Japanese, Koreans, and Vietnamese full-time workers, and were behind those of Asian Indians and Filipinos.

The 1979 median household income of immgrants was $18,544 for mainland Chinese; for those born in Taiwan, $18,271; and for natives of Hong Kong, $18,094. Among the major Asian immigrant groups in the United States, these figures were below those of Indians and Filipinos, above that of the Japanese, and similar to that of Koreans.

While no complete data are readily available on the income distribution for the households of all Chinese immigrants, we do have data for Chinese immigrant households that arrived between 1970 and 1979. As might be expected, the data indicate that the percentage of Chinese immigrant households with income below $10,000 is higher than that of U.S. households as a whole. Conversely, the percentage at the upper reaches of the income scale is much lower.

However, the spirit of enterprise of Chinese households and their ability to do well in the long run can be grasped when all Chinese households—both native and immigrants—are considered in the analysis in Table 13.12. Only 25.7% of Chinese households have an income of less than $10,000, versus 29.2% of all U.S. households; at the other end of the scale, 20.8% of Chinese households have an income of $35,000 or more, versus 13.2% of all U.S. households.

The same point is also evident in the figures for the median income of a family in relation to the number of workers in the family. The percentage of all ethnic Chinese families and those of Chinese families who immigrated between 1970 and 1979—with no worker or one worker in the family—is lower than that of U.S. families in general. However, the percentage of those families with two or more workers is higher. On the income side, while the median income of Chinese immigrant families is invariably lower—regardless of the number of workers—the median income of ethnic Chinese families (including both the U.S.- and foreign-born) is higher than U.S. families in the case of families with one or two workers, and comparable for families with three or more workers (Table 13.13).

Because of their low income-earning performance in comparison with U.S. families, the percentage of poor Chinese families, (those with income

Table 13.12

Household Income Distribution of Chinese Who Immigrated between 1970 and 1979 versus All U.S. Households and All Ethnic Chinese Households: 1979 (in percentages)

Income	U.S. Households	All Ethnic Chinese Households	Chinese Immigrant Households
Less than $5,000	13.3	12.4	15.8
$5,000 - $7,499	8.0	6.6	9.4
$7,500 - $9,999	7.9	6.7	10.1
$10,000 - $14,999	15.3	13.1	17.8
$15,000 - $19,999	14.1	12.2	14.1
$20,000 - $24,999	12.5	11.4	10.3
$25,000 - $34,999	15.7	16.8	12.3
$35,000 - $49,999	8.6	12.9	6.6
$50,000 or more	4.6	7.9	3.6

Sources: U.S. Bureau of the Census, *1980 Census of the Population, U.S. Summary* 1-14 and *U.S. Summary, General Social and Economic Characteristics* 1-101 (Washington, D.C.: Government Printing Office, 1981).

Table 13.13

Workers per U.S., Ethnic Chinese-American, and Chinese Immigrant Family and Median Family Income: 1979

Number of Workers Per Family	U.S. Families	U.S. Families' Median Income	Chinese American Families	Chinese-American Families' Median Income	Chinese Immigrant Families	Chinese Immigrant Families' Median Income
None	12.8 %	$ 7,791	7.1%	$ 5,056	8.0%	$ 2,580
1	33.0	16,181	27.7	17,394	25.2	10,962
2	41.6	23,058	46.8	25,176	46.2	15,970
3 or more	12.6	31,880	18.7	31,420	20.6	23,033

Source: U.S. Bureau of the Census, *1980 Census of the Population, U.S. Summary* (Washington, D.C.: Government Printing Office, 1981).

below the standards set by the federal government) is greater than the U.S. national norm. In fact, while in 1980, 9.6% of all U.S. families were considered poor on the basis of their family size and income earned in 1979, 10.5% of all Chinese families fell in the same category. Among immigrant Chinese families, the overall rate was 10% for natives of mainland China, 11.8% for those hailing from Taiwan, and 8.9% for those from Hong Kong.

As might be expected, the percentage of poor families among Chinese immigrants was directly influenced by their length of residence in the United States. Data confirming this fact are presented in Table 13.14.

While most recent Chinese immigrants (those who came between 1975 and 1980) have an extremely large percentage of families with incomes below the poverty line, their situation is not static, and they are not an institutionalized poverty class. Actually, the data show that, within a period of 1–9 years, the percentage of poor Chinese families dropped considerably— approaching or being lower than that of all U.S. familes. Furthermore, Chinese immigrant families who have been in the United States longer than ten years invariably had a smaller percentage of poor families than U.S. families in general.

Thus, while serious income and poverty problems exist within the Chinese immigrant community for the first few years of their lives in the United States, such problems appear to be resolved within a few years after their arrival—thanks to hard work, family cohesiveness, and education.

Table 13.14
Chinese Immigrant Families with Income below the Poverty Line: 1979
(in percentages)

| Year of Immigration | Place of Birth | | |
	Mainland China	Taiwan	Hong Kong
All Periods	10.0	11.8	8.9
1975–80	25.3	22.8	18.6
1970–74	9.9	6.1	9.6
1965–69	6.7	3.0	5.9
1960–64	6.3	1.5	5.7
1959 & earlier	5.5	4.6	4.4

Source: U.S. Bureau of the Census, "Foreign-Born Immigrants: Chinese—Tabulations from the 1980 U.S. Census of the Population and Housing," mimeographed report, Washington, D.C., October 1984.

ACCULTURATION

Two indexes of the degree and pace of acculturation of Chinese immigrants are their ability to speak English and their naturalization as U.S. citizens. Data on both these factors are ascertainable from the unpublished special tabulations made by the U.S. Census Bureau from information collected in 1980.

The overall figures for Chinese immigrants naturalized as U.S. citizens were 50.3% for those born on the mainland, 28.9% for those born in Taiwan, and 38.3% for natives of Hong Kong. These figures are deceptive, however, because they include the immigrants who arrived in 1975-80. By 1980, most of these immigrants could not have legally applied for naturalization, since they could not meet the five-years legal residence requirement. If these immigrants are excluded, the percentages rise to 66.9 for mainlanders, 57.9 for Taiwanese, and 55.9 for those born in Hong Kong (Table 13.15).

Predictably, length of residence in the United States positively influenced naturalization percentages. After ten years in the country, more than two-thirds of all Chinese immigrants have become U.S. citizens—an impressive percentage. Thus—just like countless immigrants from other countries—they could start to take an active part in the affairs of their new home, derive the benefits of such status, and perform the duties that it entails.

The ability to speak English—perhaps the most important factor in the acculturation of immigrants—is explored next. What is immediately noticeable is the use of Chinese in the home, even when the immigrant can speak

Table 13.15
Naturalization of Chinese Immigrants, as of 1980

Year of Immigration	Mainland Chinese Naturalized		Taiwanese Naturalized		Hong Kong Natives Naturalized	
All periods	286,120	50.3 %	75,353	28.9 %	80,380	38.3 %
1975-80	77,816	6.0	41,108	4.7	28,045	5.5
1970-74	58,213	38.7	19,979	40.1	22,184	35.3
1965-69	49,039	65.4	9,628	79.6	17,757	63.6
1960-64	28,960	76.8	3,185	90.0	7,069	76.6
1959 & earlier	72,092	86.4	1,453	88.5	5,325	88.6

Source: U.S. Bureau of the Census, "Foreign-Born Immigrants: Chinese—Tabulations from the 1980 Census of the Population and Housing," mimeographed report, Washington, D.C., October 1984.

English. We see that, even after a stay of 20 or more years in the United States, most Chinese immigrants (more than three-fourths) speak a Chinese dialect at home.

Table 13.16 shows that the percentage of immigrants born in mainland China who speak English at home and who speak it well or very well outside the home is 58.3%; this percentage fluctuates between 41% for those who immigrated between 1975 and 1980, and 69% for those who arrived before 1960. The percentage of mainlanders who do not speak English at all is 14.5%, with a variation from 25.4% for the latest arrivals (1975-80) to 6.3% for the pre-1960 immigrants.

Since they generally have more education, those born in Taiwan are more proficient in English than the mainlanders. Overall, 82% speak English well or very well. About 73.1% of those who arrived in the United States between 1975 and 1980 fall in this category; it rises to 89% for the early immigrants who came before 1960. Only 3.1% of Taiwanese immigrants do not speak English at all: The figures range from 4.8% for the latest arrivals to 1.3% for the pre-1960 group.

The immigrants born in Hong Kong also do relatively well in their ability to speak English. Overall, 85.5% speak English well or very well; this figure ranges from a low of 76.1% for those who came in the period 1975-80, to a

Table 13.16
Ability to Speak English among Chinese Immigrants over Age 5: 1980 (in percentages)

English Language Ability	Mainland Born All	1975-80	Pre-'60	Taiwan Born All	1975-80	Pre-'60	Hong Kong Born All	1975-80	Pre-'60
1. Speak only English at home	4.4	1.3	11.1	5.8	2.2	24.6	5.4	3.2	21.1
2. Speak other than English at home	95.6	98.7	88.9	94.2	97.8	75.4	94.6	96.8	78.9
A. Speak English very well	25.5	13.6	30.8	33.3	23.4	41.0	44.5	27.4	46.8
B. Speak English well	28.4	26.1	27.1	42.9	47.5	23.7	35.6	45.5	19.1
C. Speak English poorly	27.2	33.6	24.7	14.9	22.1	9.4	11.9	19.6	10.7
D. Do not speak any English	14.5	25.4	6.3	3.1	4.8	1.3	2.6	4.3	2.3

Source: U.S. Bureau of the Census, "Foreign-Born Immigrants: Chinese—Tabulations from the 1980 U.S. Census of the Population and Housing," mimeographed report, Washington, D.C., October 1984.

high of 87% for the pre-1960 immigrants. Only 2.6% of the Hong Kong immigrants speak no English.

The above data on acculturation reveal that while Chinese immigrants are linguistically and—by inference—culturally attached to their society and customs, they are slowly becoming an integral part of U.S. society, if the ability to speak English and their naturalization as U.S. citizens are taken as a measure.

14

Conclusions and Prospects for the Future

The Chinese ethnic community in the United States will continue to grow in size—primarily because of continued heavy immigration, rather than natural increase. It has been estimated that the number of ethnic Chinese in the United States will reach the 1.25 million mark by 1990, and will approach 1.7 million by the year 2000.

In 1980, more than 400,000 Chinese—or 54.4% of the total 812,178—were foreign-born, with about three-fifths from mainland China and about one-fifth each from Taiwan and Hong Kong.

While—in comparison with the U.S. norm—a higher percentage of the foreign-born Chinese were in the 14–64 age bracket, those from mainland China also had a disproportionate number over the age of 64. Apart from natives of Hong Kong, Chinese immigrants had high marriage rates and extremely low rates of divorce, as compared with the U.S. average.

Both their family and household sizes were larger than the U.S. norm, and households tended to include relatives and others in a proportion higher than American families and households.

In the realm of education, Chinese immigrants presented some paradoxes. While the percentage of those with four or more years of college was higher for natives of all three localities—reaching a high of 56% for those born in Taiwan—the percentage of those born in Hong Kong or on the mainland who had graduated from high school was lower than that for the

United States. Natives of mainland China also had a large number with less than five years of education: 15.7%.

While overall labor-force participation by Chinese immigrants was higher than the U.S. norm, this rate was considerably lower for those who had arrived between 1975 and 1980. The immigrants' unemployment rates in 1980 were lower than that of the U.S. labor force, although—excepting natives of mainland China—Chinese immigrants in 1979 were more likely to have been unemployed. The average length of unemployment for the immigrant unemployed worker was higher than the U.S. norm for natives of mainland China; and lower, for natives of Hong Kong and Taiwan.

Occupationally, all three groups of Chinese immigrants were overrepresented in the managerial/executive, professional, and technical fields. Hong Kong natives were also heavily overrepresented in the clerical field; and mainland Chinese, in both factory and service occupations. The emerging picture is that of a relatively high percentage of individuals in high-paying occupations and an even higher percentage in low-paying occupations.

In 1979, the median income for both a full-time Chinese immigrant worker and an entire Chinese immigrant family was lower than the U.S. norm. Despite the fact that Chinese immigrant households have more workers per unit than the U.S. norm, the median household income was lower.

The percentage of Chinese immigrant families with income below the poverty level was marginally higher in 1979 than that of U.S. families in general. The problem was particularly acute for those families who had immigrated in the period 1975-79: The figure for poor families in this category was more than 20% for natives of mainland China and Taiwan; and a shade below that, for Hong Kong natives. However, this problem seemed to be a temporary one, since the percentage dropped below the U.S. norm for all Chinese immigrant families who had been in the United States for ten years or longer.

The acculturation of Chinese immigrants in the United States appears to be proceeding at a rapid pace, both in terms of naturalization as U.S. citizens and in English-language proficiency. More than 50% of all Chinese immigrants who, by 1980, had been in the United States for 6–10 years were U.S. citizens; it rose to more than 75% after a residence of 16–20 years, and as high as 90% for the Taiwanese. Overall, 58.3% of all mainland Chinese immigrants spoke English well or very well, as compared with 82% of the Taiwanese and 85.5% of the Hong Kong natives. However, the mainlanders also included 14.5% who spoke no English at all.

The overall situation of Chinese immigrants in the United States in 1980 was marked by many paradoxes: high percentages of both college-educated and barely literate individuals; a large number of professionals versus an even larger number of individuals in low-skill, low-paying occupations;

high levels of English-language skills together with large numbers of persons with no knowledge of English at all; and overall lower incomes and a
higher poverty level than the U.S. norm. Clearly, Chinese immigrants have
quite a way to go—particularly on the economic level—before entering the
mainstream of U.S. society.

III

Filipino, Korean, and Chinese Immigrants: 1980-1985

The preceding analysis of immigrants in the United States was primarily based on published sources and on published and unpublished data from the U.S. Bureau of the Census, the U.S. Immigration and Naturalization Service, the U.S. Department of State, and various offices in the Philippines, Hong Kong, South Korea, and Taiwan. For the most part, the available data covered only immigrants enumerated by the U.S. Bureau of the Census in 1980 and, even then, delved only into certain sociodemographic characteristics present at the time the census was taken, in April 1980.

The following analysis is based on the results of a survey of the members of Filipino, Korean, and Chinese immigrant households who arrived in the United States in the period between January 1980 and December 1985. Among other factors, the survey sought to establish some of the socioeconomic and demographic characteristics of these immigrants prior to their arrival, their current sociodemographic characteristics, the type of problems that they encountered on settling in the United States, their tax contributions to U.S. society, and the aspects of life in the United States that they most liked or disliked at the time of their interview.

The questionaire used for the individual interviews conducted during the survey was designed by the author, and underwent a series of changes between April and November 1985 (the study's planning stage). It was vetted by several sociologists, demographers, and social scientists in the

Philippines, Korea, Hong Kong, and the United States—through whose suggestions and advice the questionnaire was considerably improved.

The original plan for the study was to select the interview sample at random from data maintained by the U.S. embassies and consulates that issue immigrant visas in Korea, Hong Kong, China, and the Philippines. Since immigrant visa operations in those U.S. diplomatic posts are computerized, it would have been feasible to obtain names and U.S. addresses of every adult issued an immigrant visa during the previous two years (1984 and 1985). Depending on the size of such listings, every fifth, tenth, or twentieth name on the list could have been selected as a subject for this survey. The plan also called for the mailing of 3,000 to 4,000 questionnaires, and the author envisioned a response rate of 10–20 percent—for a total minimum of 300 and a maximum of 800 replies.

However, it turned out to be impossible to obtain such listings from the embassies and consulates because, under privacy statutes and Section 222(f) of the Immigration and Nationality Act of 1952 (as amended), visa record information may only be used for the enforcement or amendment of the immigration laws of the United States. Therefore, a new plan of action had to be devised.

The new plan called for contacting social and ethnic organizations, diplomatic representatives, religious organizations, and academic sources in a number of cities with large immigrant groups from the three countries selected, in order to ascertain their willingness to assist in identifying prospective subjects for the study and to subsequently conduct the interviews.

Preliminary attempts to contact these sources by mail and establish rapport elicited a disappointing response. Therefore, after selecting a number of cities—nationwide—where large groups of immigrants from the Philippines, Korea, and China resided, the author traveled to six cities to pursue leads and personally make additional contacts. Where successful, he then briefed and trained the prospective assistants, who would be conducting the actual interviews.

Sources of assistance developed through these efforts may be divided into two groups: individuals—generally, graduate students—at a local university; and social/ethnic organizations. In the case of graduate students, subjects for interviews were selected by a "cascade" or "referral" method: The interviewer asked the first few persons interviewed for the name and address of other recent immigrants of the same nationality and for permission to use their name as a reference. In the case of social/ethnic organizations, subjects to be interviewed were selected at random from the files of the organization, and included members, supporters, and clients alike.

No effort was made to make the sample statistically meaningful and accurate as a reflection of the larger immigrant groups of that country in the United States. However, given the size of the sample, it is believed that generally valid conclusions can be drawn from the data collected through the survey.

The geographical areas selected for the study were: Houston, Texas; the New York City metropolitan area; the Los Angeles area; the San Francisco–Bay area; Seattle and its environs; the Chicago metropolitan area; and Jersey City, New Jersey. These seven geographical areas were selected for two reasons: (1) Each has a relatively large number of immigrants from one or all three countries selected for the study; and (2) the author was able to line up competent help to conduct actual interviews in those areas.

The total number of interviews conducted was 849—comprising 330 Filipino, 255 Chinese, and 264 Korean adults. Only heads of households, or their spouses over the age of 18, were interviewed. The other major criterion was that the person interviewed must have arrived in the United States as an immigrant between January 1980 and December 1985.

The factual data collected were then entered into a Commodore 128 computer—using a data-base program; and the output, analyzed.

As there is no reason to believe that, in their totality, the immigrants interviewed are not representative of recent immigrants from the Philippines, Korea, and China, the study should help to shed much needed light on the preimmigration sociodemographic characteristics and current status of the latest wave of immigrants from these three important sources of Asian immigration.

15

The Survey Sample

We have seen how the author arrived at the survey sampling. The number of interviews per geographical area or by place of birth of the respondent was not predetermined, but depended mainly on the ability and efforts of the person conducting the actual interviews in each particular location. Thus, the sample is not in any way proportionate to the number of foreign-born residents of the three ethnic groups living in a particular location. Apart from the information given in Table 15.1, the results of the interviews are not shown by geographical area, but only in the aggregate. Even then, as the size of the sample of respondents born in Taiwan or Hong Kong—or of Chinese born in other countries—is rather small, the findings for these groups should be approached with considerable caution.

As seen in Table 15.1, the total number of interviews was 849: 330 Filipino, 264 Korean, and 255 Chinese immigrants. All but two or three of the Filipino and Korean immigrants had resided in the Philippines and South Korea, respectively, prior to their immigration to the United States. On the other hand, Chinese immigrants born on the mainland came from a number of other localities besides China. Of the 148 mainland-born Chinese who were interviewed, 66.2% had resided in their country of birth prior to their immigration; 23%, in Hong Kong; 6.1%, in Taiwan; and 4.7%, in other countries.

Similarly, 26% of the interviewed Chinese were neither born nor resided on the mainland, Hong Kong, or Taiwan. They were born and came to the

Table 15.1
The Survey Sample of Immigrants, Showing U.S. Area of Residence

Place of Birth				Place of Residence				
	Houston	Chicago	Seattle	San Francisco	Los Angeles	New York	Jersey City	Total
Philippines	86	52	48	51	52	7	34	330
Korea	58	52	39	74	41	--	--	264
Mainland China	4	25	28	--	20	70	1	148
Taiwan	30	1	8	--	1	9	--	49
Hong Kong	--	1	13	--	3	15	--	32
Elsewhere (Chinese)	2	13	1	--	5	5	--	26
Totals	180	144	137	125	122	106	35	849

Source: Compiled by the author.

Table 15.2
The Survey Sample, Showing Year of Immigration

Year of Immigration	Total		Place of Birth					
			Philippines	Korea	Mainland China	Taiwan	Hong Kong	Elsewhere (Chinese)
1980	130	15.3%	63	38	10	12	4	3
1981	172	20.3	78	60	17	8	6	3
1982	157	18.5	69	51	19	11	7	--
1983	117	13.8	40	36	23	7	9	2
1984	100	11.8	25	35	28	2	2	8
1985	173	20.3	55	44	51	9	4	10
Totals	849	100%	330	264	148	49	32	26

Source: Compiled by the author.

Table 15.3
The Survey Sample, Showing Sex and Household Position

Place of Birth	Male – Head of Household	Household Position Female – Head of Household	Female Spouse
Philippines	161	55	114
Korea	164	22	78
China – Mainland	102	25	21
China – Taiwan	22	9	18
China – Hong Kong	16	5	11
Elsewhere (Chinese)	17	4	5
Totals	482	120	247
Percentages	56.8	14.1	29.1

Source: Compiled by the author.

Table 15.4
The Survey Sample, Showing Date of Birth

Place of Birth	Before 1910	1910–1920	1921–1930	1931–1940	1941–1950	1951–1960	1961–1970
Philippines	3	7	23	58	99	92	48
Korea	4	15	32	36	57	111	9
Mainland China	--	13	26	35	42	26	6
Taiwan	--	1	1	1	9	36	1
Hong Kong	--	--	--	4	12	14	2
Elsewhere (Chinese)	--	--	2	4	9	8	3
Totals	7	36	84	138	228	287	69
Percentage	.8	4.2	9.9	16.3	26.9	33.8	8.1

Source: Compiled by the author.

United States from such places as Vietnam, Macau, Singapore, Burma, and Malayasia. Because their background is different from the other Chinese who were interviewed, they are listed separately in all tables.

The year of immigration of the interviewed subjects is shown in Table 15.2. As can be seen, those who came to the United States in 1981, 1982, and 1985 are overrepresented and those who came in 1980, 1983, and 1984 are underrepresented, if the year of immigration is used as a criterion.

The respondent's sex and household position are shown in Table 15.3. The data indicate that 56.8% of the respondents were male heads of households, and 43.2% were females. The latter figure includes the 14.1% of females who were also heads of households.

As for age, more than two-thirds of the respondents (68.8%) were born after 1940 and, thus, were under the age of 45 in 1985. An additional 26.2%—since they were born between 1921 and 1940—were between the ages of 45 and 64. Only 5% of the respondents were 65 or older. Data on this factor are provided in Table 15.4.

16

Sociodemographic Characteristics Prior to Immigration

A number of survey questions were framed to ascertain the socio-demographic characteristics of the respondents prior to their immigration to the United States. Through their replies, this chapter will explore such factors as marital status, number of children prior to immigrating, educational achievement, labor force participation and occupations, property ownership, English-language knowledge and proficiency, and—lastly—reason or reasons for immigrating.

MARITAL STATUS

All 94% of the respondents who answered the question on marital status were either married or single prior to their arrival in the United States; none were divorced, widowed, or separated. Overall, 62.5% of respondents were married; and 37.5%, single. According to the data shown on Table 16.1, Chinese born in the mainland were most likely to be married; and those from Taiwan, the least likely to be married. Filipinos were as likely to be married as not, while more than two-thirds of Koreans were already married when they entered the United States.

NUMBER OF CHILDREN

All respondents answered the question on the number of children (Table 16.2). Nearly two-fifths—39.8%—had no children; an additional 32.2% had

Table 16.1
Respondents' Marital Status Prior to Immigration

Place of Birth	Married	Single	Total	No Replies
Philippines	158	151	309	21
Korea	171	78	249	15
Mainland China	118	20	138	10
Taiwan	18	30	48	1
Hong Kong	19	12	31	1
Elsewhere (Chinese)	15	8	23	3
Total	499	299	798	51
Percentage	62.5%	37.5%	100%	

Source: Compiled by the author.

Table 16.2
Respondents' Number of Children, Prior to Immigration

Place of Birth	None	1	2	3	4	5	More than 5	Total
Philippines	171	32	35	32	23	17	20	330
Korea	88	50	60	24	16	12	14	264
Mainland China	26	23	39	29	13	10	8	148
Taiwan	29	5	10	2	1	2	--	49
Hong Kong	15	7	5	2	3	--	--	32
Elsewhere (Chinese)	9	3	5	2	4	3	--	26
Total	338	120	154	91	60	44	42	849
Percentage	39.8	14.1	18.1	10.7	7.1	5.2	5.0	100

Source: Compiled by the author.

one or two children; and 10.2% had five or more children. By place of birth, 51.8% of the Filipinos, 33.3% of the Koreans, 17.5% of the mainland Chinese, 59.2% of the natives of Taiwan, 46.8% of those born in Hong Kong, and 34.6% of the "other" Chinese had no children. Conversely, 11.2% of the Filipinos, 9.8% of the Koreans, 12.2% of the mainland Chinese, 4.1% of the Taiwanese, none of those born in Hong Kong, and 11.5% of the "other" Chinese had five or more children. Thus, it appears that the immigrants from mainland China were less likely to have been childless and, conversely, more likely than the other groups to have had a large family comprising five or more children.

EDUCATIONAL ACHIEVEMENT

The educational achievements of the respondents prior to their immigration to the United States are impressive: Only 1.2% had had no formal schooling, and 46.9% were college graduates (Table 16.3). This last figure compares with 16.2% college graduates for the native U.S. population over the age of 25 in 1980.

By place of birth, Filipino immigrants appear to have been the best educated: 65.8% were college graduates, and 20.6% had some university-level training. With respect to immigrants who were college graduates, natives of Taiwan placed second; and Koreans, third. Natives of mainland China had the lowest percentage of college graduates and the highest percentage of immigrants with eight or less years of education. Surprisingly, however, the percentage of college graduates for all six groups was higher than the comparable figure for the U.S. population at large. The above data

Table 16.3
Respondents' Years of Schooling, Prior to Immigration

Years of Schooling	Philippines		Korea		Mainland China		Taiwan		Hong Kong		Elsewhere (Chinese)		Total	
	No.	%	No.	%	No.	%	No.	%	No.	%	No.	%	No.	%
None	--	--	6	2.3	3	2.0	--	--	--	--	1	3.8	10	1.2
1-5 Years	4	1.2	8	3.0	17	11.5	--	--	--	--	3	11.6	32	3.7
6-8 Years	8	2.4	17	6.4	29	19.6	3	6.1	2	6.3	2	7.7	61	7.2
9-12 Years	33	10.0	76	28.8	59	39.9	7	14.3	15	46.9	12	46.2	202	23.8
1-3 Years University	68	20.6	49	18.6	14	9.4	7	14.3	7	21.8	1	3.8	146	17.2
4 or More Yrs. University	217	65.8	108	40.9	26	17.6	32	65.3	8	25.0	7	26.9	398	46.9
Totals	330	100	264	100	148	100	49	100	32	100	26	100	849	100

Source: Compiled by the author.

make it clear that the United States is still attracting to its shores some of the best-educated citizens of the surveyed countries.

LABOR FORCE STATUS AND OCCUPATIONS OF EMPLOYED

Of the 849 interviewed immigrants, 705—or 83%—were employed prior to their immigration to the United States (Table 16.4). This percentage of labor force participation is considerably higher than that of the U.S. labor force as a whole—which, in 1980, was 63.8% of all those over the age of 16. By 1983, this figure had risen only marginally, to 64%.

Of the total number of those interviewed, 95 (or 11.2%) had been self-employed in their previous country of residence—a percentage that is approximately double that of self-employed persons in the U.S. labor force. Chinese immigrants from the mainland had the largest percentage of persons who had been employed prior to emigration—followed by the "other" Chinese. Immigrants from Hong Kong and Korea had the largest number of persons who had not been employed prior to their entry into the United States. The "other" Chinese also had the highest percentage of entrepreneurs—followed by the Koreans; in this category, Chinese born in Hong Kong placed last.

Occupationally, the sample of interviewed immigrants who had been

Table 16.4

Respondents' Labor Force Status and Occupations of Employed, Prior to Immigration

Labor-Force Status	Philippines		Korea		Mainland China		Taiwan		Hong Kong		Elsewhere (Chinese)		Total	
	No.	%	No.	%	No.	%	No.	%	No.	%	No.	%	No.	%
Not Employed	58	17.6	62	23.5	5	3.4	10	20.4	8	25.0	1	3.9	144	17.0
Self-employed	32	8.7	38	14.4	13	8.8	4	8.2	1	3.1	7	26.9	95	11.2
Emp. by Others	240	73.7	164	62.1	130	87.8	35	71.4	23	71.9	18	69.2	610	71.8
Occupations Professional	130	47.8	57	28.2	21	14.7	18	46.1	12	50.0	5	20.0	243	34.5
Manager/Exec.	21	7.7	29	14.4	16	11.2	1	2.6	1	4.2	2	8.0	70	9.9
Sales	30	11.0	18	8.9	11	7.7	2	5.1	2	8.3	5	20.0	68	9.6
Factory Worker	11	4.1	16	7.9	30	20.9	1	2.6	3	12.5	4	16.0	65	9.2
Service	11	4.1	33	16.3	23	16.1	4	10.3	1	4.2	5	20.0	77	10.9
Clerical	64	23.5	41	20.3	14	9.8	12	30.7	5	20.8	4	16.0	140	19.9
Farmer	5	1.8	8	4.0	28	19.6	1	2.6	--	--	--	--	42	6.0
Totals	272	100	202	100	143	100	39	100	24	100	25	100	705	100

Source: Compiled by the author.

employed prior to immigration included 34.5% who were engaged in the professions then and 19.9% who were employed in clerical jobs. Farmers comprised only 6% of the total.

By place of birth, Filipinos had the second-largest number of professionals (47.8%) and the smallest number of farmers (1.8%). By contrast, mainland Chinese had the smallest number of professionals (14.7%) and the largest number of farmers (19.6%). Taiwanese had the highest percentage of clerks (30.7%); and those born in Hong Kong, the highest percentage of professionals (50%). Koreans included the highest number of persons who had held managerial and executive positions (14.4%). In no instance was the percentage of persons engaged in the professions lower than the percentage in the U.S. labor force as a whole (which was 12.7% in 1983).

PROPERTY OWNERSHIP

Table 16.5 presents data on the property ownership status of the sample, prior to their move to the United States.

Of the 849 persons interviewed, 522—or 61.5%—owned at least one of the following in their own country: house or apartment, some land, or an automobile. Slightly more than 50% owned their residence; 18.3% owned some land; and 19.3% owned an automobile.

By place of birth, Koreans had the highest percentage of residence ownership (61.0%)—followed by nearly half of the Filipinos and mainland Chinese. Close to one-third of the Filipinos also owned some land and an automobile, before emigrating.

Table 16.5
Respondents' Property Ownership, Prior to Immigration

Owned One or More of the Following:	Philippines		Korea		Mainland China		Taiwan		Hong Kong		Elsewhere (Chinese)		Total	
	No.	%	No.	%	No.	%	No.	%	No.	%	No.	%	No.	%
	214	64.8	181	68.6	81	54.7	16	32.7	13	40.6	17	65.4	522	61.5
1. Residence	161	48.8	161	61.0	73	49.3	12	24.5	10	31.3	8	30.8	425	50.1
2. Land	99	30.0	36	13.6	15	10.1	2	4.1	--	--	3	11.5	155	18.3
3. Automobile	102	30.9	34	12.9	6	4.1	8	16.3	3	9.4	11	42.3	164	19.3
Did not own any of above	116	35.2	83	31.4	67	45.3	33	67.3	19	59.4	9	34.6	327	38.5

Note: Percentages of those owning residence, land, or automobile—out of total number of persons interviewed—exceed 100%, since some respondents owned more than one of these items.

Source: Compiled by the author.

ABILITY TO SPEAK ENGLISH

While, overall, close to one-fifth of the interviewed immigrants had no speaking knowledge of English and nearly one-third spoke only a little English prior to immigration, substantial variations in English-speaking ability were found when the place of birth was taken into account. In fact, while less than 1% of Filipinos did not speak any English, 58.8% of the mainland Chinese were in this category. Conversely, only 3% of the Koreans spoke English fluently, as compared with 58.5% of the Filipinos. (See Table 16.6).

REASONS FOR IMMIGRATING TO THE UNITED STATES

One of the questions in the survey questionnaire attempted to ascertain why the respondents had chosen the United States as their country of immigration. Respondents were given a choice of five replies, and were directed to pick a maximum of two.

Overall, as shown in Table 16.7, 52.8% of the 849 respondents indicated that they chose the United States in order to join family members; 49.6% chose the United States because of the better employment opportunities that its economy offers; and 35.6% checked better educational opportunity as one of their reasons. Only 14.4% of the respondents indicated that one of their reasons for coming was the climate of political and religious freedom to be enjoyed in the United States. Additionally, 5.4% indicated reasons other than those given in the questionaire.

As shown in Table 16.7, Filipinos most frequently indicated better employment opportunities as their reason (69.4%); Koreans placed family reunification first (50.3%)—as did those born in mainland China (81.1%), natives of Hong Kong (62.5%), and the "other" Chinese (46.1%). Natives of Taiwan chose educational opportunity most often (65.3%) as their reason for coming to the United States.

Table 16.6
Respondents' Ability to Speak English, Prior to Immigration

	Philippines		Korea		China Mainland		Taiwan		Hong Kong		Elsewhere (Chinese)		Total	
	No.	%	No.	%	No.	%	No.	%	No.	%	No.	%	No.	%
No English	3	.9	61	23.1	87	58.8	7	14.3	4	12.5	4	15.4	166	19.5
A little	27	8.2	152	57.6	46	31.1	23	46.9	10	31.2	15	57.7	273	32.2
Well	107	32.4	43	16.3	9	6.1	14	28.6	12	37.5	2	7.7	187	22.0
Fluently	193	58.5	8	3.0	6	4.0	5	10.2	6	18.8	5	19.2	223	26.3
Totals	330	100%	264	100%	148	100%	49	100%	32	100%	26	100%	849	100%

Source: Compiled by the author.

Table 16.7
Respondents' Reasons for Immigrating to the United States

	Philippines		Korea		Mainland China		Taiwan		Hong Kong		Elsewhere (Chinese)		Total	
	No.	%	No.	%	No.	%	No.	%	No.	%	No.	%	No.	%
1. Better Employment Opportunities	229	69.4	113	42.8	55	37.2	11	22.4	3	9.4	10	38.5	421	49.6
2. Political and Religious Freedom	42	12.7	31	11.7	34	23.0	--	--	7	21.9	8	30.8	122	14.4
3. Better Educ. Opport.	90	27.3	114	43.2	40	27.0	32	65.3	17	53.1	10	38.5	303	35.6
4. To Join Family Members	142	43.0	133	50.3	120	81.1	21	42.9	20	62.5	12	46.1	448	52.8
5. Other Reasons	10	3.0	16	6.1	11	7.4	2	4.1	5	15.6	2	7.7	46	5.4

Note: *All percentages refer to the number of respondents who chose each reason. As a maximum of two reasons could have been chosen, percentages do not add up to 100.

Source: Compiled by the author.

17

Current Sociodemographic Characteristics in 1985

The majority of survey questions were directed toward ascertaining the sociodemographic characteristics of the immigrants at the time their interviews took place: December 1985 through March 1986. This chapter will look at such factors as family size, household size, property ownership, employment, income, size of residence, educational activities, proficiency in spoken English, the extent of membership in organizations, major problems encountered in settling in the United States, sources of assistance in the settling process, taxes paid, and remaining ties to the country of origin (as measured by plans to remain in this country, trips made to their country of last residence, and petitions filed to have eligible family relatives join them in the United States).

FAMILY SIZE AND HOUSEHOLDS

Overall, the size of the respondents' families—if they were married—were somewhat larger than U.S. families in general. While 18% of the respondents were living by themselves, the balance (82%) were living in a family setting (Table 17.1). If one excludes individuals living alone, 16.4% of the respondents lived in family units of two persons; 45%, in family units of three or four persons; 30.3%, in families with five or six members; and 8.3%, in families with seven or more members. Comparable 1983 U.S. census data for all U.S. families show 23.8% with two family members, 31.5%

Table 17.1
Size of Respondents' Families (if any): 1986

Family Size (# persons)	Philippines No.	%	Korea No.	%	Mainland China No.	%	Taiwan No.	%	Hong Kong No.	%	Elsewhere (Chinese) No.	%	Total No.	%
1	92	27.9	27	10.2	16	10.8	12	24.5	2	6.3	4	15.4	153	18.0
2	38	11.5	45	17.1	12	8.1	12	24.5	6	18.7	1	3.9	114	13.4
3 to 4	98	29.7	119	45.1	59	39.8	17	34.7	14	43.7	7	26.9	314	37.0
5 to 6	79	23.9	60	22.7	47	31.8	8	16.3	8	25.0	9	34.6	211	24.8
7 or more	23	7.0	13	4.9	14	9.5	--	--	2	6.3	5	19.2	58	6.8
Totals	330	100%	264	100%	148	100%	49	100%	32	100%	26	100%	849	100%

Source: Compiled by the author.

with three or four members, 17.9% with five or six members, and 6.2% with seven or more persons. Thus, we see that the respondents' families were larger than the U.S. norm.

As indicated above, 18% of the respondents lived by themselves; the comparable figure for households of one person in the U.S. population at large in 1983 was 19.3%—only marginally higher.

By the respondent's place of birth, the Filipinos had the largest percentage of individuals living alone (27.9%); and immigrants from Hong Kong, the largest percentage of respondents living in a two-person family (24.5%). Koreans had the largest percentage of persons residing in a three or four person family; and the "other" Chinese, the largest percentages of those living in families of both five or six and seven or more persons. On the other hand, Taiwanese had the smallest percentage of five or six person families, and none of the 49 respondents lived in a family unit with seven or more persons.

As seen in Table 17.2, a large number of the interviewed immigrants' households lodged other persons, in addition to nuclear family members. While 64.1% of the households contained only nuclear family members, 35.9% had one or more other persons residing in the household—including 8.1% with four or more persons who were not nuclear family members. In this respect, the "other" Chinese were the most likely to have taken in relatives and friends, while immigrants from mainland China turned out to be the least likely to have done so.

PROPERTY OWNERSHIP

Even though they had been in the United States from just a few months to a full five years, more than one-fourth of the interviewed immigrants had purchased a home (Table 17.3). Furthermore, close to three-fourths owned at least one automobile by early 1986—with 34% owning two or more. Im-

Table 17.2
Persons Other Than Nuclear Family Members in Respondents'
Households: 1986

Others in Household	Philippines		Korea		Mainland China		Taiwan		Hong Kong		Elsewhere (Chinese)		Total	
	No.	%	No.	%	No.	%	No.	%	No.	%	No.	%	No.	%
None	201	60.9	183	69.3	107	72.3	33	67.3	13	40.6	7	26.9	544	64.1
1	35	10.6	30	11.4	9	6.1	7	14.3	10	31.2	7	26.9	98	11.6
2	34	10.3	29	10.9	12	8.1	2	4.1	2	6.3	2	7.7	81	9.5
3	29	8.8	10	3.8	9	6.1	4	8.2	1	3.1	4	15.4	57	6.7
4 or more	31	9.4	12	4.6	11	7.4	3	6.1	6	18.8	6	23.1	69	8.1
Totals	330	100%	264	100%	148	100%	49	100%	32	100%	26	100%	849	100%

Source: Compiled by the author.

migrants from Hong Kong were the most likely to have purchased a home—with a percentage of 46.9%—followed by Filipinos and Koreans. The mainland Chinese were the least likely to have done so. With reference to the ownership of automobiles, Korean immigrants were most likely to have acquired one or more. On the other hand, mainland Chinese were the least likely to own automobiles: In fact, 71.6% had none.

EMPLOYMENT

The survey instrument posed a number of questions on employment status within the respondent's household: first, whether the respondent was employed; second, whether other persons in the household held full-time jobs; third, whether other persons in the household had part-time em-

Table 17.3
Respondents' Property Ownership: 1986

Home	Philippines		Korea		Mainland China		Taiwan		Hong Kong		Elsewhere (Chinese)		Total	
	No.	%	No.	%	No.	%	No.	%	No.	%	No.	%	No.	%
Rents	224	67.9	189	71.6	129	87.2	37	75.5	17	53.1	21	80.8	617	72.7
Owns	106	32.1	75	28.4	109	12.8	12	24.5	15	46.9	5	19.2	232	27.3
	300	100%	264	100%	148	100%	49	100%	32	100%	26	100%	849	100%
Automobiles None	72	21.8	36	13.6	106	71.6	5	10.2	10	31.3	44	42.3	240	28.3
1	137	41.5	102	38.6	35	23.6	23	46.9	13	40.6	10	38.5	320	37.7
2	82	24.9	106	40.2	6	4.1	19	38.8	4	12.5	5	19.2	222	26.1
3 or more	39	11.8	20	7.6	1	.7	2	4.1	5	15.6	--	--	67	7.9
	330	100%	264	100%	148	100%	49	100%	32	100%	26	100%	849	100

Source: Compiled by the author.

ployment; fourth, whether the *head of household* was unemployed, self-employed, or employed by others; and lastly, the occupation of the head of household who was employed by others.

Of the total number of 849 respondents, 628 (or 74%) indicated that they were employed—a rate considerably higher than the 64% rate of labor force participation for the U.S. population over the age of 16. Filipino respondents had the highest percentage of employed persons (82.1%), and the "other" Chinese had 34.6%—the lowest. (See Table 17.4).

Additionally, as shown in Tables 17.5 and 17.6, 54.3% of the respondents indicated that at least one other person in their households was employed full-time, and 33% reported that at least one other person in the household was employed part-time.

A total of 192 Filipino respondents (58.2%) indicated that at least one other person in their household was employed full-time. Additionally, 39.1% on the 330 interviewed Filipinos indicated that at least one person in their households was employed part-time. While households of the "other" Chinese had the smallest percentage of other persons employed part-time, the households of Taiwanese immigrants contained the smallest number of persons employed part-time: In fact, only 12.2% had one or more persons in this category.

Turning to the respondents' heads of households (as shown in Table 17.7), we find that 84.2% were employed at the time the survey was taken—with 75.8% employed by others and 8.4% self-employed, mainly in retail and service businesses. The highest percentage of employed heads of households was found among the Taiwanese respondents; the lowest percentage, among the "other" Chinese. Korean immigrants had the highest percentage of heads of households who were self-employed (16.3%)—followed by those from Hong Kong (12.5%). On the other hand, Filipino immigrant households contained the smallest percentage of self-employed heads of households (3.7%).

As for occupation, the respondents' heads of households who were employed by others compare favorably with the occupational distribution of all employed persons in the United States in 1983. In fact, 31.1% were professionals (U.S.: 12.7%); 6.7% were managers or executives (U.S.: 10.7%);

Table 17.4
Respondents' Employment Status: 1986

	Philippines		Korea		Mainland China		Taiwan		Hong Kong		Elsewhere (Chinese)		Total	
	No.	%	No.	%	No.	%	No.	%	No.	%	No.	%	No.	%
Employed	271	82.1	192	72.7	98	66.2	33	67.3	25	78.1	9	34.6	628	74.0
Unemployed	59	17.9	72	27.3	50	33.8	16	32.7	7	21.9	17	65.4	221	16.0

Source: Compiled by the author.

Table 17.5
Other Persons Employed Full-Time, in Respondents' Households: 1986

	Philippines		Korea		Mainland China		Taiwan		Hong Kong		Elsewhere (Chinese)		Total	
	No.	%	No.	%	No.	%	No.	%	No.	%	No.	%	No.	%
None	138	41.8	121	45.8	66	44.6	31	63.3	15	46.9	17	65.4	388	45.7
At Least 1	192	58.2	143	54.2	82	55.4	18	36.7	17	53.1	9	34.6	461	54.3

Source: Compiled by the author.

10.2% were employed in sales occupations (U.S.: 11.7%); 18.2% in clerical/administrative-support jobs (U.S.: 16.3%); and 18.3% in service occupations (U.S.: 13.7%).

The largest number of professional heads of household was found among the Taiwanese respondents (51.2%)—followed by those from Hong Kong (43.5%) and the Filipinos (40.5%). Only in the case of mainland Chinese did the percentage (11.6%) dip below that of the United States (12.7%).

On the other hand, the mainland Chinese respondents had the largest percentage of heads of households in service occupations (52.7%); and Filipinos, the highest percentage in clerical jobs (26.3%).

FAMILY INCOME

As some of the respondents and members of their families had arrived in the United States in 1985 and had not yet had the opportunity to receive a full year's income, they were not required to answer the income question. Additionally, some others declined to reply. Instead, the questions asked in the survey related to 1984 gross income. The remaining 657 respondents—or 77.4% of the total—provided replies; the results are shown in Table 17.8.

Overall, 20.5% of the respondents had an income of less than $10,000 in 1984; 34.8%, between $10,000 and $19,999; 39.5%, between $20,000 and $49,999; and 5.2%, $50,000 or more. These figures may be compared with

Table 17.6
Other Persons Employed Part-Time, in Respondents' Households: 1986

	Philippines		Korea		Mainland China		Taiwan		Hong Kong		Elsewhere (Chinese)		Total	
	No.	%	No.	%	No.	%	No.	%	No.	%	No.	%	No.	%
None	201	60.9	181	68.6	99	66.9	43	87.8	25	78.1	20	76.9	569	67.0
At Least 1	129	39.1	83	31.4	49	33.1	6	12.2	7	21.9	6	23.1	280	33.0

Source: Compiled by the author.

Table 17.7
Labor Force Status and Occupations of Heads of Respondents'
Households: 1986

Labor Force Status	Philippines		Korea		Mainland China		Taiwan		Hong Kong		Elsewhere (Chinese)		Total	
	No.	%	No.	%	No.	%	No.	%	No.	%	No.	%	No.	%
Unemployed	44	13.3	39	14.8	30	20.2	4	8.2	5	15.6	12	46.2	134	15.8
Self-Employed	12	3.7	43	16.3	6	4.1	4	8.2	4	12.5	2	7.7	71	8.4
Employed by Others	274	83.01	82	68.9	112	75.7	41	83.6	23	71.9	12	46.1	644	75.8
Occupations of Those Employed By Others														
Professionals	111	40.5	41	22.6	13	11.6	21	51.1	10	43.5	4	33.3	200	31.1
Manager/Executive	20	7.3	17	9.3	2	1.8	2	4.9	2	8.7	--	--	43	6.7
Sales	27	9.8	34	18.7	2	1.8	3	7.3	--	--	--	--	66	10.2
Factory Worker	20	7.3	34	18.7	27	24.1	--	--	1	4.4	3	25.0	85	13.2
Service	21	7.7	24	13.2	59	52.7	7	17.2	5	21.7	2	16.7	118	18.3
Clerical	72	26.3	27	14.8	5	4.4	5	12.2	5	21.7	3	25.0	117	18.2
Other	3	1.1	5	2.7	4	3.6	3	7.3	--	--	--	--	15	2.3
Farmer	--	--	--	--	--	--	--	--	--	--	--	--	--	--
Totals	274		182		112		41		23		12		644	100%

Source: Compiled by the author.

Table 17.8
Income of Respondents' Families: 1984

Income	Philippines		Korea		Mainland China		Taiwan		Hong Kong		Elsewhere (Chinese)		Total	
	No.	%	No.	%	No.	%	No.	%	No.	%	No.	%	No.	%
Less than $5,000	15	5.6	11	5.2	20	19.8	2	5.1	--	--	4	30.8	52	7.9
$5,000 – $9,999	21	7.9	17	8.0	36	35.7	4	10.3	4	16.0	1	7.7	83	12.6
$10,000 – $14,999	44	16.5	42	19.7	19	18.8	7	17.9	4	16.0	--	--	116	17.7
$15,000 – $19,999	33	12.4	49	23.0	18	17.8	4	10.3	8	32.0	--	--	112	17.1
$20,000 – $29,999	62	23.3	45	21.1	7	6.9	13	33.3	3	12.0	5	38.4	135	20.5
$30,000 – $50,000	64	24.1	44	20.7	1	1.0	8	20.5	6	24.0	2	15.4	125	19.0
Over $50,000	27	10.2	5	2.3	--	--	1	2.6	--	--	1	7.7	34	5.2
Totals	266	100%	213	100%	39	100%	39	100%	25	100%	13	100%	657	100%
No Reply	64		51		47		10		7		13		192	

Source: Compiled by the author.

the income level distribution for all U.S. families in 1983 (which are the latest available figures): less than $10,000, 15.9%; between $10,000 and $19,999, 23.4%; between $20,000 and $49,999, 48%; and $50,000 or more, 12.6%. Thus, we see that, as a group, the income of the families of the immigrants interviewed in the survey was below that of U.S. families in general. This result was to be expected, given the fact that—of the 676 respondents who had come between 1980 and 1984—only 19.8% had been in the United States four years, by 1984; 26.2% had been in residence three years, by then; 24.9% two years; 17.8%, one year; and 15.2% had arrived during the year in question.

Variations among the several groups were more striking than the differences between the surveyed group as a whole and U.S. families in general. In fact, the percentages of Filipino, Korean, and Taiwanese immigrant families with an income of less than $10,000 were lower than the U.S. percentage—and only marginally higher, for families of Hong Kong immigrants. On the other hand, 55.5% of the families of immigrants from mainland China and 38.5% of the families of the "other" Chinese had 1984 incomes under the $10,000 mark. Similarly, while 53.8% of the "other" Chinese and Taiwanese families had incomes between $20,000 and $49,999—along with 47.4% of the Filipino families, 41.8% of the Koreans, and 36% of those from Hong Kong—only 7.9% of the families of mainland Chinese fell in this middle category.

In the over-$50,000 income category, the highest figures were for Filipino families (10.2%) and the "other" Chinese (7.7%), while none of 101 immigrants from mainland China or the 25 from Hong Kong were in this group.

At least in terms of family income, Filipino immigrant families are better off than all the other groups, while the mainland Chinese are the worst off. The "other" Chinese present a paradox: While a very large percentage had very low family incomes in 1984, an even higher percentage enjoyed good incomes. These results are probable due to the small size of the sample and the fact that the "other" Chinese include both refugees from Vietnam and wealthy merchants from Singapore.

SIZE OF LIVING QUARTERS

The size of the living quarters in which the immigrants were living at the time of their interview is given in Table 17.9. As can be observed, a great majority of the total number (57%) lived in housing units of fewer than 4 rooms. A little more than one-third lived in units of 4–6 rooms, and 7.7% had spacious quarters with 7 or more rooms. By comparison, of the total occupied housing units in the United States in 1983, 23% had 7 or more rooms. Therefore, in general, the immigrants resided in quarters that had less living space per person than the U.S. standard. While their families

Table 17.9

Size of Respondents' Living Quarters: 1986

	Philippines		Korea		Mainland China		Taiwan		Hong Kong		Elsewhere (Chinese)		Total	
	No.	%	No.	%	No.	%	No.	%	No.	%	No.	%	No.	%
Less than 4 rooms	146	44.2	197	74.6	97	65.5	22	44.9	7	21.9	15	57.7	484	57.0
4 to 6 rooms	144	43.7	57	21.6	46	31.1	26	53.1	19	59.4	8	30.8	300	35.3
7 or more rooms	40	12.1	10	3.8	5	3.4	1	2.0	6	18.7	3	11.5	65	7.7

Source: Compiled by the author.

were generally larger and their households more likely to include persons other than nuclear family members, the size of the housing unit that they occupied was smaller.

Again, variations are evident among the surveyed groups. Hong Kong immigrants were—by far—better off than all the others, followed by Filipinos. Korean and mainland Chinese groups were worse off, in this respect.

EDUCATION

Several questions in the survey dealt with educational activities. One question sought to ascertain the number of respondents' families with at least one member attending school, and another asked the average grades received by these students. Two other questions dealt with adult education—asking how many in the family aged 18 or over attended school full-time; and how many, part-time.

Overall, as seen in Table 17.10, 59% of respondents indicated that their family included at least one person attending school. This percentage was highest for the "other" Chinese (88.5%), and lowest for the Taiwanese (40.8%).

Of all respondents with someone in their family in school, 35.9% reported that the students' average grades were excellent. Conversely, only 3.4% reported students getting poor grades. Filipino respondents reported the highest percentage of excellent grades (44.7%), with none getting poor grades.

With reference to family members aged 18 or over attending school full-time, 26.6% of the respondents fell into this category, and 23.2% indicated that at least one member of their family attended school part-time. Within the various groups, 50% of the "other" Chinese had family members aged 18 or over going to school part-time. (See Table 17.11). By comparison, statistics published by the U.S. National Center for Education indicate that,

Table 17.10
Respondents' Families with Members Attending School, and Average Grades of Students: 1986

School Attendance	Philippines		Korea		Mainland China		Taiwan		Hong Kong		Elsewhere (Chinese)		Total	
	No.	%	No.	%	No.	%	No.	%	No.	%	No.	%	No.	%
No one	160	48.5	111	42.0	39	26.4	29	59.2	6	18.8	3	11.5	348	41.0
At Least One	170	51.5	153	58.0	109	73.6	20	40.8	26	81.2	23	88.5	501	59.0
Average Grades														
Excellent	76	44.7	59	38.5	24	22.0	7	35.0	7	26.9	7	30.5	180	35.9
Good	79	46.5	76	49.7	30	27.5	12	60.0	13	50.0	11	47.8	221	44.1
Satisfactory	15	8.8	11	7.2	45	41.3	1	5.0	6	23.1	5	21.7	83	16.6
Poor	--	--	7	4.6	10	9.2	--	--	--	--	--	--	17	3.4
Totals	170		153		109		20		26		23		501	

Source: Compiled by the author.

in 1981, 12.8% of the total U.S. population over the age of 17 was enrolled in school.

ABILITY TO SPEAK ENGLISH

Table 17.12 shows the average ability of respondents, and their family members to speak English. The data indicate that, overall, 2.7% of the respondents (and members of their families) did not speak any English; 14% stated that they spoke a little English; and 82.5% of the respondents indicated that they and their family members spoke English well or fluently. Among the surveyed groups, Filipinos appear to be the most fluent in English, to the point of nearly 100%. (Since, by population, the Philippines is

Table 17.11
Respondents' Families with Members over Age 18 Who Are Attending School: 1986

Full-Time Attendance	Philippines		Korea		Mainland China		Taiwan		Hong Kong		Elsewhere (Chinese)		Total	
	No.	%	No.	%	No.	%	No.	%	No.	%	No.	%	No.	%
At Least 1	75	22.7	78	29.5	45	30.4	10	20.4	5	15.6	13	50.0	226	26.6
None	255	77.3	186	70.5	103	69.6	39	79.6	27	84.4	13	50.0	623	73.4
Part-Time Attendance														
At Least 1	61	18.5	70	26.5	40	27.0	8	16.3	10	31.3	8	30.8	197	23.2
None	269	81.5	194	73.5	108	73.0	41	83.7	22	68.7	18	69.2	652	76.8

Source: Compiled by the author.

Table 17.12
Average Ability to Speak English among Members of Respondents'
Families: 1986

	Philippines		Korea		Mainland China		Taiwan		Hong Kong		Elsewhere (Chinese)		Total	
	No.	%	No.	%	No.	%	No.	%	No.	%	No.	%	No.	%
None	--	--	7	2.7	16	10.8	--	--	--	--	--	--	23	2.7
A Little	3	.9	46	17.4	61	41.2	5	10.2	1	3.1	3	11.6	119	14.0
Well	112	34.0	180	68.2	60	40.5	37	75.5	22	68.8	16	61.5	427	50.3
Fluently	211	63.9	31	11.7	9	6.1	7	14.3	9	28.1	6	23.1	273	32.2
No Reply	4	1.2	--	--	2	1.4	--	--	--	--	1	3.8	7	.8
Total	330		264		148		49		32		26		849	

Source: Compiled by the author.

the third-largest English-speaking country in the world, this result was to
be expected.) Of the natives of Hong Kong (where English coexists with
Chinese), 96.9% spoke English well or fluently, as did 89.8% of those from
Taiwan. The replies of respondents born in mainland China indicate that
their language ability—and that of their family members—is not so good as
that of the other groups surveyed: 10.8% indicated no ability to speak English; 41.2% reported that they spoke only a little English; and 46.6%, that
they spoke English well or fluently.

The data in Table 2.10 (on the respondents' English-speaking ability
prior to immigration) are not fully comparable to the figures given in Table
17.12: One deals with respondents only; and the other, with all members of
the family unit. However, if one assumes that—prior to immigration—
other family members did not speak English any better than the respondents, Table 17.12 can provide a useful yardstick for measuring progress in
the immigrants' efforts to learn English. Inasmuch as 19.5% of the respondents spoke no English and 32.2% spoke little English prior to immigration,
their progress is impressive.

MEMBERSHIP IN ORGANIZATIONS

It would seem logical that recent immigrants who have not yet developed extensive U.S. ties would prefer to join organizations devoted to
their ethnic and cultural background. Yet, the results of the survey on this
question indicate that ony half of the respondents or their family members
had joined any organization or club. The ethnic group with the highest percentage of "joiners" were the Koreans: Close to three-fourths belonged to
such organizations. Chinese—particularly those from the mainland—had
the lowest percentage (18.9%).

Except for the Filipino immigrants, the overwhelming majority of those who belonged to organizations were members of a church or other religious organization. Ethnic and social organizations—the favorite of Filipinos—were not found relevant by the majority of the other immigrants. (See Table 17.13.)

SOURCES OF DIFFICULTIES IN THE UNITED STATES

One of the survey questions tried to ascertain which of a number of factors had caused the respondents and their families the most acute problems in settling in the United States. Respondents were given a choice of five such factors to check off—plus an *other* category, where they could write in their comments. They were asked to select the three most important factors.

As seen in Table 17.14, 95.5% of the 849 interviewed persons indicated one or more problem experienced in settling into their new life, while 4.5% stated that they had not encountered any problems at all. In this respect, Chinese from Hong Kong turned out to be the least likely to have experienced any problems, while the mainland Chinese appear to have been the most likely to have problems.

In terms of the difficulties encountered, the most common problem of those who had any was "locating employment" (60.7%)—followed by "learning English" (40.3%), coping with the transportation system (31.6%), locating a house or apartment (30.7%), various other problems (6.4%), and "learning to shop" (4.2%).

Table 17.13
Membership in Organizations, on the Part of Members of Respondents' Families: 1986

	Philippines		Korea		Mainland China		Taiwan		Hong Kong		Elsewhere (Chinese)		Total	
	No.	%	No.	%	No.	%	No.	%	No.	%	No.	%	No.	%
1. Do Not Belong to Any	164	49.7	67	25.4	120	81.1	31	63.3	19	59.4	21	80.8	422	49.7
2. Belong to One1 or More	166	50.3	197	74.6	28	18.9	18	36.7	13	40.6	5	19.2	427	50.3
3. Type of Organization A. Ethnic, Social	120	72.3	38	19.3	2	7.1	1	5.6	1	7.7	1	20.0	163	38.2
B. Cultural	35	21.1	12	6.1	1	3.6	--	--	--	--	--	--	48	11.2
C. Religious	55	33.1	166	84.3	24	85.7	15	83.3	12	92.3	5	10.0	277	64.9
D. Other	21	12.6	2	1.1	1	3.6	3	16.7	--	--	--	--	27	6.3

Source: Compiled by the author.

Table 17.14

Respondents' Sources of Difficulty in Settling in the United States: 1980-85

Difficulties	Philippines		Korea		Mainland China		Taiwan		Hong Kong		Elsewhere (Chinese)		Total	
	No.	%	No.	%	No.	%	No.	%	No.	%	No.	%	No.	%
1. None	22	6.7	7	2.7	1	.7	2	4.1	4	12.5	2	7.7	38	4.5
2. Had One or More	308	93.3	257	97.3	147	99.3	47	95.9	28	87.5	24	92.3	811	95.5
3. Type of Difficulty														
A. Locating House or Apart.	107	34.7	59	23.0	56	38.1	9	19.1	8	28.6	10	41.7	249	30.7
B. Locating Employment	221	71.8	126	49.0	78	53.1	31	66.0	19	67.9	17	70.8	492	60.7
C. Learning English	10	3.2	162	63.0	117	79.6	18	38.3	12	42.9	8	33.3	327	40.3
D. Learning to Shop	9	2.9	13	5.1	9	6.1	1	2.1	1	3.6	1	4.2	34	4.2
E. Transportation	143	46.4	43	16.7	44	29.9	10	21.3	7	25.0	9	37.5	256	31.6
F. Other	21	6.8	10	3.9	13	8.8	5	10.6	2	7.1	1	4.2	52	6.4

Source: Compiled by the author.

The groups most likely to have had problems in finding living quarters were the "other" Chinese and those from mainland China. Filipinos and the "other" Chinese appeared to have had the greatest difficulty in finding employment, while the mainland Chinese and Koreans experienced more problems than the other groups in learning English. Transportation was ranked highest by Filipinos and the "other" Chinese, while the *other* category was picked most by the Taiwanese and the mainland Chinese. The surveyed immigrants with the greatest difficulty in learning to shop were the mainland Chinese.

SOURCES OF ASSISTANCE IN THE UNITED STATES

Most of the surveyed immigrants—close to three-fourths—were assisted by some person and/or organization during the process of settlement (Table 17.15). In this respect, Korean immigrants appeared to be the most self-reliant group: 31.1% stated that they had not received any help from anyone. Mainland Chinese, on the other hand, relied on assistance from one or more sources—more so than any of the other groups: In fact, 87.8% stated that they had received some type of assistance.

Overall, family members were the most likely source of assistance for the immigrants who were surveyed, and 47.9% of those who had received assistance checked this category. In order of magnitude, assistance by

Table 17.15

Respondents' Sources of Assistance in Settling in the United States: 1980-85

Assistance	Philippines		Korea		Mainland China		Taiwan		Hong Kong		Elsewhere (Chinese)		Total	
	No.	%	No.	%	No.	%	No.	%	No.	%	No.	%	No.	%
1. None	96	29.1	82	31.1	18	12.2	9	18.4	7	21.9	4	15.4	216	25.4
2. One or More	234	70.9	182	68.9	130	87.8	40	81.6	25	78.1	22	84.6	633	74.6
3. Source of Assistance														
A. Family Members	117	50.0	82	45.1	67	51.5	23	57.5	13	52.0	1	4.5	303	47.9
B. Relatives	100	42.7	86	47.3	79	60.8	15	37.5	13	52.0	7	31.8	300	47.4
C. Friends	55	23.5	48	26.4	15	11.5	12	30.0	6	24.0	2	9.1	138	21.8
D. Social/Ethnic and Religious Organizations	6	2.6	33	18.1	22	16.9	8	20.0	2	8.0	9	40.9	80	12.6
E. Government	37	15.8	27	14.8	34	26.2	2	5.0	5	20.0	10	45.5	115	18.2

Source: Compiled by the author.

family members was followed by that from relatives, friends, government, and social, ethnic, and religious organizations.

The Taiwanese relied the most on family members for assistance (57.5%), while—among the various groups who were surveyed—the mainland Chinese were assisted most frequently by relatives (60.8%). Close to one-third (30%) of the assisted Taiwanese mentioned friends as their source of help, while the "other" Chinese immigrants received assistance more frequently from government (45.5%) and from social, ethnic, and religious organizations (40.9%).

The reliance of "other" Chinese on government assistance was most likely caused by the fact that this group included a large percentage of Chinese who were born in Vietnam and may have originally left their country as refugees. The type of government assistance encompassed in this category included food stamps, medical care, aid for dependent children, supplemental security assistance for the elderly, unemployment benefits, and job training programs run by social agencies and funded by the federal or state government. Taiwanese were the least likely to benefit from government assistance: Only 5% of those who were assisted by anyone found themselves sufficiently in need to turn to this source.

TAXES PAID IN THE UNITED STATES: 1984

While 27.8% of the 849 respondents failed to answer this question, 72.2% (or 613 interviewed persons) did so—indicating their estimate of the federal, state, and local government taxes that their family had paid for 1984. Virtually all the nonrespondents were persons who arrived in the United States in 1985. Of those answering, Taiwanese and Filipinos had the highest percentage of families who paid more than $10,000 in taxes for 1984: respectively, 8.6 and 6.1. Conversely, none of the immigrant families from mainland China, Hong Kong, or the "other" Chinese fell in this category.

Mainland Chinese families also had the highest percentage of those who paid less than $1,000 (48.4%) and the smallest percentage of those who paid $5,000 or more (3.2%). On the other hand, 25.8% of the Taiwanese were in this category—followed by Filipinos, with 23.8%. (See Table 17.16.)

EXTENT OF TIES TO COUNTRY OF ORIGIN

An attempt to measure the extent of ties to the immigrants' country of origin was made through questions on the respondents' planned length of residence in the United States; trips made to their country of origin, since arrival in this country; and the number of immigrant visa petitions filed to bring eligible family members to the United States as immigrants. In the case of the latter respondents, beneficiaries of such petitions would most likely be spouses and unmarried sons and daughters.

Table 17.16
Estimated Taxes Paid by Respondents' Families: 1984

Taxes Paid	Philippines		Korea		Mainland China		Taiwan		Hong Kong		Elsewhere (Chinese)		Total	
	No.	%	No.	%	No.	%	No.	%	No.	%	No.	%	No.	%
No Reply	82	24.8	65	24.6	55	37.2	14	28.6	7	21.9	13	50.0	236	27.8
Less than $1,000	43	17.3	47	23.6	45	48.4	10	28.5	6	24.0	3	23.1	154	25.1
$1,000 – %1,999	72	29.0	54	27.1	26	28.0	3	8.6	5	20.0	3	23.1	163	26.6
$2,000 – $2,999	42	17.0	38	19.1	13	14.0	4	11.4	5	20.0	1	7.7	103	16.8
$3,000 – $4,999	32	12.9	30	15.1	6	6.4	9	25.7	7	28.0	4	30.7	88	14.4
$5,000 – $6,999	35	14.1	20	10.1	2	2.1	3	8.6	1	4.0	1	7.7	62	10.1
$7,000 – $9,999	9	3.6	9	4.5	1	1.1	3	8.6	1	4.0	1	7.7	24	3.9
$10,000 Over	15	6.1	1	.5	--	--	3	8.6	--	--	--	--	19	3.1
Total	248	100%	199	100%	93	100%	35	100%	25	100%	13	100%	613	100%

Source: Compiled by the author.

While 52.3% of all respondents stated that they were planning to remain indefinitely in the United States, 37.3% did not know how long they would stay; and the balance (10.4%) indicated that their plans at the time of the interview were to remain in the United States less than ten years (Table 17.17). The "other" Chinese appeared to be the most likely to remain indefinitely (77%)—followed by those from Hong Kong (75%) and mainland China (75%). Taiwanese had the smallest percentage of those wanting to stay permanently (24.5%) and the highest percentage of those who indicated plans to stay less than ten years.

With reference to trips back to their country of origin, 33.5% of all the interviewed immigrants had returned to their country at least once since arrival in the United States. Taiwanese were the group with the highest percentage (57.1) of interviewed immigrants who had returned to their country. On the other hand, the "other" Chinese and the mainland Chinese (no doubt, because of both economic and political reasons) had the smallest percentages—11.5 and 18.2, respectively.

Apparently, the large majority of interviewed immigrants had their immediate family members in the United States. In fact, 79.9% had not filed immigrant visa petitions for any such family members (Table 17.18). In this regard, Filipino immigrants showed the highest percentage of immigrants who had filed petitions—23.6. The 78 respondents who had done so had filed at least 161 petitions, or an average of 2.1 petitions each. On the other

Table 17.17
Planned Length of Residence and Trips to Country of Origin, by Respondents or Spouses, as of 1980-85

1. Planned Length of Residence	Philippines		Korea		Mainland China		Taiwan		Hong Kong		Elsewhere (Chinese)		Total	
	No.	%	No.	%	No.	%	No.	%	No.	%	No.	%	No.	%
A. For Good	141	42.7	136	51.5	111	75.0	12	24.5	24	75.0	20	77.0	444	52.3
B. 2 to 5 Years	17	5.2	11	4.2	3	2.0	4	8.2	2	6.2	1	3.8	38	4.5
C. 5 to 10 Years	24	7.3	21	8.0	1	.7	3	6.1	--	--	1	3.8	50	5.9
D. Unknown	148	44.8	96	36.3	33	22.3	30	61.2	6	18.8	4	15.4	317	37.3
2. Trips to Country of Origin														
A. None	224	67.9	161	61.0	121	81.8	21	42.9	15	46.9	23	88.5	565	66.5
B. One	70	21.2	71	26.9	18	12.2	21	42.9	9	28.1	2	7.7	191	22.5
C. Two	21	6.4	27	10.2	6	4.0	4	8.1	4	12.5	--	--	62	7.3
D. Three	6	1.8	3	1.1	1	.7	1	2.0	4	12.5	--	--	15	1.8
E. Four or More	9	2.7	2	.8	2	1.3	2	4.1	--	--	1	13.8	16	1.9

Source: Compiled by the author.

Table 17.18

Immigrant Visa Petitions Filed for Eligible Family Members by Respondents or Spouses, as of 1980-85

Petitions Filed	Philippines		Korea		Mainland China		Taiwan		Hong Kong		Elsewhere (Chinese)		Total	
	No.	%	No.	%	No.	%	No.	%	No.	%	No.	%	No.	%
None	252	76.4	211	80.8	124	83.3	42	85.7	28	87.5	21	80.9	678	79.9
One	27	8.2	37	14.0	15	10.1	4	8.2	2	6.3	1	3.8	86	10.1
Two	31	9.4	8	3.0	6	4.1	2	4.1	1	3.1	1	3.8	49	5.8
Three	8	2.4	8	3.0	2	1.3	--	--	--	--	1	3.8	19	2.2
Four or More	12	3.6	--	--	1	.7	1	2.0	1	3.1	2	7.7	17	2.0

Source: Compiled by the author.

hand, immigrants born in Hong Kong had the lowest percentage of petition filers; only 5 out of 32 (or 12.5%) had done so—with an average of 1.6 petitions per filer.

Thus, it appears that—for the most part—interviewed immigrants from the three ethnic groups had their immediate families with them in the United States. In this sense, their ties to the mother country were not very strong, and their integration into U.S. society would not by impeded by this factor.

18

The United States in the Eyes of Immigrants: Likes and Dislikes

Among the questions asked in the survey were two that were designed to be open ended, rather than to elicit a check-type response. Respondents could decline to answer one or both of these, or could make any comment or statement they wished.

The two questions were as follows: (1) "What do you like most about the United States now?"; and (2) "What do you like least about the United States now?" Some respondents were quite vocal and articulate, and indicated a number of likes and dislikes, in their replies. Other answered with one word, while still others either indicated that they had no comment or declined to reply at all.

Since all component parts of a reply were tabulated—and the respondents' answers were not limited to any specific number of likes or dislikes—the tabulated number of indicated likes or dislikes exceeds the number of respondents. Additionally, even though the original replies may have been expressed with different words, all replies were categorized for purposes of tabulation. Otherwise, the list of likes or dislikes would have been too long. For example, replies such as "plenty of food," "one can own his own home," "shopping is good," and so forth were tabulated as "economic opportunity." Similarly comments such as "free elections," "good government," and "nobody tells you what to do" were tabulated under "freedom." However, certain replies that appeared frequently—even though they could have been tabulated under a different heading—were accounted for separately. One such category is "cheap food," which—although it could have been incorporated in the "economic opportunity" category—was left by itself because of the considerable number of replies indicating this as the facet of U.S. life that some immigrants liked most.

Table 18.1 gives the number of persons interviewed and the number of respondents to each of these two questions, by ethnicity and percentages. As the information indicates, Chinese immigrants were fairly open and forthcoming in expressing what they like or dislike in U.S. society. Koreans were the least open, particularly on dislikes: More than half did not answer that question. While most Filipinos answered the question on likes, close to two-fifths chose not to identify features of U.S. life and practices that they did not like.

Not surprisingly, when all three ethnic groups are taken together, "freedom"—political, religious, and of the press—and democratic government institutions constitute the facet of U.S. life these interviewed immigrants liked best (Table 18.2). Freedom was mentioned in 34.6% of all replies to the question on likes. "Economic opportunity"—facility in finding employment, the rewards that such employment offers, and the abundance and affordability of consumer goods—took second place, at 33.7%. "Educational opportunity"—the ability to attend school, particularly higher education—was third, with 12.4% of all replies falling in this category. Surprisingly, "cheap food" (its abundance, variety, and cost)—a category that could have easily fit into the "economic opportunity" category—garnered 5.9% of the responses by itself.

However, differences are apparent when each of the three interviewed groups is taken separately. Filipinos, for example, appear to place a higher importance on economic opportunity than on freedom; and, relative to the other two groups, they do not value education opportunities as highly. In

Table 18.1
Likes and Dislikes: Number of Interviews and Responses

Ethnicity	Total number of Interviews	Answered "Likes" Question		Answered "Dislikes" Question	
Filipinos	330	281	85.2%	198	60.0%
Koreans	264	172	65.2	130	49.2
Chinese	255	216	84.7	195	76.5
Totals	849	669	78.8	523	61.6

Source: Compiled by the author.

Table 18.2
Replies to "What Do You Like Most about the United States Now?"

Likes	Total		Filipinos		Koreans		Chinese	
Freedom (political, religious, press, etc.)	185	34.6%	113	33.4%	68	34.9	104	35.7%
Economic Opportunity	278	33.7	136	40.2	59	30.2	83	28.5
Educational Opportunity	102	12.4	20	5.9	26	13.3	56	19.3
Clean Physical Environment	39	4.7	4	1.2	14	7.2	21	7.2
Climate (weather)	21	2.5	4	1.2	12	6.2	5	1.7
Government Social Assistance Programs	17	2.1	3	.9	5	2.6	9	3.1
Recreational Opportunities	12	1.5	4	1.2	5	2.6	3	1.0
People and Culture	21	2.6	11	3.3	4	2.0	6	2.1
Cheap Food	49	5.9	43	12.7	2	1.0	4	1.4
Totals	824	100%	338	100%	195	100%	291	100%

Source: Compiled by the author.

fact, educational opportunity drew only 5.9% of responses, while the low price of food garnered 12.7%. This is perhaps due to the fact that, for the largely middle-class Filipinos who are likely to become immigrants in the United States, entry into higher education facilities is not restricted in their country of origin. However, the author's personal observation and the discussions he has had with a cross-section of Filipino immigrants in the United States buttress the view that Filipino immigrants in this country are less likely to be interested in higher education—particularly, at the graduate level—than in occupational pursuits that produce economic rewards quickly.

On the other hand, Koreans value freedom most, and give a good deal of attention to educational opportunity—which is in third place, with 13.3% of responses. Both a clean physical environment — open spaces, lakes, parks, and so on—and climate rank high with Korean immigrants: These likes are in fourth and fifth places—with 7.2% and 6.2% of responses, respectively. This may be due to the fact that South Korea (from which most of the immigrants hail) is intensely populated in comparison to the United States, with more than 1,000 persons per square mile. Similarly, the climate— particularly in California, where close to one-third of these immigrants reside—is certainly milder than in Korea.

Chinese immigrants appear to value freedom more than economic opportunity, as compared with the other two groups. They also rank higher than Filipinos and Koreans in the frequency with which they mentioned educational opportunity; they placed their liking for a clean physical environment and wide-open spaces on the same plateau as the Koreans.

The perceptions of U.S. society that are shown in replies to the question on dislikes are also very interesting (Table 18.3). Taken as a group, the immigrants who were interviewed and replied to this question indicated that, among the facets they like least about life in the United States, the top three were the incidence of crime (20.7%), cultural and language differences (19.4%), and racial discrimination (13.5%).

However, the three different immigrant groups appeared to find different societal factors and problem areas of the national life more troublesome than others.

Filipinos appeared to be more concerned about racial discrimination (18.6%) than crime (13.3%)—perhaps due to the fact that, since they do not generally reside in ethnic neighborhoods but are spread out over the large cities and their suburbs, they are less likely to become victims of violent crimes. Climate and its harshness in some of the cities where the survey took place was, however, the factor most often mentioned by Filipinos— garnering a 19% response. Other factors that Filipinos mentioned as less likable aspects of U.S. society were cultural differences (8.8%); domestic government policies and practices, such as welfare eligibility, the insufficiency of trash collection, and U.S. government foreign policy (7.5%); and the public transportation system (7.1%). Most of the replies in the foreign-policy category mentioned U.S. nuclear policies and U.S. government policies toward the Philippines. As the survey was taken before the fall of the Marcos regime, it may be that the emphasis on this subject would be less now.

A notable number of Filipinos also complained about the high level of taxation in the United States (6.2%), and a few (1.8%) lamented the lack of servants. Both of these complaints are a reflection of their previous life in the Philippines, where—apparently—only fools pay taxes due in full and where most middle-class families enjoy the luxury of one or more servants (whose $10–20 monthly salary is affordable even to families with a monthly income of $200).

On the other hand, Koreans—because of their unfamiliarity with English and their traditional distinct national culture—were most concerned about

Table 18.3
Replies to "What Do You Like Least about the United States Now?"

Dislikes	Total		Filipinos		Koreans		Chinese	
Racial Discrimination	81	13.5%	42	18.6%	30	22.4%	9	3.8%
High Crime Rates	124	20.7	30	13.3	26	19.4	68	28.4
Climate	56	9.4	43	19.0	--	--	13	5.4
High Taxes	27	4.5	14	6.2	4	3.0	9	3.8
Decline of Morality	25	4.2	12	5.3	12	9.0	1	.4
Abuse of Freedoms	21	3.5	9	4.0	4	3.0	8	3.3
Economic Conditions	32	5.3	11	4.9	5	3.7	16	6.7
Cultural and Language Differences	116	19.4	20	8.8	33	24.6	63	26.4
Breakdown of Family and Kinship Ties	37	6.2	8	3.5	15	11.2	14	5.9
Domestic Government Policies	57	9.5	16	7.1	5	3.7	36	15.1
U.S. Government Foreign Policies	17	2.8	17	7.5	--	--	--	--
Lack of Servants	6	1.0	4	1.8	--	--	2	.8
	599	100	226	100	134	100	239	100

Source: Compiled by the author.

cultural and language differences. In fact, these factors were mentioned by Korean immigrants in 24.6% of instances, with racial discrimination and the incidence of crime in second and third places—22.4% and 19.4%, respectively. Korean immigrants were also concerned about the tendency of U.S. society to foster intergenerational conflicts and the breakdown of family and kinship ties, (11.2%), and the decline of morality standards (the incidence of alcoholism, use of drugs, and premarital sex: 9%).

Chinese immigrants do not perceive racial discrimination as a major problem for themselves, perhaps because most of them—at least for the first years of their life in the United States—live and work in ethnic neighborhoods and do not have extensive social contacts with members of other races or the dominant U.S. ethnic groups. Out of the 239 items mentioned by the 195 Chinese respondents to this question, discrimination was only mentioned in nine instances—a frequency of 3.8%. The incidence of crime was foremost in the minds of these immigrants, with a frequency of 28.4%—followed by cultural and language differences (26.4%) and domestic government policies (15.1%), such as public housing policies, trash collection, the undisciplined quality of education, the inadequacy of the public transportation system, and similar perceived shortcomings at the local and state levels.

While—as seen in the data—the responses of these immigrants on the features of U.S. society that they like best show a high degree of consistency and cluster primarily on freedom and economic opportunity, their replies on the features that they like least do not appear to have this tendency. In fact, while only four categories of likes were mentioned by all respondents with a frequency of more than 5%, seven categories of dislikes fall into this pattern. While there is a focus among these immigrants on the societal features that make the United States a desireable place of residence, no such harmony presents itself on the less desirable aspects of the national life.

19

Summary and Conclusions

SUMMARY BY COUNTRY OF ORIGIN

Filipino Immigrants

Among the immigrant groups examined in the survey, Filipinos had the highest percentage of college graduates—65.8%—prior to emigration, and the highest percentage of persons in the managerial, executive, and professional occupations—55.5%. Additionally, 48.8% of the Filipinos owned their residence; 30% owned land; and 30.9% owned an automobile, prior to their move to the United States. Since—by population—the Philippines are the third-largest English-speaking country in the world (approximately the same as the United Kingdom), 90.9% spoke English well or fluently. Most (69.4%) claimed to have decided to come to the United States for economic reasons—desiring to receive a better economic return for their skill and education.

In late 1985 and early 1986, 69.1% of the Filipino respondents' nuclear families comprised four or fewer persons, while 39.1% of their households included persons other than nuclear family members. By early 1986, close to one-third had purchased a residence in the United States, and nearly four-fifths owned an automobile. More than four-fifths—82.1%—of all Filipino respondents were employed, with 58.2% having at least one other person in their household employed full-time; and 39.1% counted at least one other person employed part-time. Of the 330 heads of households (respondent or spouse), 86.7% were employed, with 47.8% of those who were employed by others being in a managerial, executive, or professional position. A very small percentage—3.7%—were self-employed. As for income in 1984, only 5.6% of the respondents' families had incomes of less than $5,000; 46.3% had incomes between $20,000 and $49,999; and 10.2% enjoyed an income of $50,000 or more.

In more than half of the respondents' families, at least one person was attending school—with 91.2% reporting excellent or good grades. Less than one-quarter of the respondents reported that members of their family over age 18 were attending school full-time; and less than one-fifth, that members of their family over age 18 were attending school part-time. A little more than half of the respondents also indicated that members of their families belonged to one or more organization, with most of these showing a marked preference for social/ethnic organizations.

Most Filipino respondents indicated that, after arrival in the United States, they had serious difficulties in finding employment and with the transportation system and that they relied on assistance from family members and relatives, in the process of starting their life anew. Nearly two-fifths of the respondents indicated that they planned to remain in the United States for good; close to one-third said that they had temporarily returned to the Philippines at least once; and 23.6% had also filed immigrant visa petitions to bring eligible relatives to the United States.

One-third of the respondents stated that the feature they liked best about the United States was freedom, while 40.2% chose economic opportunity. On the other hand, 18.6% mentioned racial discrimination as a cause of concern, while 19% did not like the climate.

Korean Immigrants

Of the Korean immigrants surveyed, 40.9% had completed four or more years of university-level studies, prior to their move to the United States. Approximately 76.5% had been employed in their country, with 14.4% of the interviewed total being self-employed. The percentage who, in their own country, were practicing one of the professions or were employed in managerial/executive positions was 42.6%. Another indication that most of these immigrants belonged to the middle class in their country is the fact that 61% owned their residence; 13.6%, land, and 12.9%, automobiles. Of the total 264 immigrants interviewed, 19.3% spoke English well or fluently, while 23.1% could not speak English. Slightly more than half of these Koreans stated that their reason for immigrating to the United States was to join family members; more than 40% gave almost equal weight to better educational and employment opportunities.

The survey results indicate that, at the time it was taken, 72.4% of the respondents' families included from one to four members, and that there were one or more persons who were not close family members in 30.7% of the households. By early 1986, 28.4% of these Korean immigrants had purchased their own home, and 86.4% owned at least one automobile.

In the field of employment, 72.7% of the respondents were employed; 54.2% of their households also included at least one other person employed full-time; and 31.4% had at least another individual who was employed part-time. In these households, 85.2% of the heads of households were employed, with 16.3% engaged in self-employment activities—mostly in service or retail operations. Of the total employed by others, 31.9% were in professional, executive, or managerial positions. While 5.2% of the Korean respondents' families had incomes of less than $5,000 in 1984, 41.8% were in the $20,000–$49,999 range, and 2.3% had incomes of $50,000 or more.

Close to 60% of the respondents stated that members of their families were attending school, with 88.2% indicating that the average grades of such students were good or excellent; 29.5% of the respondents also indicated that at least one member of their family aged 18 or over was attending school, as did 26.5% with reference to part-time school attendance. By early 1986, 79.9% of the respondents said that members of their family spoke English well or fluently, and only 2.6% indicated that no one in their family spoke any English.

Nearly three-fourths of the Korean respondents belonged to one or more organizations: Most of these (84.3%) were members of religious organizations—generally, Protestant churches. On the other hand, only 19.3% of the respondents stated that members of their families belonged to ethnic/ social organizations. Virtually all of the respondents cited one or more difficulties in settling in the United States: Learning English (63%) was the cause most frequently cited—followed by difficulties in finding employment (49.0%). A little more than two-thirds also indicated that they were assisted by one or more sources, after their arrival: Relatives and family members—in that order—were the two sources of assistance chosen most often by those who had help.

While 51.5% of the respondents stated that they were planning to remain in the United States indefinitely, 12.2% indicated that their plans were to return to Korea after a stay ranging from two to ten years; 39% of the respondents had also returned to Korea at least once, since arrival in the United States; and 20% had filed petitions to allow family members to apply for U.S. immigrant visas.

Slightly more than one-third of the Korean immigrants cited "freedom" as the facet of U.S. society they liked most—followed by "economic opportunity" (30.2%) and "educational opportunity (13.3%). Significant numbers of these respondents disliked having to cope with cultural and language differences (24.6%), racial discrimination (22.4%), and high crime rates (19.4%).

Chinese Immigrants

Chinese immigrants were not a homogeneous group, and their socio-demographic characteristics varied according to their place of birth and last residence. For the purposes of this survey, Chinese immigrants were divided accordingly to their place of birth. Mainland Chinese showed the lowest percentage of individuals who had university degrees prior to their emigration (17.6%). On the other hand, Taiwanese (with 65.3%) had the highest, while the "other" Chinese (26.9%) and those born in Hong Kong (25%) fell somewhere in between the two extremes.

With reference to work activities prior to arrival in the United States, the mainland Chinese had the highest level of labor force participation (96.6%)—followed by the "other" Chinese (96.1%), those from Taiwan (79.6%), and natives of Hong Kong (75%) More than half of the immigrants born in Hong Kong and close to half of those born in Taiwan were engaged in professional, executive, or managerial activities; these percentages for those from mainland China and the "other" Chinese were 25.9 and 28, respectively.

Prior to emigration from their country of residence, nearly half of the mainland-born Chinese owned their residence—as did close to one-third of the "other" Chinese and of those born in Hong Kong, and less than one-fourth of those from Taiwan. An astonishing 42.3% of the "other" Chinese also owned automobiles. In their ability to speak English well or fluently, those born in Hong Kong (with 56.3%) were first, while the mainland-born (with 10.1%) fared worst.

While most mainland-born Chinese (81.1%) stated that their primary reasons for immigrating to the United States was to join family members (as did 62.5% of those from Hong Kong and 46.1% of the "other" Chinese), Taiwanese chose the better educational opportunities as their principal reason (65.3%). Those from Hong Kong also picked this last reason in large numbers—making it their second-most important reason.

By the time the survey was taken, 83.7% of Taiwanese respondents' families comprised four or fewer members; the corresponding figures for those from Hong Kong was 68.7%; for those from mainland China, 58.7%; and for the "other" Chinese, 46.2%.

In addition to having the largest families, the "other" Chinese respondents also had the largest percentage of households that included persons other than nuclear family members (73.1%). Conversely, a small proportion (27.7%) of the household of those born in mainland China included such persons.

While 46.9% of those born in Hong Kong had purchased their residence by early 1986, only 12.8% of those born in mainland China had done so. Most of those born in mainland China (71.6%) also did not own any automobile, while 89.8% of those born in Taiwan had at least one.

The highest level of employment among the respondents was found among the natives of Hong Kong (78.1%), while the "other" Chinese had the lowest level (34.6%). The households of mainland Chinese respondents accounted for the largest percentages of those having at least one other person employed full-time and part-time—55.4 and 33.1, respectively. The "other" Chinese households showed the lowest percentage of those having other full-time workers (34.6); and the Taiwanese, the lowest percentage of those having part-time workers (12.2).

The highest percentage of head of households who were employed was among the Taiwanese (91.8); the lowest was among the "other" Chinese (53.8). Those born in Hong Kong seemed the group that was most gifted with entrepreneurial daring: In fact, 12.5% were self-employed. Occupationally, more than half (56.1%) of the Taiwanese heads of households were employed in professional, executive, or managerial jobs—as were 52.2% of those born in Hong Kong, 33.3% of the "other" Chinese, and only 13.4% of those born in mainland China. Conversely, 52.7% of the heads of households of respondents born in mainland China were engaged in service occupations (in restaurants and in building maintenance); and 24.1%, as factory workers (principally, in the garment-making industry).

Income for 1984 showed a high degree of correlation with work-force status and occupation. In fact, 19.8% of the families of mainland Chinese respondents had incomes of less than $5,000; only 7.9% had incomes between $20,000 and $49,999; and none of the 101 respondents to this question reported a 1984 income of $50,000 or more. On the other hand, only 5.1% of the families of Taiwan-born respondents had incomes below $5,000, while 53.8% were in the $20,000 to $49,999 range—and 2.6%, in the over-$50,000 bracket. The "other" Chinese presented a picture of extremes: 30.8% of their families had incomes of less than $5,000, while 53.8% were in the $20–49,999 bracket; and 7.7% had made $50,000 or more, during the year.

While the percentage of the "other" Chinese respondents who reported members attending school was the highest (88.5)—and Taiwanese had the lowest (40.8)—Taiwanese reported that 95% of those attending school in their family had grades that were either excellent or good. Apparently, family members of the mainland Chinese respondents were the poorest students: 41.3% reported "satisfactory" grades, and 9.2% reported poor grades. Also, while 50% of the "other" Chinese reported having family members aged 18 or over who were attending school full-time—and 30.8%, as having members 18 or over who were attending school part-time—only 15.6% of those born in Hong Kong indicated that members of their family aged 18 or over were going to school full-time, and only 16.3% of the Taiwanese reported part-time attendance.

By early 1986, the average ability of family members to speak English well or fluently was also varied among the four groups. On this point, the families of the Hong Kong respondents were the star performers (at 96.9%), while those of mainland Chinese had the poorest showing (with 46.6%).

Chinese immigrant families did not appear to be great joiners in organizations. In fact, the best showing was that of the families of the Hong Kong respondents (40.6%), and the worst was that of the mainland Chinese (18.9%). More than four-fifths of those who were members of any organizations had joined religious groups.

Excluding natives of Hong Kong, more than 90% of the interviewed Chinese immigrants had experienced some difficulties in the process of adapting to life in the United States. Most mainland Chinese indicated that their most significant problem was learning English (79.6%), while the "other" Chinese stated that finding employment had been most troublesome for them (70.8%)—a problem that was also indicated as most serious by those from Hong Kong (67.9%). The latter also reported that 21.9% of them had not received any help from anyone in settling here, while the mainland Chinese—with 12.2% of the respondents in this category—had the lowest percentage receiving no help.

Of the mainland Chinese who reported receipt of assistance, 60.8% indicated that they had been helped by relatives. Those from Taiwan mentioned family members most often (57.5%), while Hong Kong immigrants said that the top two sources of assistance for them were relatives and family members (52%), equally. The "other" Chinese—probably because most of them were originally refugees from their own countries—reported that government was their primary source of assistance: This was true for 45.5% of these respondents.

While only 24.5% of the Taiwanese respondants indicated a commitment to remain in the United States permanently—and 14.3% indicated that they would return to Taiwan within ten years—three-fourths of the other three groups of Chinese immigrants expressed their conviction to remain in the United States indefinitely. More than 50% of the Taiwanese and those born in Hong Kong had also made one or more trips back to their country, but only 11.5% of the "other" Chinese and 18.2% of those born on the mainland had done so. In all cases, less than 20% of respondents indicated that they or their spouses had filed immigrant visa petitions to bring eligible family members to the United States.

With reference to their likes and dislikes of facets of our society, Chinese respondents placed the highest importance on freedom, economic opportunity, and educational opportunity—on one side of the ledger—and the high crime rates and cultural and language differences on the other.

CONCLUSIONS

Recently, some demographers and immigration experts have contended that, while—following passage of the Immigration and Nationality Act of 1965—the United States attracted a large number of Asian immigrants who were exceedingly well educated and whose skills were highly competitive in the U.S. labor market, this was not true for the more recent Asian immigrants. The majority of these—coming under family reunification provisions—were not believed to be as highly educated as their predecessors; and their skills and earning power, not as great. Such immigrants—they claim—may be imposing increasingly heavy burdens on the U.S. society.

To ascertain whether these charges have any basis in fact, it may be useful to look at selected sociodemographic characteristics of the surveyed immigrants and to compare these characteristics with those of Asian immigrants who were in the United States in 1980, with all ethnic Asians (whether immigrants or U.S.-born) in the United States in 1980, and with the U.S. population at large in 1983. Table 19.1 affords such a comparison.

While this data may not be fully comparable, it is evident that—in terms of college education and occupation—both the survey sample and all Asian immigrants who came to the United States between 1970 and 1980 enjoy the advantage. In fact, while—in 1983—only 18.8% of persons who were 25 years of age and over had four or more years of college, 35.9% of the Asian immigrants did so (in 1980)—as did 46.9% of the survey sample.

Similarly, while 23.4% of all persons over the age of 16 were employed in managerial/executive or professional occupations in the United States in 1983, 27.6% of the 1970–80 Asian immigrants were so occupied in 1980—as well as 37.8% of the survey-sample heads of households. As for income, the survey-sample participants' families did not do so well in 1984 as U.S. families at large did in 1983. As can be seen, their income distribution was at a level similar to that of U.S. families in 1979. However, considering that 84.1% of all survey respondents who answered the income question had been in the United States for three years or less, their income achievement is no mean feat. Thus—on balance—the evidence is that Filipino, Chinese, and Korean immigrants (at least) are as well or better educated than those who came in the past, include a higher percentage of more highly skilled and trained individuals, and are catching up fast in terms of income—contributing their skills and taxes to their own betterment and that of U.S. society.

The picture that has thus emerged from *Filipino* respondents is of a highly educated and skilled group who like to work hard, who enjoy relatively good incomes, and who possess an acquisitive nature. However, recent Filipino immigrants do not appear to be risk-takers or entrepreneurs; they prefer white-collar, salaried jobs. Comfortable, acquisitive—but "playing it safe"—these Filipino immigrants do not appear to have the

Table 19.1
**Selected Characteristics and Years: U.S. Population at Large, All Ethnic Asians,
Asian Immigrants, and Survey Sample (in percentages)**

Education	U.S. Population 1980	U.S. Population 1983	Ethnic Asians 1980	Asian Immigrants 1970–1980	1985–86 Survey Sample
(Persons 25 or Over) High School Graduate	67.7	72.1	74.8	73.0	64.1
4 or More Yrs. College	16.3	18.8	32.9	35.9	46.9
Occupation					
Manager/Exec. Professional	22.7	23.4	23.8	27.6	37.8
Family Income	(1979)	(1983)	(1979)	Household Income (1979)	(1984)
Less than $5,000	7.3	5.7	7.6	18.4	7.9
$20,000 – $49,999	36.8	48.0	48.5	34.2	39.5
$50,000 – Over	5.6	12.6	9.1	5.1	5.2

Sources: U.S. Bureau of the Census, Various reports from the *1980 Census of the Population* (Washington, D.C.: Government Printing Office, 1981) and *Statistical Abstract of the United States, 1985* (Washington, D.C.: Government Printing Office, 1985).

degree of ambition, drive, or forward vision that will place them in leadership positions in the foreseeable future.

On the contrary, *Korean* immigrants—while not as well educated or highly skilled as the Filipinos—appear to be headed for a bright future with assurance. Energetic, hard-working, and willing to take risks (witness the 16.3% self-employment of household heads in this sample), these Koreans are building for the future, rather than living for the day. Thus, while—in respect to income—they may not be as well-off as Filipinos, they may be significantly better-off in the future. Infused by a spirit of achievement, they—or perhaps their children—may become what the Jewish immigrants turned out to be in the past: businessmen and professionals whose relatively low numbers belie their importance and influence.

Chinese immigrants present a mixed picture. While Taiwanese have "arrived" (in terms of occupational status and income) and those born in Hong Kong are at their heel, the mainlanders are far behind—educationally, occupationally, and economically. Perhaps it will take a generation for them to catch up. The "other" Chinese are a group too varied for easy categorization: Some are educated and wealthy; others, poor and hopeless.

However, as a group, the sociodemographic characteristics of the surveyed sample make it abundantly clear that, for the most part—unlike immigrants to the United States from other countries or other times—recent Filipino, Korean, and Chinese immigrants have not been the poor, uneducated, unskilled "wretched refuse" of their societies. On the contrary—examined by any measure—these immigrants form a picture of social stability, impressive educational and occupational achievement, English-language ability, and middle-class status in their own countries. In fact— as we have seen—62.5% were married, and 72% had either no children or only one or two. Furthermore, 46.9% were college graduates, and 34.5% were engaged in the professions in their own countries. More than 60% were also property owners—with 50.1% owning their residence; 18.3%, land, and 19.3%, automobiles. While 48.3% spoke English well or fluently before arriving in the United States, only 19.5% did not.

Thus, their immigration promises the addition of valuable human capital assets to U.S. society: a well-educated, enterprising, highly mobile group of immigrants who came to the United States to fulfill their potential and contribute to society's well-being, while improving their own lot.

Notes

PART I. IMMIGRANTS IN THE UNITED STATES

Chapter 1. The Ebb and Flow of Immigration

1. Robert Warren and Ellen Percy Kraly, "The Elusive Exodus: Emigration from the United States," Population Reference Bureau Bulletin No. 8, Washington, D.C., March 1985.
2. William S. Bernard, "Immigration: History of U.S. Policy," in Oscar Handlin, ed., *Harvard Encyclopedia of American Ethnic Groups* (Cambridge, Mass.: Belknap Press, 1980), p. 486.
3. Richard A. Easterling, "Immigration: Economic and Social Characteristics" in Handlin, *Harvard Encyclopedia,* p. 479.
4. Warren and Kraly, "Elusive Exodus", p. 5.
5. Moldwin A. Jones, *Destination America* (New York: Holt, Rinehart, and Winston, 1976), p.12.

Chapter 2. Sociodemographic Characteristics of U.S. Immigrants

1. Easterling, "Immigration Characteristics," pp. 476-86.
2. Morton D. Winsberg, "1980 Rates of Emigration to the United States," *Population Today* (February 1985): 5-6.

3. U.S. Bureau of Census, *Social Indicators, 1980* (Washington D.C.: Government Printing Office, 1981).

4. Easterling, "Immigration Characteristics," p. 479.

5. Ibid. p. 481.

6. Ibid. p. 482.

7. U.S. Bureau of the Census, *Social Indicators, 1980.*

8. U.S. Bureau of the Census, *1980 Census of the Population, U.S. Summary* (Washington, D.C.: Government Printing Office, 1981).

9. Barry C. Chiswick, "The Economic Progress of Immigrants: Some Universal Patterns" in Barry R. Chiswick, ed., *The Gateway: U.S. Immigration Issues and Policies* (Washington, D.C.: American Enterprise Institute, 1982).

10. Ellen Seghal, "Foreign Born in the U.S. Labor Market: The Results of a Special Survey," *Monthly Labor Review* (July 1985).

11. David S. North, *Seven Years Later: The Experiences of the 1970 Cohorts of Immigrants in the United States,* R&D Monograph No. 71, U.S. Department of Labor, 1979.

12. Seghal, "Foreign Born in the Labor Market."

13. U.S. Bureau of the Census, *1980 Census, U.S. Summary.*

PART II. ASIAN IMMIGRANTS: FILIPINO, KOREAN, AND CHINESE

1. Robert W. Gardner, Bryant Robey, and Peter C. Smith, "Asian Americans: Growth, Change, and Diversity," Population Reference Bureau Bulletin Vol. 40, No. 4, Washington, D.C., October 1985, p. 3.

THE PHILIPPINES

Chapter 3. A Short History of Filipino Immigration to the United States

1. Information on early Filipino settlements in Lousiana was published in a series of articles by Carlos Quirino in *The Graphic* (Manila, Philippines, March 23, March 30, and April 6, 1933).

2. Ruben Alcantara, "1906: The First Sacada" in J. C. Dionisio, ed., *The Filipinos in Hawaii: The First 75 Years* (Honolulu: Filipino News Specialty Publications, 1981), p. 25.

3. Howard Brett Melendy, *Asians in America: Filipinos, Koreans, and East Indians* (Boston: Twayne Publishers, 1977), p. 37.

4. Howard Brett Melendy, "Filipinos" in Handlin, *Harvard Encyclopedia,* p. 360.

5. Monica Boyd, "Oriental Immigration: The Experience of Chinese, Japanese, and Filipino Population in the U.S.A.," *International Migration Review* (Spring 1971): 48-60.

Chapter 4. Current Emigration Trends and Problems in the Philippines

1. *Bulletin Today,* Manila, May 25, 26, and 27, 1985; and *Times Journal,* Manila, May 8, 1985.

2. Unpublished data obtained by the author from the Commission on Filipinos Overseas, Manila.

Chapter 5. Social and Demographic Characteristics of Filipino Immigrants: 1980

1. Leon F. Bouvier and Anthony Agresta, "Projection of the Asian American Population, 1980-2030," quoted in Gardner, Robey, and Smith, "Asian Americans".

2. U.S. Bureau of the Census, "Foreign-Born Immigrants: Filipinos—Tabulations from the 1980 Census of the Population and Housing," mimeographed report, Washington, D.C., October 1984.

3. U.S. Bureau of the Census, *1980 Census, U.S. Summary.*

4. Gardner, Robey, and Smith, "Asian Americans," p. 26.

5. U.S. Department of Justice, *1983 Statistical Yearbook of the U.S. Immigration and Naturalization Service* (Washington D.C.: Government Printing Office, 1984).

6. Rene E. Mendoza, "Immigration to the U.S.: Is It in Our National Interest?" *Foreign Service Institute Record 3,* Ministry of Foreign Affairs, Manila, 1982, p. 15.

7. Ricardo G. Abad and Elizabeth Eviota, "Reproducing Development Inequalities: Some Effects of Philippine Emigration to the U.S.," unpublished paper presented at the Conference on Asian–Pacific Immigration to the United States, East/West Population Institute, Honolulu, September 1984.

8. Franklin Goza, "Income Attainment among Native and Immigrant Asians in the United States: 1960-1980," unpublished report, University of Wisconsin, Madison, 1984.

9. Morrison G. Wong, "The Cost of Being Chinese, Japanese and Filipino in the United States: 1960, 1970 and 1976," *Pacific Sociological Review* (January 1982): 58-78.

KOREA

Chapter 7. A Short History of Korean Immigration to the United States

1. Hyung-Chan Kim, "Some Aspects of the Social Demography of Korean Americans," *International Migration Review* (Spring 1974): 23-42.

2. Hawaiian Sugar Planters' Association Files, quoted in Dionisio, ed. *The Filipinos in Hawaii,* p. 46.

3. Illsoo Kim: "Korean Emigration Connection to Urban America: A Structural Analysis of Pre-emigration Factors in South Korea," unpublished paper presented at the Conference on Asia–Pacific Immigration to the United States, East/West Population Institute, Honolulu, September 1984, p. 4.

4. Ibid., pp. 5 and 6.

5. Jung Keun Kim, "The Trends and Policies of Korean Emigration," unpublished paper presented at the Conference on Asia–Pacific Immigration to the United States, East/West Population Institute, Honolulu, September 1984.

6. Pyong Gap Ming, "A Structural Analysis of Korean Business in the United States," *Ethnic Groups* (June 1984).

7. Kwang Chung Kim and Won Moo Hurth, "Ethnic Resource Utilization of Korean Immigrant Entrepreneurs in the Chicago Minority Area," *International Migration Review 19* (Spring 1985).

8. Pyong Gap Min and Charles Jaret, "Ethnic Business Success: The Case of Korean Small Business in Atlanta," *Sociology and Social Research* (April 1985).

9. Won Moo Hurth and Kwang Chung Kim, "Cohesive Sociocultural Adaptation of Korean Immigrants in the U.S.: An Alternative Strategy of Minority Adaptation," *International Migration Review* 18 (Summer 1984):188-216.

Chapter 8. Current Emigration Trends and Problems in Korea

1. Kwong-Kyun Ro, "International Labor Migration: Economic Theory and an Analysis of Korean Data," unpublished paper presented at the Expert Group Meeting on International Migration in Asia and the Pacific, Manila, December 6-12, 1984.

2. J. K. Kim, "Trends and Policies of Korean Emigration."

3. Ro, "International Labor Migration: Korean."

4. Priority date is the date on which a petition or other documents that entitle a person to registration as an intending immigrant are filed with the U.S. Immigration and Naturalization Service or a consular office. Preference is the category under which a prospective immigrant is registered. This category depends on the immigrant's degree of relationship to a U.S. citizen or permanent resident or in case of immigration based on skills or occupations, such skills or occupations.

Chapter 9. Social and Demographic Characteristics of Korean Immigrants: 1980

1. Bouvier and Agresta, "Projection of Asian American Population," p. 37.

2. Gardner et al., "Asian Americans," p. 26.

Chapter 10. Conclusions and Prospects for the Future

1. Bouvier and Agresta, "Projection of Asian American Population," p. 37.

CHINA

Chapter 11. A Short History of Chinese Immigration to the United States

1. Stanford M. Lyman, *The Asians in North America* (Santa Barbara, Calif.: ABC-CLIO, 1977), p. 40.

2. Ibid.

3. H. M. Lai, "Chinese" in Handlin, *Harvard Encyclopedia,* p. 218.

4. Lyman, *Asians in North America,* p. 40.

5. Lai, "Chinese," p. 218.

6. Lyman, *Asians in North America,* p. 42.

7. James A. Banks, *Teaching Strategies for Ethnic Studies* (Boston: Allyn and Bacon, 1975), p. 324.

8. U.S. Immigration and Naturalization Service (INS), *Annual Report, 1983* (Washington, D.C.: Government Printing Office, 1984) table 177–1.2, p. 2; and U.S. Bureau of the Census, *1980 Census.*

9. Lyman, *Asians in North America,* p. 43.

10. Betty Lee Sung, *Mountains of Gold: The Story of the Chinese in America* (New York: Macmillan, 1967), p. 39.

11. Lai, "Chinese," p. 219.

12. Ibid.

13. Jack Chen, *The Chinese in America* (San Francisco: Harper and Row, 1980), p. 138.

14. Betty Lee Sung, "Mountains of Gold," reprinted in Melvin Steinfield, *Cracks in the Melting Pot* (Beverly Hills, Calif.: Glencoe Press, 1970), p. 125.

15. Carey McWilliams, "Brothers under the Skin," reprinted in Steinfield, *Cracks.*

16. Lyman, *Asians in North America,* pp. 55 and 56.

17. Thomas Sowell, *Ethnic America* (New York: Basic Books, 1981), p. 138.

18. Lai, "Chinese," p. 223.

19. Sowell, *Ethnic America,* p. 144.

20. Lai, "Chinese," p. 226.

21. U.S. Department of Justice, *1983 Statistical Yearbook,* pp. 4 and 5.

Selected Bibliography

PART I: IMMIGRANTS IN THE UNITED STATES

Books

Archdeacon, Thomas J. *Becoming American: An Ethnic History*. New York: Free Press, 1983.

Ashabrenner, Brent. *The New Americans*. New York: Dodd, Mead, and Company, 1983.

Banks, James A. *Teaching Strategies for Ethnic Studies*. Boston: Allyn and Bacon, 1975.

Briggs, Vernon M., Jr. *Immigration Policy and the American Labor Force*. Baltimore: Johns Hopkins University Press, 1984.

Bryce-La Porte, Roy Simon, et al. (editors). *Sourcebook on the New Immigration: Publications for the United States and the International Community*. New Brunswick, N.J.: Transaction Books, 1980.

Carlson, Lewis H., and George A. Cobburn (editors). *In Their Place*. New York: John Wiley and Sons, 1972.

Chiswick, Barry R. *The Employment of Immigrants in the United States*. Washington, D.C.: American Enterprise Institute, 1982.

———— (editor). *The Gateway: U.S. Immigration Issues and Policies*. Washington, D.C.: American Enterprise Institute, 1982.

Ethnic Information Sources of the United States. Detroit: Gale Research Company, 1983.

Fellner, W. (editor). *Contemporary Economic Problems.* Washington, D.C.: American Enterprise Institute, 1979.

Glazer, Nathan (editor). *Clamer at the Gates: The New American Immigration.* San Francisco: ICS Press, 1985.

Handlin, Oscar (editor). *Harvard Encyclopedia of American Ethnic Groups.* Cambridge, Mass.: Belknap Press, 1980.

_____ (editor), *Immigration as a Factor in American History.* Englewood Cliffs, N.J.: Prentice-Hall, 1959.

Hansen, Marcus Lee. *The Immigrant in American History.* New York: Harper and Row, 1964.

Higham, John. *Send These to Me.* New York: Atheneum, 1975.

_____ *Strangers in the Land.* New York: Atheneum, 1981.

Jones, Moldwin A. *Destination America.* New York: Holt, Rinehart, and Winston, 1976.

Kennedy, John F. *A Nation of Immigrants.* New York: Harper and Row, 1964.

Kritz, Mary M. *U.S. Immigration and Refugee Policy: Global and Domestic Issues.* Papers presented at conferences sponsored by the Rockefeller and Ford Foundations in August and November, 1981.

Levine, Daniel B., Kenneth Hill, and Robert Warren (editors). *Immigration Statistics, A Story of Neglect.* Washington, D.C.: National Academy Press, 1985.

Muller, Thomas, et al. *The Fourth Wave—California's Newest Immigrants.* Washington, D.C.: Urban Institute, 1985.

North, David S. *Seven Years Later: The Experiences of the 1970 Cohorts of Immigrants in the United States,* R&D Monograph No. 71.

Robey, Bryant. *The American People.* New York: E.P. Dutton, 1985.

Sowell, Thomas. *Ethnic America.* New York: Basic Books, 1981.

Steinfield, Melvin. *Cracks in the Melting Pot.* Beverly Hills, Calif.: Glencoe Press, 1970.

U.S. Bureau of the Census. *Census of the Population* (various volumes). Washington, D.C.: Government Printing Office, 1980-83.

_____ *Statistical Abstract of the United States, 1985.* Washington, D.C.: Government Printing Office, 1985.

U.S. Department of Justice. *1983 Statistical Yearbook of the U.S. Immigration and Naturalization Service.* Washington, D.C.: Government Printing Office, 1984.

U.S. Department of State. *Report of the Visa Office, 1978.* Washington, D.C.: Government Printing Office, 1985.

Vialet, Joyce. *U.S. Immigration Law and Policy: 1952-1979.* Washington, D.C.: Government Printing Office, 1979.

Weiser, Marjorie P.K. (editor). *Ethnic America.* New York: H.W. Wilson Company, 1978.

Ziegler, Benjamin M. (editor). *Immigration: An American Dilemma.* Boston: D.C. Heath and Company, 1953.

Other Sources

Adams, Willy Paul. "Immigration and the American Experience," *The Wilson Quarterly* (New Year's 1983).

Bean, Frank D., and Teresa A. Sullivan. "Confronting the Problem," *Society* (May–June 1985): 67-73.

Church, George J. "We Are Overwhelmed," *Time Magazine* (June 25, 1984): 16-17.

Esphenshade, Thomas J., and Tracy Ann Goodis. "Recent Immigrants to Los Angeles: Characteristics and Labor Market Impact," *The Urban Institute* (May 1985), PDS-85-1.

Fallows, James. "Immigration—How It's Affecting Us," *The Atlantic Monthly* (November 1983): 45-61.

Goodman, Walter. "Message of Immigration Bill Is Disputed," *New York Times*, October 12, 1984.

"Illegal Immigrants: The U.S. May Gain More Than It Loses," *Business Week* (May 14, 1984): 126-29.

Irwin, Richard. "Changing Patterns of American Immigration," *International Migration Review* 6 (Spring 1972): 18-31.

Lane, Chuck. "Open the Door," *The New Republic* (April 1, 1985): 20-25.

Matthews, Jay. "Economic Says Illegal Aliens Cost the U.S. Jobs and Taxes," *Washington Post*, April 19, 1985.

Miller, Mark J. "President Reagan and a Humane U.S. Immigration Policy," mimeographed byliner paper commissioned by the United States Information Agency (USIA), October 1982.

Morganthau, Tom. "Closing the Door?", *Newsweek* (June 25, 1984): 18-24.

Morrison, Thomas K. "The Relations of U.S. Aid, Trade and Investment to Migration: Pressures in the Major Sending Countries," *International Migration Review* 16(Spring 1982): 4-26.

Portes, Alejandro, and A. Douglas Kincaid. "Alternative Outcomes of Reform," *Society* (May–June 1985): 73-76.

"Proposed Immigration Reform and Control Legislation—Pro and Con," *Congressional Digest* (August–September 1983).

Roucer, Joseph S. "Some Historical Trends in Acculturation of American Minorities and Their Descendants," *Sociologia Internationalis* (West Germany) 16 (1978): 137-151.

Segal, Aaron. "The Current Scene," *The Wilson Quarterly* (New Year's 1983).

Seghal, Ellen. "Foreign Born in the U.S. Labor Market: The Results of a Special Survey," *Monthly Labor Review* (July 1985): 18-24.

"U.S. Immigration Policy," mimeographed staff paper of the Economic Policy Council, September 1981.

Warren, Robert, and Ellen Percy Kraly. "The Elusive Exodus: Emigration from the United States," Population Reference Bureau Bulletin No. 8, Washington, D.C., March 1985.

Weiss, Julian. "A Fair and Realistic Policy," Interview with INS Commissioner Nelson, mimeographed byliner paper commissioned by USIA, May 1982.

Winsberg, Morton D. "1980 Rates of Emigration to the United States," *Population Today* (February 1985): 5-7.

PART II. ASIAN IMMIGRANTS: FILIPINO, KOREAN, AND CHINESE

Books

Fawcett, James, Benjamin V. Carino, and Fred Arnold. *Asian–Pacific Immigration to the United States—A Conference Report.* Honolulu: East/West Population Institute, 1985.

Lyman, Stanford M. *The Asians in North America.* Santa Barbara, Calif.: ABC-CLIO, 1977.

Melendy, H. Brett. *Asians in America: Filipinos, Koreans, and East Indians.* Boston: Twayne Publishers, 1977.

_____. *The Oriental Americans.* New York: Twayne Publishers, 1972.

U.S. Civil Rights Commission. *Civil Rights Issues of Asian and Pacific Americans: Myths and Realities,* Washington, D.C.: Government Printing Office, 1980.

U.S. Department of Health. *Asian American Reference Data Directory.* Washington, D.C.: Government Printing Office, 1976.

Welty, Paul T. *The Asians.* Philadelphia: J.B. Lippincott, 1970.

Young, Jared J. *Discrimination, Income, Human Capital Investment, and Asian Americans.* San Francisco: R&E Research Associates, 1977.

Other Sources

"Asian-Americans Reported Doing Better Than Whites," *Hartford Courant,* October 9, 1985, A-9.

Bell, David A. "The Triumph of Asian-Americans," *The New Republic* (July 15 and 22, 1985): 24-31.

Boyd, Monica. "The Changing Nature of Central and Southeast Asian Immigration to the United States: 1961-1972," *International Migration Review* 8 (Winter 1974): 507-520.

Goza, Franklin. "Income Attainment among Native and Immigrant Asians in the United States: 1960 to 1980," unpublished report prepared under contract for the U.S. Department of Health and Human Services, at the University of Wisconsin, Madison, June 1984.

Hirschman, Charles, and Morrison G. Wong. "Trends in Socioeconomic Achievement among Immigrant and Native-Born Asian-Americans, 1960-1976," *The Sociological Quarterly* 22 (Autumn 1981): 495-514.

Kuo, Wen H. "Colonized Status of Asian-Americans," *Ethnic Groups* 3(1981): 227-51.

Lindsey, Robert. "Asian Immigrants," *New York Times Magazine,* May 9, 1982, 25-42.

Mariante, Benjamin R. "How Have They Fared in Paradise? A Reconnaissance of Lifestyle Indicators among Hawaiian Ethnic Groups," *Ethnic Groups* 5(1984): 227-53.

Matthews, Jay. "Hard Work Not Foreign to These Collegians," *Hartford Courant,* November 29, 1985, 14-15.

Sullivan, Teresa A. "Special Studies of Immigrants: A Comparison of Work on

Asian and Hispanic Immigrants to the United States," Paper b.022, Population Research Center, University of Texas at Austin, August 1984.
Wong, Morrison G. "The Cost of Being Chinese, Japanese and Filipino in the United States: 1960, 1970, and 1976," *Pacific Sociological Review* 25 (January 1982): 58-78.

THE PHILIPPINES

Books

Aquino, Valentin. *The Filipino Community in Los Angeles,* San Francisco: R&E Research Associates, 1974.
Dionisio, J.C. (editor). *The Filipinos in Hawaii: The First 75 Years, 1906-1981.* Honolulu: Filipino News Specialty Publications, 1981.
Kim, Hyung-Chan. *The Filipinos in America, 1898-1974.* Dobbs Ferry, N.Y.: Oceana Publications, 1976.
Manot, Patricio R. *Filipino Physicians in America.* Bloomington: Indiana University Foundations, 1981.
Munoz, Alfred N. *The Filipinos in America.* Los Angeles: Mountain View Publishers, 1971.

Other Sources

"Anti-U.S. Stance Not Popular," *Malaya,* Manila, April 24, 1985.
"Documenting the Three Waves of Filipinos Who Came to America," *San Francisco Examiner,* January 23, 1985, A-3.
"Filipino Immigrants," mimeographed reports of the Commission on Filipino Overseas, Manila, May 1985.
"Filipinos Flood to U.S.—Legally or Not," *Pacific Stars and Stripes,* June 19, 1985.
Keely, Charles B. "Philippine Migration: International Movement and Emigration to the United States," *International Migration Review* 7 (Summer 1973): 177–187.
Melendy, H. Brett. "Filipinos in the United States." *Pacific Historical Review* 43 (1974): 520-47.
Mendoza, Rene E. "Immigration to the U.S.: Is It in Our National Interest?" *Foreign Service Institute Record* 3, Ministry of Foreign Affairs, Manila, 1982.
Okamura, Jonathon Y. "Filipino Voluntary Associations in Hawaii," *Ethnic Groups* 5 (1984): 279-305.
Parazo, Chito. "Filipino Nurses in U.S.," *Bulletin Today,* Manila, May 25, 26 and 27, 1985.
Pernia, Ernesto M. "The Question of the Brain Drain from the Philippines," *International Migration Review* 10 (Spring 1976): 63-72.
Quirino, Carlos. "Louisiana's Filipino Fishing Village of St. Malo," "Manila Village," and "A Promised Land for Paisonos," *The Graphic,* Manila, Philippines, March 23, March 30, and April 6, 1933.
Smith, Peter C. "The Social Demography of Filipino Migration Abroad," *International Migration Review* 10 (Fall 1976): 307-354.

U.S. Bureau of the Census. "Foreign-Born Immigrants: Filipinos—Tabulations from the 1980 U.S. Census of the Population and Housing," mimeographed report, Washington, D.C., October 1984.

KOREA

Books

Choi, Bong-Youn. *Koreans in America.* Chicago: Nelson-Hall, 1979.
Hurth, Won Moo. *Assimilation Patterns of Immigrants in the U.S.: A Case Study of Korean Immigrants in the Chicago Area.* Washington, D.C.: University Press of America, 1978.
Hurth, Won Moo. *Comparative Studies of Korean Immigrants in the United States.* San Francisco: R&E Research Associates, 1977.
Kim, Hyung-Chan (editor). *The Korean Diaspora.* Santa Barbara, Calif.: ABC-CLIO, 1977.
Kim, Hyung-Chan, and Wayne Patterson (editors). *The Koreans in America, 1882-1974.* Dobbs Ferry, N.Y.: Oceana Publications, 1974.
Kim, Illsoo. *New Urban Immigrants: The Korean Community in New York.* Princton, N.J.: Princeton University Press, 1981.
Korea–USA Centennial—1882-1982. Seoul, Korea: Yonhap News Agency, 1982.
Yu, Eui-Youg, Earl H. Phillips, and Eun She Yan (editors). *Koreans in Los Angeles.* Los Angeles: Koryo Research Institute, California State University, 1982.

Other Sources

Houchins, Lee, and Chang-Su Houchins. "The Korean Experience in America," *Pacific Historical Review* 43(1974): 548-75.
Hurth, Won Moo. "Toward a Korean–American Ethnicity: Some Theoretical Models," *Ethnic and Racial Studies* 3(October 1980): 444-64.
Hurth, Won Moo, and Kwang Chung Kim. "Cohesive Sociocultural Adaptation of Korean Immigrants in the U.S.: An Alternative Strategy of Minority Adaptation," *International Migration Review* 18(Summer 1984): 188-216.
Kim, Hyung-Chan. "Some Aspects of the Social Demography of Korean Americans," *International Migration Review* 8(Spring 1974): 23-42.
Kim, Kwang Chung, and Won Moo Hurth. "Ethnic Resource Utilization of Korean Immigrants in the Chicago Minority Area," *International Migration Review* 19(Spring 1985).
Kim, Kwang Chung, and Won Moo Hurth. "An Exploration in the Success Image of Asian Americans: A Case Study of Korean Immigrants," paper presented to the American Sociological Association Conference, 1983.
Kim, Kwang Chung, Hei Chu Kim, and Won Moo Hurth. "Division of Household Tasks in Korean Immigrant Families in the United States," *International Journal of Sociology and the Family* 9(July–December 1979): 161-75.
Kim, Kyong-Dong. "Koreans in America: Their Cultural Adaptation and Con-

tributions," conference paper in *Reflections on a Century of United States–Korean Relations.* New York: University Press of America, 1985.

Ming, Pyong Gap. "A Structural Analysis of Korean Business in the United States," *Ethnic Groups* (June 1984).

Ming, Pyong Gap. "From White-Collar Occupations to Small Business: Korean Immigrants' Occupational Adjustment," *The Sociological Quarterly* 25 (Summer 1984): 333-52.

Ming, Pyong Gap, and Charles Jaret. "Ethnic Business Success: The Case of Korean Small Businesses in Atlanta," *Sociology and Social Research,* April 1985.

Ro, Kong-Kyun. "International Labor Migration: Economic Theory and an Analysis of Korean Data," unpublished paper presented at the Expert Group Meeting on International Migration in Asia and the Pacific, Manila, December 6-12, 1984.

U.S. Bureau of the Census. "Foreign-Born Immigrants: Koreans—Tabulations from the 1980 U.S. Census of the Population and Housing," mimeographed report, Washington, D.C., October 1984.

CHINA

Books

Chen, Jack. *The Chinese in America.* San Francisco: Harper and Row, 1980.

Dillon, Richard H. *The Story of the Tong Wars in San Francisco's Chinatown.* New York: Coward and McCann, 1962.

Kud, Chia-Ling. *Social and Political Change in New York Chinatown: The Role of Voluntary Associations.* New York: Praeger, 1977.

Lan, Dean. *Prestige and Limitations: Realities of the Chinese–American Elite.* San Francisco: R&E Research Associates, 1976.

Lee, Rose Hum. *The Chinese in the United States of America.* Hong Kong: Hong Kong University Press, 1960.

Li, Peter S. *Occupational Mobility and Kinship Assistance: A Study of Chinese Immigrants in Chicago.* San Francisco: R&E Research Associates, 1978.

Steiner, Stan. *Fusang, The Chinese Who Built America.* New York: H.W. Wilson Company, 1978.

Sung, Betty Lee. *Mountains of Gold: The Story of the Chinese in America.* New York: Macmillan, Books 1967.

——. *A Survey of Chinese–American Manpower and Employment.* New York: Praeger, 1976.

Other Sources

Cheung, Freda, and Marlene Dobkin De Rios. "Recent Trends in the Study of the Mental Health of Chinese Immigrants to the United States," *Research in Race and Ethnic Relations* 3 (1982): 145-63.

King, Haitung, and Francis B. Locke. "Chinese in the United States: A Century of

Occupational Transition," *International Migration Review* 14(Winter 1980): 511-24.

U.S. Bureau of the Census. "Foreign-Born Immigrants: Chinese—Tabulations from the 1980 U.S. Census of the Population and Housing," mimeographed report, Washington, D.C., October 1984.

Wong, Morrison G. "Changes in the Socioeconomic Status of Chinese Population from 1960-1970," *International Migration Review* 14(Winter 1980): 511-24.

Yao, Ester Lee. "The Assimilation of Contemporary Chinese Immigrants," *The Journal of Psychology* 101(January 1979): 107-13.

Index

About the Author

LUCIANO MANGIAFICO is a U.S. diplomat who has served as a consular officer in Canada, Italy, Romania, the Philippines, and Barbados. He is currently consul general of the U.S. Embassy in Barbados. Born in Italy, Mr. Mangiafico came to the United States in 1956 and was educated at the University of Hartford where he obtained a Bachelor of Arts degree, Magna Cum Laude, in 1968. Mr. Mangiafico has previously written on immigration for numerous publications and has been a speaker on the subject throughout his diplomatic career.

DATE DUE